Konrad Lorenz

*The Man
and
His Ideas*

Konrad
Lorenz

*The Man
and
His Ideas*

RICHARD I. EVANS

Harcourt Brace Jovanovich / New York and London

75-134785-7

Printed in the United States of America

Library of Congress Cataloging in Publication Data

Evans, Richard Isadore, 1922–
  Konrad Lorenz: the man and his ideas.

  (Dialogues with notable contributors to behavioral
psychology; v. 9)
  Bibliography: p.
  Includes index.
  1. Lorenz, Konrad. 2. Psychology—Addresses, essays,
lectures.
BF109.L67E93   150   75-9581
ISBN 0-15-147285-8

First edition

B C D E

To my lovely wife and children

Contents

Contents

Acknowledgments

In the long process of filming and taping the dialogues with Konrad Lorenz and integrating them into the present volume, I am indebted to a great many people. I wish to express my appreciation to at least some of them.

Grateful acknowledgment is made to the University of Houston for permission to use the printed texts of the filmed and taped dialogue, and to Robert Cozens for his assistance in taping and filming sessions.

I also wish to express my thanks to Bette Keating for the transcription of the tapes, to Terry Rulfs for rechecking the transcription and for analyzing the materials, and to my secretary, Jan Prevatt, who assisted in completing this volume.

I am grateful for the support of the National Science Foundation, without which this project could not have been implemented.

Thanks are accorded to Donald T. Campbell of Northwestern University for his provocative paper on Lorenz, which he prepared especially for this volume.

Acknowledgments

Four of Konrad Lorenz's earlier papers are included in this book, and thanks are due to him, and to the publications in which these papers originally appeared, for permission to reprint them.

Special thanks are accorded psychology student Bettye Earle Raines, who made particularly important contributions which included editorial assistance, checking bibliographical sources, and collating and typing the final form of the manuscript.

Finally, the wonderful cooperation of Professor Konrad Lorenz cannot be emphasized enough. Not only was he willing to participate in the filming and audio-taping sessions involved in this project, but his genuine kindness and good humor during the course of these sessions will long be remembered by us all.

Introduction

*Personal Impressions of
a Controversial Scientist*

Introducing Konrad Lorenz to those interested in psychology through the medium of this dialogue could hardly be more timely. Shortly after we completed the dialogue, he and two other zoologists were awarded the 1973 Nobel Prize, the first time any contributors in the behavioral sciences had been so honored. More than any of the three, Dr. Lorenz has been popularly identified with the behavioral sciences in general, and with psychology in particular.

The experience of being with Professor Lorenz in the taping and filming of these dialogues was most rewarding. As I walked into the International Arrival Area of the Vienna Airport, I wondered whether I'd recognize him, or if he would still be waiting for me, as my plane from London was almost an hour late. My concern was short-lived, for the man at the front of the waiting crowd—face pressed against the glass enclosure—was surely Konrad Lorenz. There was no mistaking the tall heavy man with the bold features and the celebrated thatch of white hair and beard. Wearing a black-and-white checked shirt, a well-worn brown corduroy work suit and knee-high rubber boots, his erect bearing and aggressive gait belying his seventy years, he could easily have passed for a robust farmer. The sense of vitality which he generated made it difficult to believe that he considered himself ready to retire from the Max Planck Institute to his home in Altenberg, near Vienna. This enthusiasm was to prove one of the joys of being with him in the succeeding days.

Responding to my signal of recognition with a warm smile, he insisted on helping me load my baggage into his sleek Mercedes-Benz. I reminded him that the film crew and my son, a medical student, would be arriving the next day. My reference to my son stimulated Dr. Lorenz to speak of his own medical studies in New York and Vienna and his continued contact with the field of medicine. He completed his medical degree primarily to please his father, a prominent Viennese surgeon. The family home is located on Adolphlorenzgasse, a street named in honor of his father. His wife of forty-seven years, Margarethe, whom her friends call Gretl, is also a physician, specializing in obstetrics and gynecology. He recalled how important the income from her practice was during the lean years while he completed his Ph.D. in Zoology at the University of Vienna and held junior faculty appointments. He was Chairman of the Psychology Department at the University of Königsberg and served in the German army as a psychiatrist, but his first love was not clinical medicine. A remarkable research career in a bold new discipline culminating in a Nobel Prize supports his self-evaluation.

The evolution of Lorenz the ethologist began with his activities as a child in Altenberg, where he spent long hours observing waterfowl. His passionate love of nature and his fascination with the behavior of the organism in its natural environment grew with each succeeding year.

Oskar Heinroth, one of the pioneers of behavior studies, helped focus this interest in natural behavior. Lorenz was impressed with Heinroth's observation that graylag geese, reared from the egg by humans, would follow them as they would their natural parents. Lorenz was even more intrigued when Heinroth noted that as the geese grew sexually mature, humans became the objects of their "social" attention even while they were involved in normal mating with other geese. Obsessed with these observations, Lorenz had to extend them. He performed experiment after experiment, checking and rechecking this seemingly bizarre phenomenon with geese, shell parakeets, muscovy ducks, and his old "experimental subject," the jackdaw. He confirmed Heinroth's observations and fixed the precise period in development and conditions under which this "imprinting" would occur.

He extended these observations further as they related to programing in the genome. Are a fixed number of responses "innate"? How rigid are they? Which stimuli in the environment trigger them? What about gross behavior such as aggression? What about territoriality? What are the parameters within this "innately" programed sequence? Naturally, such a re-examination of the importance of biological determinism against a backdrop of radical behaviorism and its environmental determinism prevalent in the United States in the 1940's and 1950's led to consistent discrediting of Lorenz's observations by many psychologists, still evident today.

His book, *On Aggression* (1966) brought this theory to the attention of an even wider audience, incurring much criticism, as he asked: Is aggressivity "innate" in man? Will it occur without provocation? Can territoriality really explain man's complex behavior?

He responded to the critic he respected the most, Daniel Lehrman, in a publication of which he is enormously proud, *The Evolution and Modification of Behavior* (Lorenz, 1965).

Other concerns were beginning to preoccupy him. He could cope with the effects of genetic programing, instinctive behavior, and natural selection as he continued his remarkable observations of lower organisms in their natural setting. But what about man? What has gone wrong? Unconvinced by growth in technology, science, and the healing arts, Lorenz increasingly feels that the problem involves the evolution of man's values rather than his biological structure. He believes these distorted values are leading to overpopulation, the threat of nuclear destruction, genetic decay, the waning of deep emotions, increased vulnerability to authoritarian control, ecological crises, war and hatred among men in general. In his most recent book, *Civilized Man's Eight Deadly Sins* (1974), he lays this out in a dramatic, didactic tone that will surprise the readers of his gentle *King Solomon's Ring* (1962) and *Man Meets Dog* (1964).

He believes that science no longer has time to work these problems out methodically. He feels that the scientist must take a stand—and take a stand he does! Understandably, this book, too, will evoke considerable criticism, as he attacks behaviorism and speculates on the impact of phylogenetically derived behavior patterns on man.

One perplexing problem which Professor Lorenz mentioned to me at dinner one evening was the charges of racism leveled against him in recent years.

An article in the *Journal of the New York Academy of Sciences* (1973) summarized the dispute. Psychiatrists Peter Breggin and Frederic Wertham criticized

the award, while anthropologist Margaret Mead defended Lorenz, charging that he was the victim of systematic persecution. Elizabeth Hall, in *Psychology
Today* (1974), summed up the issue:

> Lorenz has never denied that at one time he found some
> of the Nazi theories attractive. He told journalist Vic Cox, "Of
> course I believed that some good might come of the Nazis.
> Much better, more intelligent men than I believed that,
> among them my father. That they meant murder when they
> said 'selection' was beyond the belief of anyone. I never
> believed the Nazi ideology, but like a fool I thought I could
> improve them, lead them to something better. It was a naïve
> error."

This leads us to the disturbing question: To what
degree can the involvement of the scientist in a political movement be held against him when he subsequently admits that the involvement was naïve?

I asked Professor Lorenz to respond to questions
concerning his own involvement with the Nazis. Exhausted by the repeated stirring of reactions, particularly after he received the Nobel Prize, he apparently
feels that further comment is useless. In a letter to me
dated August 13, 1974, concerning this issue for inclusion in this volume, he illustrates his dismay in the following comment:

> On the other hand, I definitely do not want to answer in
> public the questions you raised. If I do, it will appear as if I
> feel the need to apologize, which I do not. If my stupidity of
> trying to appeal to the Nazis can be atoned for by anything,
> it is by standing for opinions which I believe correct, even if
> they make me highly unpopular with present-day readers.

To add to Professor Lorenz's remarks, I can only say
that I sense that he passionately believes in the values
he espouses today. I feel that he will stand up to this
criticism, and all criticism—not engaging in *ad homi-
nem* attacks on his critics, perhaps rethinking or even

changing some of his ideas in light of criticism—but he will go on to attack what he considers dangerous and destructive and to stand up for his beliefs. Being one of the first behavioral scientists to become a Nobel laureate has in no way affected Lorenz, even in unpopular resolves. Perhaps that is characteristic of Nobel Prize laureates. Certainly, it is characteristic of Konrad Lorenz.

Some Observations on the Dialogue Technique and an Overview

The present book is the ninth in a series based on dialogues with some of the world's outstanding contributors to psychology. To avoid possible misunderstanding of the goals of the dialogue style used in this volume, some perspective may be of value. Designed as an innovative teaching device, the series was launched in 1957 with completion of dialogues with the late Carl Jung and Ernest Jones, supported by a grant from the Fund for the Advancement of Education. The series is being continued under a grant from the National Science Foundation. A basic purpose of the project is to produce for teaching purposes a series of films which introduce the viewer to outstanding contributors to the field of psychology and human behavior. We hope that these films may also serve as documents of increasing value to the history of the behavioral sciences.*

The books in this series are based on edited transcripts of the dialogue, including audiotaped discussions as well as the contents of the films. These dialogues are designed to introduce the reader to the contributor's major ideas and points of view, conveying

* The films are distributed by Macmillan Films, Inc., 34 Mac Questen Pkwy. So., Mt. Vernon, New York 10550.

through the extemporaneousness of the dialogue style a feeling for the personality of the contributor.

When we completed the first book in the series based on dialogues with Jung and Jones (Evans, 1964) we thought the word "conversation" could best be used in the title to describe the process and content. We soon discovered that this implied to potential readers something a bit more casual and superficial than we had intended. Even though we emphasize spontaneity in our dialogues, this should not detract from the significance of the content. A more detailed description of the philosophy and techniques of this project is reported elsewhere (Evans, 1969c).

Since the questions are intended to reflect many of the published writings of the interviewee, it might be expected that a comprehensive summary of his work is evoked. The selectivity necessary in developing the questions within a limited time interval does not always provide the basis for an inclusive summary, such as are found in many secondary sources. But we are using this teaching technique in an effort to discourage so many of our students today from becoming increasingly dependent on secondary sources. The material—films and books—resulting from our dialogues provides a novel "original source" exposure which may, in turn, stimulate the viewer or reader to go back to the original writings.

It is my intention that these "dialogues" reflect a constructive, novel method of teaching with my role as interviewer not being primarily one of critical challenger. Using such dialogues primarily as a background for critical examination of the views of the participants must be left to another type of project. In fact, I expect that some of the interviewees in this project would not have participated if they had sensed that it would become primarily a critical attack on their work.

As was the case with subjects of the earlier books in

the series, Jung and Jones (Evans, 1964), Fromm (Evans, 1966), Erikson (Evans, 1969a), Skinner (Evans, 1968), Arthur Miller (Evans, 1969b), Allport * (Evans, 1970), and Piaget (Evans, 1973), it is hoped that the dialogue presentation allows the reader to be introduced to or to re-examine some of Konrad Lorenz's ideas in a relatively informal situation. It should be pointed out, however, that in his writings he has the opportunity to rewrite and polish until he deems the finished product satisfactory. In the spontaneity of our discussion, he is called upon to develop his ideas extemporaneously, and in a language that is not his native tongue. I hope that this element of spontaneity may present more of the "man behind the book" while losing none of the ideas central to his thought.

Preservation of this naturalness of communication is essential to the purposes of each volume of this series, and few liberties have been taken with the basic content of Professor Lorenz's responses. However, some editorial license had to be exercised to shift effectively from oral to printed communication in the service of accuracy, readability, and clarity. In spite of the editing, it was a pleasant surprise to review our hours of discussion and realize how few deletions and alterations were required.

To expand the reader's knowledge of Lorenz and his ideas, a section has been included of previously published papers, perhaps less well-known, and approved by Professor Lorenz for inclusion. This section is introduced by Donald Campbell, Professor of Psychology at Northwestern University and currently President of the American Psychological Association. Dr. Campbell has written a challenging paper which integrates the entire section and adds much to our understanding of Lorenz and his work.

* We were very pleased when one book in this series, *Gordon Allport: The Man and His Ideas*, was honored by receiving the 1971 American Psychological Foundation Media Award in the Book Category.

I / *Ethology and Imprinting*

Overview | *In this section, Professor Lorenz
and I discuss the evolution of his contributions to
ethology for which he received the Nobel Prize. He de-
fines ethology and tells how he first became interested
in this approch to studying organisms. We also discuss
his observations on imprinting and conclude this section as he reacts to how fetishisms and even Erik Erikson's identity construct might be analogous to imprinting in some respects.*

EVANS: You, Nikolaas Tinbergen, and Karl von
Frisch, of course, have been heralded for your innovative approach to the study of behavior known as ethology. The ethologist observes the characteristic behavior patterns of an animal as it forages for food, defends
itself, courts its mate, and rears its young. This research
is carried on unobtrusively, in the animal's natural environment. At this point, Professor Lorenz, it might be
very interesting to hear exactly what you mean by the
term "ethology."

LORENZ: Ethology is nothing new. In method, in
approach, in the questions it asks, it is a comparative

3

science; the same as all other branches of biology, except that it focuses primarily on behavior. Why these questions have not been applied to behavior much sooner is a good question.

EVANS: The thing that is intriguing is the way you use the term "behavior." Of course, in psychology, we usually consider behavior as being an observable and a measurable response. That is, when we talk about a unit of behavior, we are focusing on something that is observable. When you're discussing behavior, you're also focusing on the observable responses of the organism, are you not?

LORENZ: Yes. But, I should say that observable is entirely different from measurable. Observing comes first; measuring comes later. Suppose you try to describe the workings of a very complicated machine which you have never seen. Let's suppose a Martian arrives on earth and sees a car—to him, a strange sight. He would first make an inventory of the parts—the crankshaft, the carburetor, the pistons, and so on. He wouldn't start measuring until he knows the interaction of the parts. The German philosopher Windelband (1894) said that every science, every natural science, proceeds in three phases: the idiographic, the systematic, and the nomothetic. Idiographic means describing the individual's outer form, the picture. The second stage is systematizing what you have seen—counting the recognizable behavior patterns, for instance. The nomothetic phase refers to discovering the laws which prevail in the multiplicity of phenomena and determine the regularities which you find in systematizing. There has been much too much emphasis lately on developing methods of quantification; in fact, to the point of forgetting the observations that must come first.

EVANS: So, when you use the phrase "behavioral biology" you are arguing for observation in the tradition of Darwin.

LORENZ: Certainly.

EVANS: Being a bit more precise now, what is uniquely characteristic of ethology as a branch of biology?

LORENZ: I wouldn't know of a single question or one single method applied to a pattern of behavior which could not be applied in exactly the same form to the structure and function of an order. Of course, this attitude implies that we are quite convinced that everything we see in the overt behavior of the animal is the function of an internal structure; a structure and function of the central nervous system. And, as you know, even in terms of definition, you cannot draw a sharp line between structure and function. The two concepts merge into each other, and the harder you try, the less you succeed in distinguishing the two. And so I have given up trying to define what behavior is. For instance, if you watch a baboon trying to solve an insight problem, you will see him looking at the box, looking around, scratching his head. Mostly, he thinks by moving. In a young chimp, you may only see his eyes moving. He also scratches himself. And in an old, experienced chimp, you may see that he just sits and thinks about it. So much goes on internally, which comes out five minutes later in the form of overt, observable behavior. Now, I wouldn't know where to draw the line between internal thought, which is not directly observable, and behavior, which is observable and is the result of that thinking. This dilemma results from a highly complicated biological process.

EVANS: You mentioned the methods of ethology. What are some of the specific methods that the ethologist uses as he gathers his data?

LORENZ: Perhaps I can illustrate this by the way I became interested in ethology. When I was a small boy of about ten, I was interested in evolution. I read a book by Wilhelm Bölsche which mentioned the first bird—the archaeopteryx—the bird with wings like a bird, with a tail like a lizard, with a pair of feathers on each vertebra—and I realized that this evolution idea might fit anywhere; that perhaps insects with their cemented bodies were derived from earthworms. I guessed quite correctly, in fact. I thought then that the most interesting thing on earth was the study of evolution. And as I read Bölsche's book, I concluded zoology and paleontology were the things to study. My father wanted me to study medicine, and, being a nice obedient boy, I did study medicine. That turned out to have been my good luck because the professor of anatomy was a really great comparative anatomist and an even greater comparative embryologist. I learned from him how to reconstruct the genealogical tree of animals by comparing the similarity and dissimilarity of characteristics of modern forms, of recent forms. Even then I knew a lot about animal behavior, particularly about ducks—I was crazy about ducks from early childhood. I knew a lot about duck behavior. I would have been very stupid indeed not to have seen that this comparative method could be applied to behavior as well. Certain courting movements of the drake, for instance, are characteristic of a species, of a genus, of a family, even of an order of ducks, and are distributed in exactly the same way as morphological characteristics, as characters of form and structure. I became fascinated with this kind of study of behavior, and thought I had invented it, discovered it. Much later, I found that old Oskar Heinroth knew all about it, but neither of us at the time knew that Charles Otis Whitman had applied exactly the same methods ten or fifteen years before Heinroth. So the first real comparative ethological study of the phylogeny of behavior by comparative methods was a paper published by Charles Otis Whitman in Woods Hole, Massachusetts, in the year 1898.

This was actually my way of discovering how ethology originated, because neither Heinroth nor Whitman were psychologists. They were just plain zoologists and taxonomists. They wanted to find out the blood relationship between two species of pigeons, in Whitman's case; or ducks, in Heinroth's. They used all forms of behavior—courtship, signal movements, and so on—as taxonomic characters to show that the mallard and the American black duck are much more closely related to each other than they are to others of their own kind. Neither Heinroth nor Whitman fully realized the importance of their discovery that behavior patterns are characteristic of a species and also of larger taxonomic orders. They were very sure of the validity of their discovery even without realizing that it went head-on against the theories of the great psychological schools, the instinct school of psychology, as well as against the behaviorists. They just didn't know that. It is often said that I am the father of ethology, but that's not true. I only know there is considerable merit in discovering an over-all law of nature, and some smaller merit in discovering its importance. My scientific merit lies in discovering Whitman and Heinroth.

EVANS: One infers, in reading your work, that you always focus on studying the organism in its natural habitat. Is that a correct inference?

LORENZ: That is a correct inference. You cannot understand any form of life, any structure, without understanding its use and its interaction with the environment. You cannot understand the streamlined form of a shark without knowing that this form is made to cleave through the water with minimum resistance. You cannot understand the bill of a shoveler duck unless you know what the duck feeds on. And that's true of any system—the organism and its environment are one system. You cannot understand the structure of the piston of an automobile engine unless you know that it contains valves, and you cannot understand the valves unless you know how the cam shaft lifts the valve—the inlet valve in the top of the cylinder that sucks mix through the carburetor—in other words, the parts of a system can be understood *in toto* or not at all. I'm often accused of being against quantification, not able to measure, not able to experiment, and so on. My assertion is only that you have to start with the complete system and work your way down to the parts, and not focus on one part or remove that part from the engine to study it. Again, to use my simile of the automobile engine, that's like dismantling the part easiest to dismantle, see a nut and a bolt, then turn your back on the system and try to resynthesize the system out of the nut and the bolt. That can't be done.

EVANS: The methodological problem we have in naturalistic observation is the objectivity of the observer and verification of the observer's response.

LORENZ: Yes.

EVANS: And of course, scientists are always interested in verifying observation. If you moved into a natural setting to observe an animal, and then reported on your observations, would that be satisfactory? Would that be considered satisfactory data in the field of ethology, or must there be some form of verification of your observation?

LORENZ: Quantification is always the last word in verification. Just seeing a thing, discovering a thing as a function of sight perception is what you might call a hunch producer. It produces an inspired guess, but this remains a guess until you have verified it. That's where the whole logic of scientific discovery comes in—in verification. The discoverer is often a poet. Great poets discover a lot of things, but that's still only poetry and not science. And it's in verification that the experiment, and, particularly, quantification, comes in. To prove something, you have to quantify. In our most holistic approaches to the social behavior of geese—which is quite a complicated system—we have already arrived at the point where we have to feed our data into computers. We can no longer calculate it by simple recording. In particular, motivational analysis in turn requires correlational analysis. It is the only reliable way to verify relationships. But verify what? Verification means that you prove something you suspect, or guess, or have seen.

EVANS: There are a lot of different ways of verifying. Are you not confronted with a variety of verification procedures in ethology?

LORENZ: There are many different ways of verification, and there are many kinds of experiments you can conduct. However, one point that Tinbergen always makes is to change as little as possible of the normal environment so you know that the one thing you have changed is really the cause of the change in behavior you have observed. That's what Hess (1962) has called the unobtrusive experiment. The Tinbergen school excels in the unobtrusive experiment. Their work on the digger wasp, and Tiet Sevensten's work on the stickleback, are exact physiological experiments involving quantifiable verification of observed phenomena.

EVANS: Donald Campbell (1966) has demonstrated the importance of unobtrusive measures in human research in social psychology. He has focused on this very heavily, arguing that the observer can affect the environment. Now the real question is: are there enough unobtrusive measures to really get at the process of validating observation? Isn't it difficult to determine useful unobtrusive measures? Certainly it's true in studying human behavior. Finding good unobtrusive measures is very difficult.

LORENZ: I should say that the ethologist uses what you might call a detour—a cowardly evasion of difficulties by concentrating on simple elements. You know it's always a good rule, in studying behavior, to investigate

9

the phenomenon in its simplest form. That's why we study aggressivity in some species of fish which, although comparatively simple creatures, are still very aggressive, or we study bond behavior in geese. Of course, if things become as complicated as they do in human social behavior, I wouldn't know of any method other than statistically drawn samples, hoping that individual differences would thereby be eliminated. But I still feel that the statistical approach to understanding phenomena is only a substitute for determining the real cause and effect; because if you can directly affect the cause and directly observe the effect, you don't need statistics. The prediction ought to fit 100 per cent, and in our simple element, it often does.

EVANS: Now, getting back to a point you made earlier: you mentioned that the philosopher Windelband talks about idiographic, systematic, and nomothetic approaches. It's interesting that an American psychologist, Gordon Allport (Evans, 1971), took Windelband very seriously and focused specifically on the distinction between the idiographic and nomothetic approaches. He saw the idiographic approach as searching for the unique characteristic of the individual organism in contrast to the nomothetic approach, which involves searching for general laws that apply to a larger group. In studying animal behavior, can you really focus on idiographic patterns? In other words, are there certain behaviors that are unique to a *single* animal?

LORENZ: It is very interesting that you should ask that question, because this is exactly what we are now trying to do. It's wrong to arrive at the general law first, but every textbook covers the general part first and the special part later. We now know enough about the range of behavior patterns of normal geese to concentrate on the differences between individuals, which, of course, becomes idiographic in the most special and pure sense of the word. And you find that what emerges from this study is something like a very simplified model of characterology. For two years now, one of my students has been studying communication patterns among four geese and counting behavior patterns evident among them as they relate to each other. By making histograms of how often one goose threatens and another goose escapes, you find there are quantitative differences; although the behavior patterns themselves are all the same, one goose may excel in bond behavior and in fearlessness, but be very weak in aggressivity. It's a placid goose. And it's a very likable goose. To illustrate this, one goose has a very low threshold of both escape behavior and aggressive behavior. It's a funny combination—an aggressive coward—and this chap is what many normal persons would term vicious because he attacks suddenly from behind, bites, and runs away, and is very poor in bond behavior. He is a loner but he breeds. This combination of quantitative differences gives you a very clearly described character of a goose, but describing the character of this goose is confoundedly anthropomorphic. And this, of course, is only a very simple model. But we think that by using the same method you could perhaps study some other highly social creatures, particularly mammals, of which very few species have been investigated thoroughly. For instance, a highly interesting and easily accessible animal is the wild pig. In my new location, we have a large pen of wild pigs and we shall try to repeat the same studies on them as were done on geese. That's our program.

EVANS: So, in a sense, the search that the psychologist makes for the unique characteristics of the individual—arguing that it destroys individuality to try to apply general principles to all individuals—is a parallel to your observations at the lower animal level. When you say you're being anthropomorphic here, you're really finding measurable, unique characteristics of lower organisms that make them uniquely identifiable.

LORENZ: My young pupil Jane Packard has done that very thing in another interesting experiment with geese. We compared the judgments made on four geese by persons gifted in Gestalt perception with the quantitative measures of the same four geese. The individual observers merely stated their subjective impressions: this goose was nice and placid, or vicious, and so on. And as a control, of course, they were unaware of the judgments of the other observers using objective quantifiable measures. When they compared notes, it was very interesting to find how precisely the individual subjective judgments corresponded to the quantitative judgments. This was fascinating work.

EVANS: Professor Lorenz, I believe that you introduced a very intriguing term into the language of ethology: the term "imprinting." What exactly do you mean by imprinting?

LORENZ: Before giving a definition, I'd better tell you how the phenomenon of imprinting was discovered. Whitman and Heinroth reared young birds. They were both particularly interested in the ontogeny of behavior, so they studied young birds reared by "foster parents." Some were reared by them personally, some by other related species. They found that in many cases these birds could not be bred because they reacted sexually only to the species of the "foster parent," not to their own. This proved to be absolutely irreversible. I observed this in my own third jackdaw. I occupied myself a great deal with that bird while it was young, and later it turned out to be sexually fixated on humans. So the fixation of an innate behavior pattern is one characteristic of imprinting. The second is its irreversibility. And the third is that it is effected during a comparatively short phase in the individual life of the animal. For instance, as Hess (1973) has shown, the "following" response of a duckling is fixated on its object at about the seventeenth hour after hatching. The curve of imprintability is a very steep one with a maximum at seventeen hours. At twenty and twenty-three hours it is already down. Imprinting has been studied extensively in the "following mother" response of ducklings and chickens. There's a great difference between the two because imprinting merges into any kind of learning which can be restricted to a period. I'm sorry to say that domestic chickens, on which many experiments have been done, are not good subjects for the demonstration of imprinting. The term "imprinting" was coined mainly with sexual behavior in mind. All of the characteristics of imprinting I described were validated by a number of investigators. However, some of my observations have been particularly challenged by Patrick Bateson's (1964) observations of the following mother response in chicks. I grant you that the following mother response in chicks is not a typical example of imprinting and is more or less learned. In fact, there are other examples of behaviors which have some of the same characteristics as imprinting: Mark Konishi (1964) has demonstrated that song learning in birds is also restricted to a very short period of time and is irreversible. It cannot be repeated later, nor caught up with if that period is missed. Nor can it be changed. So there again, you cannot give an all-inclusive definition because some of the characteristics of imprinting are visible in any given instance, while others are not. The typical imprinting, restricted to a certain period and irreversible, is sexual imprinting. But, contrary to Bateson's assertion, I've never said that all birds imprint. In fact, in my very first mention of imprinting (I looked it up recently) I called attention to the fact that while it is relatively easy to sexually fixate jackdaws on humans, it is nearly impossible to do it with magpies, even though they are closely related to jackdaws.

EVANS: You're really saying then that imprinting as a phenomenon is limited to certain species and to a certain specific time period during the developmental process.

LORENZ: Yes.

EVANS: And only to specific objects. And you feel primarily this has been demonstrated as a sexual area. Is that correct?

LORENZ: Exactly. And you know that before imprinting was called imprinting, very long ago—I think it was about 1900—Brun, a Swiss physician, called attention to imprinting in ants. The slave-keeping hinges on the fact that the ant gets imprinted on the species present when it hatches out of its chrysalis. You can transplant chrysalises of one species of ants into the nest of another ant species, and if the chrysalis is accepted and the ant hatches out in that strange ant hill, it responds to that species, and not its own. That's a typical case of imprinting. Imprinting has also been demonstrated in various parasitic wasp species. Caterpillars of certain moths are parasitized, and if the larva from one caterpillar is transplanted into the species of another, the wasp emerging will eventually lay its eggs into the species of the caterpillar out of which it emerged. If you wish, you can call it a tradition. Thorpe (1956) produced strains of Hymenoptera which, after many generations, laid their eggs into the wrong kind of moth.

EVANS: Are there any implications of this concept for human behavior? That's a very, very big leap, of course, I realize that.

LORENZ: That is a big leap. I think that this is an unverifiable statement, but if you read the work of a very old and almost forgotten psychiatrist, Krafft-Ebing

(1950), on fetishisms, you get the impression that some of his patients' behaviors were analogous to imprinting. You can't validate such observations, of course.

EVANS: Would you expand the concept of imprinting to something like the follower-leader relationship sociologists have studied? For example, weak members of the gang will attach themselves to a strong member of the gang, follow him around, and always do his bidding.

LORENZ: Well, one of the most interesting aspects of imprinting is that the process doesn't fixate on an individual, but on a species. In Dr. Schutz's (1963b) experiments with ducks, in which he reared mallards with shelldrakes, for instance—the mallards later tried to mate with shelldrakes, but not with their foster siblings, because these species have an incest-inhibiting taboo. I don't think imprinting ever affects the responses to an individual, except perhaps in the case of follow-the-mother responses of ducklings and goslings. But if you carry this phenomenon to the human level, I think the closest you get to imprinting is that critical phase when the adolescent gets skeptical about the parental culture and casts around for new causes to embrace. He attaches himself to some ideal cause, but as in imprinting, his ideal cause leads him to disappointment. Such frustration affects this young person to the extent that he never again attaches himself to another ideal with the same emotional strength which he exhibited toward his first love.

EVANS: This is, in a way, analogous to what Erik Erikson (1963, 1968) talks about in the adolescent's striving for identity.

LORENZ: Very much so. I think that in this particular respect, Erik Erikson has some of the most profound insights ever gained into human nature. In my opinion, Erik Erikson is one of the great seers of truth about human nature. But these are truths which can't be verified. You can only understand them and say, "Yes, yes, it is so, I feel that myself." But just try to verify them by quantification! I defy you to do that!

EVANS: I'm afraid that really can't be done.

II / *Ethological Interpretations of Motivation*

Overview / *In this section, Professor Lorenz
and I discuss how the ethological approach to motivation differs from the more traditional psychological interpretation. We discuss the source of social motivation
such as social approval (learned or unlearned), instincts, and the work of Harry Harlow in this field.*

EVANS: As you know, Professor Lorenz, throughout
the history of psychology, motivation has been an area
of considerable interest to psychologists. In our typical
introductory psychology textbooks we define motivation as "all conditions which arouse, direct, and sustain
the organism." Most psychological theories of motivation center around the homeostatic model—which really comes from physiology—that as needs develop ten-
sions, there is a movement in the organism toward
tension reduction: a state of balance or equilibrium is
sought. In our motivational theories we talk about the
so-called primary drives. A primary drive is part of the
inherited nature of the organism, it is universal, and has
a physiological component whose satisfaction is necessary for the maintenance of the organism. Hunger and

19

thirst are examples of such drives. Other layers of motivation develop through learning, to which we refer as secondary or tertiary motives. These are usually social in nature, and include achievement, social approval, and affiliation. How do you feel about such a model? Does that make any sense to you?

LORENZ: Well, I'm afraid the ethological model of motivation is basically different. One of the great-grandfathers of ethology, Wallace Craig (1918), distinguished between appetites and aversions. There are two different types of behavior, one of which is motivated by the animal's (I'll put it anthropomorphically) wanting to do something. Practically every fixed motor pattern, every instinctive movement, as we call it, wants out. A dog that hasn't run for a long time will run. A rat in the activity wheel will run without getting anywhere, because the motor pattern which lies unused for some time irritates the animal. Not releasing a motor pattern for some time, "damming it up," as we say, not only lowers the threshold of releasing stimuli, but it also excites the animal to seek that stimulus situation. This fact was first discovered by Charles Otis Whitman and later confirmed by Wallace Craig, who, as I indicated, coined the concept of appetites and aversions. Now, with regard to appetites—for instance, the appetite for copulation—it seems to me a rather farfetched explanation to say that the animal copulates in order to get rid of the internal stimulus and that the reinforcing reward lies in the relief of tension. On the other hand, with the type of behavior which Wallace Craig calls aversions, the reinforcing reward does lie in the relief of tension. You can speak of appetite for quiescence, as Monika Meyer-Holzapfel did, to account for much animal and human behavior. Although the concept that the main reinforcing factor is relief of tension may be true of a large portion of animal and human actions, it's not the whole story.

Ethological Interpretations of Motivation

EVANS: Are you referring now to the late Clark Hull's (1943) drive reduction model?

LORENZ: Yes. There are, of course, a multiplicity of motives, both internal and external. For example, while aggressivity, in my opinion, is something coming from within, it can also be triggered from without by, let's say, general frustration and repression of the organism by its environment. There's no doubt that the individual is more aggressive in a hostile environment than in a kindly and permissive one. However, as I said earlier, it is dangerous to conceptualize in an oversimplified manner.

EVANS: For discussion purposes, let's consider hunger, a single primary drive, so I can illustrate the application of the criteria of some psychologists for a primary drive. First of all, hunger is physiological in nature; secondly, the organism must satisfy the hunger drive or perish; thirdly, it's universal—found in all organisms regardless of species or culture—and finally, it is part of the inherited nature of the organism. So hunger meets all the particular criteria of a single primary drive. Do you find this a useful way of classifying primary drives?

LORENZ: No, I don't. Not even hunger is as simple as such criteria would indicate—particularly with animals—because the motor patterns in acquiring food have their own specific measurable motivations. If you feed mice to a cat, the cat will stalk, jump upon, kill, and eat four or five mice to satisfy its eating drive. However, under normal conditions, a cat stalks for hours, misses a great number of "kill" attempts and waits—sitting before a mousehole, perhaps—for hours and hours. The animal needs such activities much more than the actual death bite, the killing bite. A large number of these activities must be abreacted—I don't like the word, but it's the best that comes to mind to define this. However, if you feed that cat a great number of mice, you will find that after repeating that sequence four times it will still kill a certain number of mice. And then, surprisingly enough, it will go on stalking mice at a distance while other mice are running over its paws. And it will not kill any more, but will go on stalking for a long time—sitting and watching. These activities express a whole range of motives that involve what you would call the hunger drive. These behaviors are, of course, enhanced if the cat is hungry, but if the cat's hunger is satisfied, the drives for jumping, killing, and stalking are still not extinguished.

EVANS: Motivation at the human level is even more complicated, especially when we are concerned with secondary or learned social motives. For example, if we watch the development of a child, we find that his eating behavior is conditioned by many cultural patterns. The hunger drive becomes less and less a natural response. We see the modification of a primary drive by learning. Don't you believe that the need for social approval marks an even bigger jump away from primary motivation?

LORENZ: I would say less of a jump, because the need for approval, the need for being accepted, is on a much lower level of complexity. It's much more like the primary hunger drive than a socially conditioned variation of such a primary drive. You can attach to any primal sense the rewarding functions of a number of conditioned responses of first, second, third, or fourth order in this complex system of motivations. For example, just think how powerful motivations such as money are. Yet money is only a conditioned stimulus in that you have learned that you can get some primal satisfaction out of it. But the need for social approval is obviously very deeply seated, and is, I am quite sure, instinctively programed. For example, the need for social approval is diabolically exploited as the approved method of brainwashing. The first thing the brainwasher does is to withhold social approval, so that everything the victim says causes astonished disapproval. This disturbs the individual emotionally to such an extent that after a while he'll do anything to obtain a kindly smile. He will go to any length—even to the point of sacrificing his most cherished beliefs—to get this kind of social approval. We can observe analogous responses in many animals. For example, it has been demonstrated that chimpanzees will actually die if they don't get the feedback of social bond behavior.

EVANS: This introduces an important distinction between what some psychologists believe and what the ethologist observes. They would argue that the need for social approval evolves through learning in the development and socialization of the child. You're suggesting that this is part of the inherited nature of the organism. Earlier you used the term "anthropomorphism." Isn't there danger of anthropomorphism in the perception of social approval in animals? What appears to be social approval-motivated behavior in an animal might be merely a function of attributing human qualities to the animal.

LORENZ: Well, this is a very fundamental question and, of course, much can be said on this subject. But I'd say that this need for social contact begins at the moment the child recognizes its mother as an individual. René Spitz (1965) has shown conclusively that if an infant is deprived of a personal bond with the mother, which is established a few months after birth, the child will resent strangers. If, in an orphanage, where nurses serve as mother figures, this bond is broken in the course of the routine change of duty, the child will try to form a new bond with the second nurse. Then the second mother figure is rotated and the infant tries to establish the bond a third time. When it loses the third mother figure, the child withdraws and loses the faculty to form further social contacts. This is certainly on a precultural level, and may result in the development of autistic children. The symptoms of this acquired mental illness are very similar to what is generally called infantile schizophrenia. Social animals treated in similar ways yield exactly the same results. Early social isolation can easily produce an autistic goose which will later refuse to form social contacts. If you put two such birds in a pen together, they sit in opposite corners, back-to-back, ignoring each other. This may not be homologous, but it is at least analogous.

EVANS: Of course, some psychologists believe the work of René Spitz suggests that the infant, in a situation of this kind, is responding to lack of maternal affection rather than to lack of "social contact."

LORENZ: Yes.

EVANS: The jump, however, is a very subtle one: from the need for maternal affection, or even social contact, to social approval. Now, you're suggesting that this need for affection, or social contact, is a very early form of social approval. Is that correct?

LORENZ: Yes. I'd say that one merges with the other, because, as the child moves out of the family, breaks away from the mother, and begins to develop relationships with other adults and children, its need for social contact merges imperceptibly with the increasingly complex social involvements and commitments.

EVANS: As you know, we often use the phrase "socialization process" to describe the organism's movement from being dominated by primary physiological drives to being dominated by various types of social needs. You're arguing here that the roots of socialization are innate.

LORENZ: Yes. I would say the widespread belief of innumerable psychologists and sociologists that everything social in the human organism is cultural and that the instinctive level is intrasocial is a fallacy. If I am convinced of anything at all, it is that this is absolutely untrue, and that, before they became human, our ancestors were social animals—highly social animals—with very much the same response to the conspecifics that we have. I think it highly probable that social intercourse is a prerequisite for reflection. Seeing your own hand, and recognizing that the other person has the same kind of hand, may be the root of thinking, "Well, I'm the same kind of thing as the man over there." I entirely disbelieve the theory that all social responses are cultural and learned. On the other hand, there is a predisposition for learned cultural response, upon which the whole cultural superstructure is built.

EVANS: So you're really saying then that the need for affection and other social needs, like approval, are inherent in the organism and have a physiological base.

LORENZ: Yes. Maybe even a homologous base.

EVANS: So we should not hesitate to suggest that what we broadly might call the hunger drive is no less primary than what we might broadly call the need for social approval.

LORENZ: Certainly not, certainly not. All these needs are programed in the same central nervous system.

EVANS: If so, we'd better start rewriting some of our introductory psychology textbooks. You've already used the term "instinct." You probably realize that, in our early efforts in psychology to come up with terms that are useful in understanding motivation, we used "instinct," but have been increasingly cautious with its use in recent years.

LORENZ: Yes, a dangerous term!

EVANS: In the 1920's, in American psychology, almost every act, every response, was termed instinctive. In fact, L. L. Bernard (1925), the sociologist, counted the various types of behavior described as instinctive, and came up with over fourteen thousand! It reached the point where, if someone twiddled his thumbs, they would say he had a thumb-twiddling instinct, and if he didn't, they would say he had a thumb-not-twiddling instinct. "Instinct" means too many things. As a result, most psychologists stopped using the term and switched to words like "drive" or "need," which they considered more definitive. Yet the term "instinct" persists in the literature. Would you drop this term? What is an instinct, as you see it?

LORENZ: First, I wouldn't drop the term, but I would use it as approved by the ethological conference to describe observable fixed motor patterns, not to define the organism's motives. Tinbergen's (1951) earlier definition of the hierarchical organization of appetitive behaviors and single motor patterns came pretty near to what was generally called an instinct, but it was considered too loose a definition. As to what you said about the assumption of instinct as a motive, like any sweeping assumption of a simple explanatory factor, it is inadmissible. However, it might be helpful to describe a fixed motor pattern in any behavior for which the origin is not clear. If the pigeon "homes"—flies home—this can be labeled a homing instinct. However, there may be a multiplicity of motor patterns operating. For instance, a bird of prey may have a bird-grabbing instinct, a bird-plucking instinct, and so on. There are many specific motivations involved in any instinct or fixed motor pattern. But they must not be labeled in terms of the function. They must be specifically observed and counted. Otherwise, the so-called explanations of a behavior are circular. As you pointed out, some of the earlier psychologists, and that goes for McDougall (1908), I am sorry to say, were guilty of making such circular assumptions very freely. If their explanations are scientific, then the next time my grandson asks me what makes the railroad train go, I'll say, "My dear child, that's the locomotive power."

EVANS: I notice that ethologists have attempted to eliminate the use of the term "innate," perhaps for the same reasons that psychologists have stopped using the term "instinct." Is that a fair assumption?

LORENZ: There is one thing to which the term "innate" can be applied and that's the information underlying behavior adapted to an environmental exigency. This means that information about this external stimulus has been set, and fed into the organism to build up the correlated adapted behavior form of ethological structure.

EVANS: Let's be a bit more specific. You talk about information being "fed" into it. Are you beginning at the level of the genome?

LORENZ: Yes.

EVANS: And you're saying there's a kind of programing here?

LORENZ: Yes. If the animal "knows" how to deal with an environmental exigency, he has "information," or is programed to respond to it.

EVANS: When you use the word "know," you don't mean it anthropomorphically. You are suggesting that a "message" is present in the DNA or subsequently in the RNA which programs the animal's reaction. Is that correct?

LORENZ: Yes. I have a message or information as to how this situation is structured, which assures my response to it. There are only two ways of getting this information into the organism. By the trial-and-error method—"tried-and-success" propensity in the genome—it incorporates the successful and eliminates the unsuccessful, or it can be fed into the organism by individual modification or learning.

EVANS: Let's go back for a moment. You refer to incorporating the successful and eliminating the unsuccessful. A response is made, it's unsuccessful and it's eliminated. What does this elimination and incorporation process consist of? Is this an adaptation process? Are we talking now of adaptation in Darwinian terms, which is reflected biochemically, in the sense that Darwin would have speculated had DNA been discovered in his time?

LORENZ: Yes, we are talking strictly in Darwinian terms, with adaptation responses reflected biochemically. This process of incorporating little bits of information which in about ten to the power of eight times reflects unsuccessful behavior. One in ten to the power of eight refers to something slightly more adaptive. The individual endowed with this new information has an enormous advantage in his efforts to adapt to the environment and in his survival potential.

EVANS: A problem the ethologist has in using the term "innate" is that he finds it insufficiently precise. So you've attempted to look at seemingly innate behavior in terms of information or programing in the genome. The organism "knows" or senses this "message" and begins to behave in terms of it. Is that correct?

LORENZ: Yes. Also, nothing is entirely innate, because however fixed the program or form of behavior in the genome, it needs the environment for its development. Only information appears to be entirely innate. The presumption is that when a form of behavior fits into a given environment, the organism has been fed information about this particular environment. Let me restate what I said earlier in a slightly different form. There are only two ways in which this can be performed: first, by an interaction of the species with its environment, the process generally called adaptation, which means forming, constructing the organism via mutation selection in Darwinian terms to make it fit the environment; or, secondly, to fit behavior to the environment by modification. Modification of behavior is learning in the widest sense of the word. So this information is either phylogenetic in origin or it originates in the learning process. The precise nature of these processes, of course, is still being researched. To my mind, it is of immense importance to know what source of information underlies the adaptive nature of a specific form of behavior. This applies to human behavior as well, because if the normal survival value of a behavior pattern is disrupted, it is highly pertinent to ask whether the disturbance is genetic, or derived from learned behavior or the conditioning, of the individual, since the measures to be taken against the disturbance are very different in the two cases.

EVANS: Let me pursue this just a little further. "Disturbed" human behavior described as schizophrenia might suffice for this purpose. There are several views currently held on the origin of schizophrenia. The genetic view is that there is an inherited predisposition to schizophrenic behavior. If an individual grows up in a schizophrenia-eliciting environment he is more likely to develop schizophrenia than the individual brought up in the same environment who is not schizophrenia-prone. Another theory holds that schizophrenia is entirely learned—as a result of environmental influences—and that there is no question of genetic proneness. Still a third point of view involves a biochemical disruption in the organism, a disruption which sets off the schizophrenia, whether it was environmentally triggered or genetically programed. But the main thing is the interplay of genetic predisposition, environmental effects, and learning in these theories. How would you apply what you just said to these views of schizophrenia?

LORENZ: I just can't say with any certainty. Of course, there are many possibilities of malfunction. Even if an individual's survival function or potential is of the highest order, there's nothing in his innate programing you cannot spoil. You can spoil it at its roots by institutionalizing a child. You can produce a complete replica of schizophrenia in an institutionalized child, as René Spitz has conclusively shown. On the other hand, how the functions of adaptation, of adaptiveness, arise, is a much more specific question. Asking how this applies to a complex illness is a difficult question altogether.

EVANS: Let's see if we can follow a similar analogy in animal behavior, like the one you used in the work of Spitz, in discussing how the need for affection leads to the need for approval, and so on. The immobility response, which some say is adaptive behavior, is certainly well known in animals and has been the subject of much research. Is it possible that we are talking here about programing for immobility—about the likelihood that this type of response is now phylogenetically carried over to the human level and becomes transposed in the form of one symptom of schizophrenia, catatonia? This would be consistent with R. D. Laing's (1965) view that some schizophrenic responses may be adaptive rather than maladaptive.

LORENZ: I simply don't know. There certainly are immobility responses of high survival value in many animals. The overt case of playing possum is a reaction of the highest survival value and many insects and higher mammals have it as well. Whether this response relates in any way to the catatonic stupor in human beings, however, I simply don't know. I find this kind of speculation difficult, anyway.

EVANS: Another area of research related to what we've been discussing is the work of Harry Harlow (1958, 1965, 1966). The whole idea of Harlow's work, as you know, was to learn something about the roots and nature of affection in the developing organism. He studied the reactions of rhesus monkeys to surrogate wire mothers and terry-cloth mothers, in contrast to the real mother. He came to the conclusion that while he could create an effective substitute mother with the use of terry cloth and a feeding mechanism, in the long run the monkeys with the substitute mothers were impotent. How do you feel about Harlow's work?

LORENZ: I think Harlow's work is excellent and ought to be pursued further. I have one criticism to make, though, which is based on my experience with mother-child relationships in geese. Harlow concludes that the rhesus babies cling more strongly to the terry-cloth mother than to their natural mother. I think this is due to the exclusively tactile nature of the contact, to a lack of vocal communication. If the surrogate mother answered the baby's questioning cry, I'm sure the baby would venture a greater distance from the mother. If the "mother" says nothing, you have to cling to "her"— that's the only comfort she provides. We came up with some very interesting information in our analogous experiment with substitute mothers for goslings. These substitute mothers had everything a mother can have— soft feathers, heat on the underside, and a large beak with an audio tape recorder planted inside reeling off goose noises. The goslings absolutely refused to react to it. I took a gosling that had rejected a dummy mother in my hand and sat with it. The gosling then started to weep, to give the distress cry, "Beep, beep, beep." I immediately said, "Come, come, come." So the baby responded with its greeting note, "Bibip, bibip." In the next experiment, we used the same dummy mother, but not with a continuous tape automatically saying "Caca, caca, caca." Instead we had a girl with a microphone responding for the dummy mother. When the gosling came out and began to weep, the dummy said "Come, come, come," in response. This was it—the simple answer to why the gosling did not respond to the continuously quacking dummy. Then Fisher and I conducted a very simple experiment. We took two goslings, marked one with a red spot on its head and the other with a yellow spot. I responded to one gosling, Dr. Fisher to the other. We repeated the experiment four times for ten minutes, and then walked away. The goslings each followed the person who had responded to its distress calls. Both heard both calls; the only difference between the two was that each gosling had received another person's voice in answer to its distress signal. So I should like to expand on Harry Harlow's terry-cloth models and make a terry-cloth model which responds when the baby goes away and asks for help.

III / *Aggression Reconsidered*

Overview / *In this section Professor Lorenz and I discuss his interpretation of the concept of aggression, or aggressivity, as he prefers to call it, and he reacts to misinterpretations of his book,* On Aggression. *We discuss his analysis of the presidential commission reports on pornography and violence, the effects of models of violence, and the reasons for the limited impact of peace models. Finally, Lorenz offers some proposals for deterring violence in today's society.*

EVANS: I would like to begin this part of our discussion with your book *On Aggression.* The word "aggression" is an emotionally loaded term—it implies violence, something extreme. Is this really what you meant to communicate in that title?

LORENZ: Your question explains why so many people have reacted emotionally and think I have written an apology for violence. When the French translation of my book came out, I realized that it ought not to have been titled *On Aggression,* but rather *On Aggressivity;* the same applies in a lesser degree to the title in English. In Freud's writing this word was translated into

35

English as "aggression" and not "aggressivity." In German, the two words are more or less synonymous; in English and French they are not. So the title should have been *On Aggressivity,* not *On Aggression,* and certainly not *On Violence!* Most of the book deals with the question of how animals avoid actual violence, actual killing, and so on. Now let's forget about that word and turn to what I once referred to, in a lecture in Honolulu, as "I-can-lick-you" behavior. If you put two little boys, two fish of one species, two roosters, two monkeys together, they will behave in the way Mark Twain described in *Tom Sawyer:* at the first meeting of Tom and his rival, Alfred Temple, they measure forces by pushing shoulders. And then one of them says "I can lick you." In a large number of species, aggression is concealed in the ritual of threat, of measuring forces. It's not the drive to kill another person, but to drive him into submission. It has to do with rank or territory, not with killing. There's no destructive instinct in that. If you observe yourself phenomenologically—what you feel when you are really, really furious at a man—you'll find that you don't want to kill him, you want to lick him until he cries "uncle"; that's not killing. In aggressive behavior, killing is always more or less an accident. There are only two species now known in which rival fighting actually results in killing the adversary. One is a species of lizard and the other is the Indian elephant. Real killing in a territorial fight has been recorded, on film, in only one other animal: the diver, a loon, a northern diver waterbird. The scarcity of the examples demonstrates very well how rare it is.

EVANS: In talking about aggressivity, we can raise the question of the degree to which the same model we've been discussing—information or programing in the genome—applies. In terms of aggressivity, would you say this same genetic programing is present?

LORENZ: If I were to write my book on aggression

again, I would make a much stricter distinction between individual intrasociety aggressivity and the collective aggressivity of one ethnic group toward the other. These may well be two very different programs. You can even see that in animals. Behavior patterns of individual animals seeking status and fighting for rank are entirely different from the behavior patterns of the group fighting a rival group. So I may have been wrong in not defining these two factors precisely enough because they are of a very different nature and a very different value. As you know, I think both kinds of aggressivity in themselves have survival value. If you are devoid of personal aggressivity, you are not actually an individual—you are everyone else's man, you have no pride in yourself. I think my friend Antony Storr (1968) has demonstrated very well the consequences of the pathological lack of individual aggressivity. On the other hand, collective militant enthusiasm, which is a prerequisite for war, is also a prerequisite for all higher human endeavor. Our enthusiasm for science is based on the same primeval instinctive roots. A man devoid of the collective-enthusiasm instinct is actually an emotional cripple. He cannot get involved in anything. But people need careful guidance in collective enthusiasm. The danger of extreme nationalism—a local bond resulting in hatred of other nations—is always present. Feelings like "I am an American" or "I am a Frenchman but he's a German" characterize this local bond. Extreme nationalism is dangerous because a man can be wholeheartedly French or English or German. But he can also be broader than that. He can be a scientist or a biologist as well as an enthusiastic musician or philanthropist. You can have many different causes, or identities, narrow ones and broad ones, in which you are deeply involved. I think that a narrow national enthusiasm, or nationalism, is a particular danger nowadays.

EVANS: You are suggesting that there is programing leading to individual aggressivity that is different from the one relating to collective, or group, aggressivity. A layer of social reinforcement is also involved in directing the pattern of aggressivity, or any other instinct at the human level, is it not?

LORENZ: It's always there. There's nothing in human behavior—nothing in your behavior or in mine, not a twitch of the nose, not a movement of the lips, not an intimation—that is not influenced by our cultural environment. All human behavior is ritualized; unritualized behavior is obscene. Scratching, picking one's nose, yawning, stretching—not to mention more improper things—are unritualized behaviors. If a man fails to conform to normal, prescribed social ritualization, he's obviously hostile. If a friend suddenly walks into the room without a smile, without looking at you, without taking cognizance of you, your first thought is, "My God, I've offended him because he's become hostile." In social intercourse, everything, every little motion, is ritualized. So, of course, this has become second nature to us. Man, inherently, is a creature of culture and so if I say there are innate programs underlying all our social behavior, this does not mean that there's not a culturally determined superstructure on it.

EVANS: You're really saying it's not a question of the principle of innate programing applied to aggressivity alone, but to all types of social behavior expressed in individual or collective form. In developing this notion in your book, *On Aggression,* you selected aggressivity as the focus. You could have selected status-seeking behavior, or, for that matter, any other social behavior.

LORENZ: Exactly.

EVANS: So you don't think there is anything, at least theoretically, special about the properties of aggressivity?

LORENZ: With nuclear weapons all around, aggressivity seems to me to be one of the most dangerous motivations at the present time. But, as you say, aggressivity is only one among many behavior patterns. More detrimental behavior patterns are motivated by sex than by aggressivity. Of course, the innate origins of every motive have to be understood by the responsible, cultured human being because he must know the horse on which he rides. I wrote this book about aggression because I think it's particularly important for us to know about one of our dangerous tendencies—the tendency to collective enthusiasm against other men organized by an equally collective enthusiasm. However, anxiety is at least as dangerous and as threatening. The effects of a free-floating anxiety may be incalculable. Someone who knows more about it than I do ought to write a volume on anxiety, to parallel my book on aggression.

EVANS: Let's get a little more specific concerning your work on aggression, or aggressivity. One thing that has troubled some readers of your work is that you appear to believe that aggressive behavior can be spontaneous: that aggression will appear in animals in game-like situations without actual provocation—aggressive "games." Logically, one might say that the basis for aggression would be some adaptive function such as a reaction to frustration, but you seem to be suggesting that aggressive behavior will emerge without provocation.

LORENZ: I'm convinced of that. I cannot prove it very well in man, but I can in certain animals. Aggression—aggressivity—follows all the rules of threshold-lowering and appetitive behavior. You can see an animal looking for trouble. A man can do that, too, of course. I'm quite sure that the laws, formal and informal, of human societies serve as coercive mechanisms in turning aggression into prescribed channels. Still, the same relationship—between the internal drive welling up and the higher centers sitting on it—restricts aggressivity, as it does most other instinctive behavior patterns. A strong argument in favor of this assumption can be found in observations of primitive tribes like the Maika Indians on the Orinoko or the Australian aborigines. Also, you find highly elaborate culture patterns reflected in what you call socialization of young children, which conducts aggressivity into harmless channels.

EVANS: Let's move to a contemporary scene in the United States, where two drives are singled out: sex and violence. We have had presidential commissions on pornography and on violence. It's interesting that the Commission on Obscenity and Pornography (1970) concluded that any sexual excitation aroused by pornography is, by and large, harmless, and that it would be ludicrous to endanger our system of liberties by censoring or banning most pornography. On the other hand, the National Commission on the Causes and Prevention of Violence (1969) felt that the portrayal of violence can be a very destructive model, that we should attempt to eliminate violence on television and in film. How do you regard these conclusions?

LORENZ: I would generally agree that the presentation of sex and violence has two effects. Julian Huxley wrote, nearly seventy years ago, that these activities are, at one and the same time, self-stimulating and self-exhausting. Of course, aggressivity is self-rewarding. So it's a very real question whether, by encouraging people to vicariously feel destructive aggressivity, you are increasing the probability of such aggressivity, or producing the good effect of cathartic abreacting of aggressivity. But I think the danger of removing inhibitions is the greater problem. The exposure of children to the mass media's overdoses of war, fighting, murder, and other acts of violence may lessen inhibitions to commit them. I think that the potential for aggressivity in itself is less changed by these factors than the tendency to lower inhibitions for aggressivity by creating a social climate which increasingly tolerates it. Also, the general tendency of individuals not to get involved, the estrangement of people from their neighbors, the solitary life that people live nowadays in a big city may have a lot to do with the increase in criminality and violence on the streets. In a sense, violence leads to estrangement, and estrangement leads to a climate of more violence. I think it's the removal of the inhibitions against violence that's dangerous. If you are a sexual sadist, you may also engage in violence. But on the whole, I believe that the main danger of pornography is that it deromanticizes sexual behavior. It does away with falling in love, with the beauty and ceremony of pair formation. This is at least as dangerous for our culture as violence.

EVANS: What do you mean here by the word "dangerous?" It's dangerous in a different sense from violence, isn't it?

LORENZ: Yes. I may say that destruction of people sounds very cruel, but our culture can tolerate a certain amount of it and survive. But the destruction of the higher emotions, the disappearance of love—of falling in love, being in love, loving your wife, the general multiplicity of finely adapted bond behavior—may present more danger to the survival of our culture than violence as such.

EVANS: Do you mean, then, that pornography may reinforce nonselective "instant sex," gradually extinguishing what we call love responses?

LORENZ: Yes. I think it may extinguish the finer, more sensitive, and, from a sociological point of view, more important superstructure of sexual behavior. I can give you a symptom of this: people write books about sex. The Kinsey Report (1948), for example, treats copulation as if it were the only form of sexual behavior. Much the same is true of Masters and Johnson (1966).

41

As I see it, sexual behavior begins with falling in love, with becoming conscious of the opposite sex, with the elaborate forms of courtship which are partly innate, partly culturally determined.

EVANS: Do you find courtship behavior in animals?

LORENZ: Yes, of course, but in domestic animals all these finer superstructures of sexual behavior tend to disappear in much the same way as they do in urbanized man. If you compare the behavior patterns of domestic animals with those of the wild species you will find that the need for unselective mating, for that form of unselective instant copulation which we call bestial, is not characteristic of wild animals, but rather of domestic animals.

EVANS: Going back to aggression again, an interesting departure from some of the views you have expressed is described in a study by Mallick and McCandless (1966). They examined the question of whether allowing children to engage in aggressive activity discharges their need for aggression. An experiment was set up in which a group of children who had an opportunity to play aggressive games first and other games later was compared with a group of children who had not been allowed to join in aggressive games. They found, interestingly enough, that engaging in aggressive games did not seem to discharge their need for aggression. Quite the contrary; when they were once again given an opportunity to be aggressive, they were more aggressive than ever. This would suggest that engaging in aggression doesn't necessarily discharge the need for it. It may in fact reinforce the need. How do you feel about that experiment?

LORENZ: I think that there may be a misunderstanding here of my views. I never intended to imply that you cannot reinforce aggression. Of course you can. An excess of aggressive activity in certain situations may lead to even more aggressive behavior. We know that fish can be trained to be more aggressive than they normally are. Which does not mean that the same fish, deprived of the opportunity to discharge any aggression, will not become spontaneously aggressive. You see, we are talking here about two separate effects. You can create the conditions to train the organism to be more aggressive, but the converse is not true. By withholding all aggression-eliciting environmental situations you cannot deactivate aggression. You cannot hope for atrophy to occur as far as the need to discharge cumulative, built-up aggression is concerned. This is also known to psychoanalysts; persons with strong blocks of aggression can become quite suicidal. They turn the aggression against themselves. So I'm not surprised at the results of Berkowitz's studies. I never thought that you could not enhance aggression by teaching the child to discharge it more successfully. But keep in mind that this procedure may affect the inhibitions toward aggression. The process of facilitating or inhibiting aggression is much more complex than meets the eye.

EVANS: So you're saying that the very act of becoming aggressive is reinforcing. You're not surprised that, under these particular conditions, children are more aggressive later?

LORENZ: Not under these conditions. I should be surprised if cutting off all aggression-eliciting factors—for instance, complete nonfrustration or complete permissiveness—produced an unaggressive child. Do you see the difference? In fact, many studies show that children in a totally permissive, nonfrustrating environment are, on the whole, very aggressive.

EVANS: Let me review the possibilities that you are describing. One situation allows the individual to be aggressive, thereby discharging his aggression. In another, the environment allows the individual to be aggressive, but this does not discharge aggression; in fact, it seems to increase the probability of its reoccurrence.

LORENZ: Yes, particularly if you reinforce this activity by social approval. This has been substantiated very nicely by a study which compared a tribe of Indians with Bushmen. The Indians are highly aggressive and they encourage their children to be aggressive by ritualizing the aggression. They permit the children to beat each other on the head with a stick in a very expressive, but not a strong, manner. The Bushmen, who are less aggressive, channel aggression toward the child by mild but expressive disapproval. Exposure to different kinds of aggression in childhood results in striking differences between these two peoples as adults. However, if you observe the early aggressive behavior of their children, you find that its magnitude is much the same.

EVANS: The study which you mentioned stems from a paradigm which we call social learning. Albert Bandura (1969, 1965) of Stanford and Berkowitz (1962) have explored what is generally called "imitation," and, more precisely, "modeling" in social psychology. Applying this to the problem of violence on television, Berkowitz might say that if a child views violence on television, the violence becomes a model which in turn reinforces violent patterns. From what you've just said, I gather that you do not disagree with this.

LORENZ: No, not at all. Modeling—imitating—is strongly enhanced by glamorizing the model the child imitates. The highly dangerous models are figures like James Bond, professional killers who are glamorized as heroes. There's no question about discharge being beneficial in such cases. I've written something else in my aggression book which I would qualify if I wrote it again. Nowadays, I have my strong doubts whether simply watching aggressive behavior has any cathartic effect at all. That's also one of the dangers of pornography—instead of doing things, you resign yourself to watching things. This is a general trend in our culture, not to do, but to be content with watching. From that point of view, watching violence might even be beneficial. Who knows? However, all these things are two-edged swords; it works both ways.

EVANS: Let's suppose we could succeed in banishing violence from television and eliminating war toys. Suppose we could eliminate most of such models of violence from our culture. What do you think would happen? Would there be a reasonable chance of reducing overt violence in society?

LORENZ: This could at least reduce the enthusiasm for war. You cannot teach a person *not* to be enthusiastic, but you can teach him what to be enthusiastic *about:* what heroes to imitate, what heroes to be enthusiastic about. I may not get enthusiastic about Napoleon, or any war hero, but I can get highly enthusiastic about Charles Darwin, who represents the constructive side of our culture. You can teach a person what cause to embrace, what causes are worthy of embracing, even though the act of embracing is emotional and highly genetically programed. That is what I mean when I say that war is institutional, because wars in general are regarded as causes worthy of embracing. We must get accustomed to the fact that war is not functional any more. With nuclear weapons, war means suicide. I think that the elimination of war should be the major task of social education today.

EVANS: Pursuing this further, let's look at the developments that led to World War II, and observe the rise of Germany, a country thoroughly demeaned as a result of the settlement of World War I. Gradually we began to see the emergence of the fanatic nationalism which you mentioned earlier. This gave Hitler the power he needed for his tremendous assaults against mankind. In a sense, the German people themselves became Hitler's victims. How do you assess the rise of aggression in Germany that led to the fanaticism found in the

Hitler Jugend, for example? What are your feelings about this?

LORENZ: I have a very arrogant theory about that. When young people in Germany nowadays are disillusioned and blasé—grasping at straws, embracing wrong causes, juvenile criminality, and so on—it's often said this indicates the disappointment they suffered in the national ideals put forth by Hitler. I believe that the success of National Socialism was a symptom of a dearth of real ideals. Take the musical *West Side Story*, which reflects the same patterns in New York street gangs. Here we see good young men—genetically perfectly decent young men—create an adversary just to be collectively enthusiastic in fighting him. *That* is the Nazi spirit. If you realize that these young men created their own fighting community, you can realize how susceptible young people are to the views of the demagogue who proffers dummy ideals and makes them fight, much in the same way we make our sticklebacks fight, with a dummy model. I think that the success of Hitler in Germany is evidence of the dangerous lack of real ideals to embrace. I believe that the main problems that face us today are ethical and moral. There is also the question of the rebellious youth who, quite rightly, rebel against the rat race of commercial competition and against the destruction and pollution of the environment. They are perfectly justified in rebelling against quite a number of things in the establishment. I'm very much on their side. But the question is what to give them instead—what ideals—and that's very difficult to do. What we need is something like a new ethic.

EVANS: You know, it's very interesting that war models always seem more attractive than peace models.

LORENZ: Yes, because man is collectively enthusiastic, militarily enthusiastic; to be enthusiastic about peace is a complicated demand on him. But I think we can get people there. We can get them to be enthusiastic about saving the environment. I'm glad to say that, particularly here in Austria, the involvement of youth in the movement to protect the environment is rapidly growing. I've always gotten along well with students. I've told them openly what is wrong with their aims, their tribal warfare against the older generation, and of the need for directing their enthusiasm in the right channels. There are, by God, enough obstacles to be overcome, if we are to save humanity. There are enough truly significant causes young people should be enthusiastic about rather than the battle against the older generation. It's a shame that this is not communicated to them convincingly enough.

EVANS: Do you feel that symbols of aggressivity, such as Hitler, could rise again? Do you think the groundwork is still there?

LORENZ: I have a deep-rooted fear this might be so.

EVANS: Getting back to something a bit more specific in your theory of aggression: Professor Heinz raised a criticism of your work, and I think it's only fair to hear your response to it. His interpretation of your theory of aggression is 1) that aggression is a constantly building energy, demanding discharge; 2) that this aggression will be discharged, even when there is no appropriate external stimulation or object to which it can be directed. Is this criticism fair?

LORENZ: I don't know whether aggressivity builds up that way in man. But I believe that it does. Considering the high danger of collective aggressivity which we discussed earlier, with regard to the danger of individuals who go "looking for trouble," the scientist has a duty to deviate from his general rationale that he is to say only things he can prove. If the danger is serious enough, the scientist is not only legitimately justified, but he is duty bound to call attention to the danger, particularly if he knows that the horse you are riding on is wild and should be bridled before it's too late. We have done a lot of experiments with fish since I first formulated that theory, which demonstrates in a number of cases that fish "go looking for trouble." We have also observed this in geese. In fact, appetitive behavior for aggressive discharge in animals has been demonstrated quite conclusively in the Institute. It is still open to doubt, of course, whether this is true in man. But if there is even a faint probability that it is, we should take defensive measures to be on the safe side. That's my answer to that question.

IV / *Some Psychological Concepts and Issues*

Overview / *In this section Professor Lorenz and I discuss various Freudian concepts and the balance among biological, cultural, and self-determination theories. He gives his reactions to various components of the theories of Karen Horney, Erich Fromm, and particularly, Carl Jung. We discuss Skinnerian theory, and, finally, Professor Lorenz's reaction to Abraham Maslow's concept of male versus female dominance.*

EVANS: In this series, we have obtained a variety of views of Freudian theory from our distinguished participants. We would very much like to hear your reactions to Freud's ideas. Especially in his early writings, Freud postulated a broad psychic sexual energy which he called "libido." He believed that the biological development of man was characterized by the libido seeking objects—first within man himself and then outside—in which to invest itself. How do you feel about Freud's libido theory?

LORENZ: On a very basic level, ethology is very much in agreement with Freudian theory. In order to assess Freud's merits correctly, you must realize that at the time he wrote, the entire scientific world was bound up in Sherringtonian reflex theory. That is, the doctrine that responding to external stimulation is the one and only function of the central nervous system. Freud recognized the existence of an endogenous production of instinct, stimulus production, or whatever you call it. He called it libido, and if you translate libido into instincts—general drives in their full complexity—you'll find that this is true. Freud's basic discovery was the function of the central nervous system as a dualism between internal drives welling up and higher, superimposed centers repressing those drives. This model is, I think, much truer to the basic function of the central nervous system. When you come down to lower animals, like the earthworm, you find that the central nervous system—the ventral cord of the animal—continuously produces stimuli for a whole gamut of activities: for eating, creeping, and so on. If you cut off the appropriate ganglia, these activities come out in a mixture, rather like an epileptic fit, and the function of the central nervous system, obviously, is to repress it. But the central nervous system also acts as a detector—I prefer the old Pavlovian word, "detector"—which decides when one of these generally inhibited activities should be disinhibited or released. This is the basic model of the ethological approach to the physiology of animal behavior. I think that the Freudian idea of a libido welling up and the ego's keeping it down is very similar.

EVANS: The specific connotation of libido as a broad psychic sexual energy was expanded by Freud into a theory of psychosexual development. This theory, of course, suggests that the development goes through a series of stages during the first five years of human life—oral, anal, and phallic. How do you feel about this theory of psychosexual development?

LORENZ: Well, I must honestly say that I have no

use for the three phases, because the oral, anal, and phallic phases are also observed in animals that have practically no mouth, no anus, and no phallus. You still find the phallic phase in birds, which have no penis. So I really have no use for that theory. The general concept of sex as the paradigm of one instinct is all right. I agree with that. But I think Freud ignores the multiplicity—the mosaic—of numerous little independent motivations which together form, for lack of a better word, a drive. Robert Hinde (1956) has written a very good paper on the unit of drive. He came to the conclusion that the drive—parental drive or sexual drive, and so on—is actually a reification of a multiplicity of independent factors, and the drive itself doesn't exist.

EVANS: As you know, Freud later modified his libido theory quite a bit. He was seriously disturbed by the killing and brutality of World War I. The libido theory, he said, couldn't account for it, there must be some sort of death instinct in man. He enlarged his theory to include not only the life instinct or libido, but also an opposing death instinct. Out of the death instinct he postulated aggression. Do you feel that Freud was right when he said there were opposing life and death instincts in the organism?

LORENZ: I think that this is absolutely wrong. It is much more difficult to explain how animals keep alive and propagate their species than how they die. You don't have to postulate a built-in breakdown-check mechanism in your car in order to explain the fact that it does, occasionally, break down. It breaks down anyway. I don't like to seem to be patting Freud's shoulder, he's a greater man than I am, but I believe that you can justify Freud's theory about the reverting of aggression toward oneself in terms of its primary application to sexual instincts. To begin with, the infant, the young animal, the young human are themselves the objects of their own sexual instincts; then they are reflected outward. However, I think that Freud's idea of a death instinct which is primarily directed toward the individual and then reflected outward—so that instead of killing himself, he kills someone else—is questionable. When applied to the individual development of the sexual instinct, this model is valid, but when applied to the aggressive instinct I don't think it is. Aggressivity is merely one of many drives. Aggressivity may lead to violence and to death, but so may sexuality. In our civilized lives more havoc is wrought by falling in love, I think, than by aggressivity, the nonviolent aggressivity, at any rate.

EVANS: Incidentally, you mentioned suicide here. I know this may sound like an elementary question, but do animals ever commit suicide?

LORENZ: No, definitely not. To commit suicide you need reflection, and again, suicide really is aggression reverted toward the individual. It has been demonstrated by many brilliant psychoanalysts and psychiatrists that a large percentage of suicide is blocked aggressivity, mainly aggressivity against one well-beloved member of the species—loving a wife and feeling aggression toward her and having this aggression blocked by the very bond behavior that brought them together in the first place. The very love you bear such a person may frequently lead to suicide.

EVANS: We would have to argue, then, that as a behavior pattern, suicide is distinctly human.

LORENZ: It is uniquely human.

EVANS: Moving now to a slightly different area, Dr. Lorenz, looking at various foci we have in psychology today, they seem to go roughly in three directions: a theory of biological determinism, which states that man's behavior is primarily determined by a variety of biological forces; a theory of social-environmental determinism, which argues that man is primarily shaped and influenced by the social environment in which he lives; and, of course, the theory that man is primarily self-determined, that he has free will, and so on. Freud, in terms of his views, would have to be described as a biological determinist. He felt that man was largely a victim of primitive, unconscious, irrational forces within himself, part of his inherited nature, the Id. According to Freud, man developed some conscious control, a rational Ego, to cope with the irrational unconscious—seemingly a losing battle. It was very hard for man to overcome these biological influences. How do you feel about these three theories?

LORENZ: I should say all three theories are partly true. The question is only how much man is motivated by each. Freud was right about a battle between the id and the ego and, far more, the superego. Man possesses the same complex of instinctive motivations as animals, but he has a lot of superstructure as well, which is largely cultural, derived from conceptual thought. There is a certain antagonism between what the instincts—the id—instigate in a man, and what society postulates from him. Certainly in his later work, Freud delved into this problem with great precision and understanding. I should say that the demands that culture puts on the instinctive make-up of man grow with the culture, and particularly, with the population. Instincts which served well in the fifty-man-society of Maikas, or in Stone Age man, may become a very serious problem to a society of millions of people.

EVANS: One of the neo-Freudian writers, Dr. Karen Horney, made an observation to which it would be interesting to hear your reaction. She discussed three general patterns of man's behavior as he relates to his fellow-man: 1) moving *against* others, which could be defined as aggression; 2) moving *toward* others, which could be defined as love; and 3) moving *away* from others, which could be defined as fear or withdrawal. Based on your observations, do you think that these three directions are basic?

LORENZ: I feel that this is a very, very dangerous simplification. Mind you, in moving toward an object an animal may be motivated by quite a number of things. For instance, it may be motivated simultaneously by sex and aggression. When two fish meet for the first time, they don't know each other's sex. What motivates them then? Is it love, or hate, or aggressivity? It's definitely all three, and there may be many additional motivations which we haven't yet identified. But trying to put this gamut of drives, even only those we have identified positively, into three boxes strikes me as highly dangerous. They are operatively impossible to distinguish. We are objective enough not to accept a definition which cannot be put to test. Any definition of behavior requires motivation analysis, which is a subtle and complicated procedure. The more we know about motivation, the less we are inclined to conceptualize simple drives.

EVANS: Another writer often grouped with the neo-Freudian group (although this does not do justice to this particular man) is Dr. Erich Fromm (Evans, 1966). Dr. Fromm, as you know, has taken a very interesting look at several facets of behavior in a psychohistorical sense. In his classic book, *Escape from Freedom* (1941), he examined the historical development of man and his search for freedom; how man sometimes cannot cope with the responsibilities of freedom and more or less escapes by accepting dominance and dependency. In a book published in 1973 one of Dr. Fromm's topics is aggression. He observes that when man is confronted with danger, threat, or frustration, he may find withdrawal a more persuasive response than aggression. How do you feel about that idea?

LORENZ: Well, if you subsume aggression, flight, escape, withdrawal in the category of avoidance, you get to the core of this matter. Getting rid of a fellow member of the species can be done in two ways: you can chase him away, or you can run away yourself. We know that the motivations for both lie close together. You present a stickleback with a simple dummy model: if the dummy is slightly smaller than the stickleback in question, you get aggression; if it is slightly larger, you get escape. You can subject an animal to identical stimuli and if he feels out of sorts on a given day he will escape; but if he is in better condition, even slightly, he will attack. So aggression and escape lie very close together. Finally, you must think of what is sometimes called the critical response—the cornered rat fighting. When you drive an animal, which reacts primarily by running away, into a corner, you get the most dramatic all-out attack—the forebearer of aggressivity in a sense—a flip-flop switch of aggression and escape. The two are close together and wired in such a way that the switch is easily made. If you have two animals of the same species, two equal rivals, threatening each other, you can see that both are torn between aggression-attack and escape behavior. In fact, every threat, by definition, is activated by the conflict between aggression and escape. All the highly elaborate ceremonies of rival fighting in fish or birds are actually of high survival value. They serve the function of selecting the stronger organism without sacrificing an individual. But again, to my mind, simplifications in this area are dangerous.

EVANS: Of all the psychoanalytic writers, the one whose ideas, I think, would be particularly challenging to you, is Carl Gustav Jung (Evans, 1964) and his notion of the collective unconscious.

LORENZ: Yes, that's true.

EVANS: He spoke of archetypes, which are "unlearned response tendencies," as he explained to me in my dialogue with him. However, when he refers to symbols acquired through the history of man, Jung appears to speak in quasi-Lamarckian terms. For example, he refers to archetypes like "the father," "evil," "the mother," "the king," and so on. This has been a very controversial view; American psychologists find it difficult to believe that one can inherit something at the symbolic level. Judging from my discussion with Jung, he was more sophisticated than this interpretation of his ideas would suggest. He argued that the environment would activate these "symbols." Does this idea of a collective unconscious make any sense to you?

LORENZ: I'm quite convinced that there is such a thing as an innate, nonacquired, genetically programed propensity of this sort that is blueprinted into the genome. Actually, there is an innate (perhaps I should avoid the unpopular word "innate") response in man to a father figure, to a mother figure, or to an individual who behaves in a socially abnormal way. A man killing children, or maltreating them, elicits a response which is definitely unconscious, or subconsciously motivated, to say the least. This doesn't surprise the ethologist, because he knows that a highly complex internalized picturelike diagram of a certain situation can be reacted to innately. There can be a selective response to a highly complicated diagram of a situation. At first, I called that schema the innate diagram. But we've dropped that because it sounds too much as if the whole thing was innate, in the form of a picture, which it isn't in an animal. In an animal you can demonstrate very clearly that innate responses are a combination of single responses to small, simple stimulus combinations, each of which has an eliciting effect in itself; the responses to the dummy depend on the sum of the single sign stimuli, as we call them, impinging on the animal. So this is not a picture. Man has the power of visualizing things. For example, you can show experimentally that certain features of the female are innate—

a slender waist, bulging hips and breasts, and so on. If you put the releasing stimuli on a dummy of a female animal in the wrong way and in the wrong place, it will still elicit a response in the inexperienced male animal. But man has the power of visualization. He is able to fantasize the female form even if he has never encountered it. He can visualize a father figure though he has never had a father. This innate-releasing mechanism, as we call it, combined with the human faculty of visualizing—dreaming about a situation—results in phenomenal reactions which are more or less identical with Jung's concept of archetypes. I think archetypes are innate-releasing mechanisms invested in visualization, in fantasy, of the individual. Man can, in his fantasy, perform experiments within himself which an animal cannot. In fact, this may explain Jung's theory of archetypes. The same applies to the Freudian concept of lower instincts. The lower level in the central nervous system produces energy and the higher level sits on it and represses it, or else channels it into the right situations.

EVANS: In terms of your own experience, when you first began reading Freud and Jung, I imagine you were quite receptive.

LORENZ: I'm awfully sorry to admit that the exact opposite is true. I objected to Freud very strongly because he was too daring in his assertions. If you were to read my marginal notes on Freud's works, you'd be surprised how quickly I rejected him. It took the simmering down of ripe old age for me to appreciate Freud. The same was true of my initial reaction to Jung.

EVANS: In reading your *Evolution and Modification of Behavior*, I found your reaction to Clark Hull's (1943) work most interesting. I'd be very curious to hear your reactions to another behaviorist who has become quite prominent, Professor B. F. Skinner of Harvard University. As you know, in his particular model,

Skinner has increasingly questioned the value of motivational terms such as aggression. He feels that this kind of concept is irrelevant, that we can shape and modify behavior simply by arranging the contingencies in the environment. We can, in this way, increase the probability that certain specific responses will occur; we can measure, control, and predict this rate of response; why should we get bogged down with cumbersome, or, as he would call them, "black box" terms such as "aggression." How do you feel about that? Does it make any sense to you that a science of behavior which ignores concepts like aggression in the motivational sense at least, might be a better science?

LORENZ: I think I can give a very concise answer to that. For Skinner and all the other operant conditioners, as you say, only one approach is scientifically legitimate: to alter the situation by reinforcing a stimulus situation. The contingencies of reinforced behavior will certainly increase the probability of this behavior occurring more often. But practically all organisms with a higher developed nervous system have a learning apparatus—a phylogenetically programed apparatus—which feeds back the success of behavior to antecedent behavior. This learning apparatus has been evolved by squids, octopi, cephalopods, crustaceans, insects, vertebrates—all of them have independently hit upon this invention and the learning apparatus is pretty well the same in all of them. If you confine yourself to this Skinnerian technique, you study nothing but the learning apparatus and you leave out everything that is different in octopi, crustaceans, insects, and vertebrates. In other words, you leave out everything that makes a pigeon a pigeon, a rat a rat, a man a man, and, above all, a healthy man healthy and a sick man sick. In my opinion, the Skinnerian, by definition, cannot see anything except the conditioning apparatus and consequently he has no right to comment on innate behavior, on phylogenetically programed behavior like aggression. Skinnerians never admit that they are unable to condition a certain species of pigeon to perform the typical courtship behavior of bowing-and-cooing, or condition a female pigeon or rat to crouch as she does during copulation, because this is phylogenetically programed behavior that cannot be conditioned by the Skinnerian technique, by just dropping a pellet. That's impossible. You cannot condition a rat to refrain from eating certain things by any stimulus other than causing nausea, as John Garcia has demonstrated in some highly interesting and important work. He showed that punishing a rat by electric shock, or by forcing it to swim, or by inflicting pain after it has eaten a certain type of food has no effect. However, if you give it a slight X-ray shock or an apromorphine injection, both of which make it feel nauseous, the rat will cease to eat the substance in question. Garcia fed his rats a menu of some ten dishes and when he made them nauseous after one of them, they'd avoid the dish that caused them nausea. This shows you how "intelligent" such an innate program is. If you eat the same thing every day and you feel nausea after eating something new, you will blame it on the new thing, whether it was the last food you ate or not.

EVANS: I don't know if Professor Skinner would necessarily agree, but some behaviorists argue that the behavioral scientist is concerned with three aspects: prediction, control, and understanding. They are not interested in understanding behavior, but merely in predicting and/or controlling it. They would say, "All right, Professor Lorenz, you are entitled to your fascinating work on understanding behavior, but that's irrelevant to us. What we can demonstrate dramatically is how to predict and/or control certain specified behaviors with our behavior-modification, operant-conditioning methods. We will grant you some of the things you're saying. We hope that you continue this fine work. But our area of interest is modifying behavior, controlling behavior, predicting behavior. The other things are not of great interest to us." How do you react to this type of observation?

LORENZ: My answer is that you cannot control behavior until you know what the reinforcers are. You have to know your range of innate behavior patterns to know what kind of situations act as reinforcements. For example, food pellets are not necessarily effective in every situation. Garcia can control the behavior of his rats in a way that Skinner cannot, because he knows which reinforcements work and which do not. I can control behavior quite well myself. I defy anybody, using Skinnerian methods, to settle a graylag goose colony in a new locality without the loss of over four percent of the birds. We can control behavior pretty well, you know.

EVANS: But Skinnerians might say that you are merely using operant conditioning Skinnerian-style, without specifying the contingencies.

LORENZ: I do use operant-conditioning methods, but I use other methods as well, particularly other sources of information. That's the difference. I don't reject anything that Skinnerians do; I merely do a lot of other things besides.

EVANS: Perhaps we might compare the way you would train a dog to the way a Skinnerian would train a dog. Specifically, how would you housebreak a dog?

LORENZ: The dog being the same, I suspect that we should hit on very much the same methods. Seriously, though, the Skinnerians would probably not use social approval as reinforcement. Social approval plays a tremendous role in conditioning a dog. I never beat a dog; I admire it and applaud it when it makes its little puddle out of doors for the first time.

EVANS: The Skinnerians might argue that it's an empirical question. If your social approval had a reinforcing effect—if it worked—they would not necessarily care whether you labeled it "social approval" or anything else. But you're not necessarily ruling out the value of operant-conditioning methods, are you?

LORENZ: I don't disagree with the dyed-in-the-wool behaviorist in anything he does. What I reproach him for is the number of things he doesn't do: for instance, simple observation of the animal's adaptation to its natural environment. I don't think many behaviorists have considered studying a wild rat in the field just to see what it does. They might get very valuable information about reinforcers if they did.

EVANS: In other words, you feel there might be a way to combine ethological observation with operant techniques, thereby increasing the knowledge of reinforcers.

LORENZ: I don't doubt the Skinnerian results, not in the least. They are correct.

EVANS: But I guess you could give them some pretty good tips on what reinforcers to use.

LORENZ: Yes, I could.

EVANS: Not unrelated to this general area of discussion is the work of an American psychologist, the late Abraham Maslow (1954), who became quite well known as a leader of the so-called Third Force, or Personal Growth movement. He conducted a very interesting research study involving several married couples and found that the real source of the conflict between most husbands and wives was not sexual or economic, but rather a subtle fight for dominance. Do you feel that this is the real source of marital conflict and that sexual and economic conflicts are merely surface manifestations?

LORENZ: It could be. First, let me describe briefly how dominance relates to pair formation in fishes and birds. In species that show no great external difference in size or appearance between the sexes, each can potentially dominate the other. This was actually a finding of my daughter-in-law's doctoral dissertation. She conducted a simultaneous motivation analysis of fighting, attack-avoidal responses, and sexual responses. At the same time, she tried to find out how the sexes recognize each other, because in these fishes among which both sexes look exactly the same, you rarely get homosexual pairs, as you often do in birds. She found that when you put two sexually mature fish of equal size together, both are sexually aroused in an aggressive way, and are slightly afraid of each other. These elements—aggressivity and fear, aggression and escape—mix equally in males and females. Every threat, by definition, is a conflict behavior between aggression and fear. However, aggression and sex, and fear and sex mix differently in the two sexes. The male can be highly aggressive and sexually motivated at the same time. He can beat the female so that its scales fly around, and then at the next moment engage in sexual movements. But the male cannot be sexually aroused and afraid of his partner at the same time. If he's even a little afraid of her, his sexuality flops completely. In the female, exactly the opposite is true. The female can be deadly afraid of the male and still be sexually aroused. What she cannot do is be aggressive and sexually aroused at the same time. If he's such a weakling, such a coward that she dares be aggressive toward him, he becomes completely uninteresting as a sexual partner and she will kill him even if it means that she will die of spawn retention. The intensity of her sexual motivation does not avert this. The same mechanism works in many birds: the stronger one acts the role of the male, the more dominated one acts the role of the female. Being *dominating* suppresses female sexuality; being *dominated* suppresses male sexuality. But in man, neither pure male nor pure female exists. There's a female element in every man and male elements in every woman. I don't think that in human married couples the relationship is that simple, one dominated and the other dominating. For example, in some respects I submit to my wife. She has a much better knowledge of people. Her assessment of strangers is much better than mine, so I trust her in that respect. In other respects, she submits to my judgment. I think that is true of many friends. To what extent the "maleness" objects to being dominated is a good question. There are pure males and pure females who are very beautiful and rather stupid at the same time. The "he-man," the film-actor ideal, is nearly always stupid. If I meet a man who is too handsome, I often doubt his intelligence. I know a lot of "male" men who object to intelligent women, who like their women stupid, don't you?

V / *Reflections on Contemporary Issues, His Critics, and the Future*

Overview / *In this section, Professor Lorenz and I discuss such contemporary issues as the Women's Movement, population control, the controversy surrounding the alleged "inferiority" of blacks as interpreted by Arthur Jensen from IQ scores. We also discuss some of the major influences on Lorenz's career, his feelings about the work of Robert Ardrey and Desmond Morris, and, finally, his assessment of his most important contributions, and his future plans.*

EVANS: Many aspects of dominance that we discussed are also concerns of the Women's Movement, such as the belief of some men that they should be dominant, and that women should be submissive. In animals, is the male always the dominant one and the female always the submissive one?

LORENZ: I'm sorry to have to tell the ladies of Women's Lib that in most animals I am familiar with, there's a clear male dominance. And in the fish I described earlier, the female is sexually frigid in response to the nondominant male. There are a few exceptions. In some species of waders, in which the female is decidedly more beautiful than the male, the male is dominated by this female, and he sits on the eggs and incubates them. The same is true of a few species of fish.

EVANS: I'd now appreciate your comment on another interesting contemporary development: the Gay Liberation Movement. This movement, of course, is characterized by both male and female homosexuals who believe that society has been discriminating against them and that they have a right to engage in any sexual activity of their choice. They question society's right to determine what's right for them. They also object very strongly to the notion that homosexual behavior is deviant. From your observations of animal pairings, would you define homosexual behavior as deviant?

LORENZ: That's an interesting question. In those animals, birds, and fish in which males and females are of the same size, appearance, and form, there is usually, in the normal make-up of the animal, the capacity for homosexual behavior. Any two male pigeons or two female pigeons, thrown together, will engage in sexual activities. The dominant bird will play the male role, and the dominated bird will play the female role. You are unaware that you've got a homosexual pair until you observe the absence of eggs in the nest—or double the number. The eggs may be fertile because both lesbian pigeons are having an affair with a male pigeon. This is one type of homosexuality. There is another type of homosexual relationship, found in geese, in which pair formation, falling in love, can be disassociated from copulation, much as it can in man. In geese, you may find a very strong homosexual bond between two males who behave like a pair—they keep together, they defend each other, they participate in the so-called triumph ceremonies together—though they cannot copulate. They never do. They try every spring. They forget that they both refuse to be mounted. They both behave in a perfectly normal male way. If he could speak, this goose would say, "I love my wife very much, but she's quite frigid." Such male pairs can acquire a mutual female. They are superior in fights to every normal pair, because the fighting potential of two males is superior to the fighting potential of a pair. And so they rise very high in the ranks of a goose colony. They are admired by unmarried females. Very often when they try to copulate and they can't because both want to mount and neither will crouch, a loving female gets between them and is copulated by one or both of them. This female is gradually accepted by the two males, but she is not respected. Nobody offers her a triumph ceremony. But when she succeeds in getting a nest and laying eggs, she may awaken both males' parental-care response and they will stand guard near the nest, accept the young, and give them the triumph ceremony. Then you have a family, a *ménage à trois*, but not the usual *ménage à trois* of two men in love with a female, but rather two males in love with each other and a female who loves one of them. This cannot be called deviant or errant behavior. Peter Scott has shown that among the wild pink-footed geese of Iceland there is a large incidence of triangular relationships which are particularly successful in rearing their young. Two males are better able to defend the babies against such dangers as the gyrfalcons. Here homosexuality is of survival value. Getting back to your question about the Gay Liberation Movement, I don't think there can be any moral objection to homosexuality. Many feel a certain aesthetic or emotional aversion to homosexual behavior. I once saw two boys embracing in a bathroom, kissing each other. Why shouldn't they? There's no moral objection, yet I was offended. I found it slightly repulsive. But in moral terms, why shouldn't they? In an overpopulated world, increased homosexuality might be a very good thing. From that point of view, perhaps homosexuality may even be desirable.

EVANS: Overpopulation is considered a very serious problem in the United States, where the problem may not even be as serious as in other parts of the world. There are those who argue that something must be done to cut down the size of the family. Have you observed the behavior in animal groups where overpopulation has occurred and some solution to it was attempted?

LORENZ: Yes, certainly. There are numerous arrangements of behavior patterns regulating population. Overpopulation is bad economics. If you overexploit the animal or plant on which you depend for your livelihood, you destroy your own means of sustenance. It is in the interest of the species not to overexploit. Territoriality—territorial behavior—has a definite survival value in limiting the number of individuals or pairs and distributing them equally over the available habitat. Wynne-Edwards (1962) covers this problem in his very illuminating book, *Animal Dispersion in Relation to Social Behavior.* Population-limiting mechanisms exist in some animals, but not in all. There's definitely a population-limiting factor in lions, but not in jackals and hunting dogs.

EVANS: At the human level, those concerned with overpopulation argue that it's not just a question of dispersal, but of economic capabilities, of food and energy resources. In other words, dispersal is not the only answer. Are there situations where the options become limited for animal groups as well—where there just isn't enough food to support the animal population? When the options run out in animals groups, do they simply perish?

LORENZ: In animals population control by starvation is the exception. As a rule there are mechanisms which prevent overpopulation long before a food shortage sets in as the limiting factor. I believe our planet, the earth, can feed many more people than it can support in dignity and freedom. In order to live a mentally healthy life the human couple has spatial requirements which are much greater than those which would be allotted to them if food production alone acted as the limiting factor. You mentioned drastic measures. We cannot take drastic measures. All our problems today stem from overpopulation. But if a solution is attempted by any means other than educational, we're back in the wildest kind of authoritarianism. If it isn't done voluntarily, it cannot be done at all. The main danger of voluntary efforts is that you may end up with ᵗhe wrong kind of selection—in the sense that intelligent and responsible people engage in family planning whereas irresponsible people don't.

EVANS: Is there such a thing as family planning in animal groups—not consciously, of course?

LORENZ: There are a lot of mechanisms doing just that. Let me cite one example. If wolves are having a hard time finding food and they have to kill big game in order to survive, as they do on Lake Superior, they must get together in large packs. In such packs only the alpha female, the dominant female, breeds. In fact, she prevents all other females from copulating. If killing big game is not necessary for the food supply, the pack dissolves into single pairs and every female can breed. In short, if a pack of fourteen is necessary to kill a big moose, out of seven females only one breeds. This has been confirmed repeatedly by different observers. So you have a mechanism there which very clearly adjusts the rate of reproduction to the available food.

EVANS: There's an important controversy going on among American psychologists and educators today, to which I would very much like to have your reaction. The principles in this argument are a Nobel Prize-winning physicist by the name of William Shockley, an American educational psychologist named Arthur Jensen, and a Harvard psychologist, Richard Herrnstein. Essentially their position is that even though blacks are exposed to culturally enriched environments with opportunities to overcome the deprivation they have suffered, they cannot rise intellectually to the level of whites because they are genetically inferior in at least one kind of intellectual potential. For example, Jensen found that in spite of early exposure to a culturally enriched environment, blacks were not able to perform as well as the whites in a test measuring a supposedly more abstract type of intelligence. Jensen has been much maligned on this point. He argues that he has been misinterpreted. He feels that he has reopened the question of individual differences, including the question of race-related genetic intellectual differences. I'm sure you're familiar with this controversy. How do you see it?

LORENZ: I'd like to quote my friend John Garcia on Jensen's black and white IQ tests. The IQ intelligence test was developed in terms of white, middle-class culture and is unfair to those of a different race and culture. No man can deny the fact that races are different. However, it is absolutely stupid to contend that this implies a difference in value. You and I are genetically more different from each other than the pintail duck is from the mallard. Now I ask you which is the better, more valuable duck, the pintail or the mallard? This is a ridiculous question. Regarding the intelligence test, Garcia quotes the findings of Tryon (1940) who tried to breed rats that were particularly bright in running through a maze. This maze had a trap door that shut whenever the rat took the right turn. After selecting for many generations, he finally learned that he was selecting rats insensitive to trap doors shutting behind them rather than maze-bright rats. Immune-to-trap-door rats did best in this particular situation, and Garcia argues that there's exactly the same danger in intelligence measures. While not denying the essential and indubitable differences between the races, I deny the right of anyone to say that one race is better or more valuable than the other. Which race is the higher? You might even go so far as to say that blacks and yellows and whites are subspecies. You might go beyond the concept of race. But to ask which subspecies is better is absurd!

EVANS: Moving to another area now, I'd like to hear your reaction to some of the recent developments in psychology and neurophysiology which touch directly on the question of genetic transfer of information in the organism. This line of work has been pursued by such American scientists as James McConnell (1959), A. L. Jacobson (1959), and George Unger (1970). They have been able to hypothesize the basis for what is a remarkable phenomenon, memory transfer. McConnell's early work was with the planaria, or flatworm. It was trained to react to light when normally it does not. He could cut this flatworm into small pieces and the tail of the worm would continue this particular response. Pieces of the flatworm that had learned this response could be fed to another flatworm that had not "learned" the response. This nontrained flatworm now "learned" it quickly. Later, Jacobson (1965) did some research with mice. The mouse would be taught a certain response, and then RNA extract from the mouse would be injected into another mouse which had not been taught this particular response. The mouse with the RNA injection would learn much more quickly than a mouse that had not been injected. In terms of your conceptualizations of the mechanisms which trigger off behavior, is this sort of research of interest to you?

LORENZ: I feel deeply doubtful about these results. I rely in my judgment on the authority of various biochemists. I believe that these chemically transferable propensities to a certain response refer to sensitization or desensitization. I find it hard to believe that anything more specific is involved here. Let's say the information—the flatworms learn to react to light when normally they do not react to light—is explicable in terms of sensitization. They simply become more sensitive to light, not really forming an association. No real reinforcement of the response is involved. The criticism by my biochemist colleagues is that in order to code a learned memory, you first have to assume that there is an apparatus that records a chain molecule of the information coming in—tack, tack, tack—like a telegraph on the paper tape. Then you have to assume that there is another apparatus that reads the molecule and transfers it back into nervous impulses. How long does an RNA messenger need to build a molecule? All of this takes much too much time—I don't know exactly how much—but probably by powers to ten to explain this transfer of information on the basis of chemistry. Authorities contend that many of the experiments with planaria could not be reproduced. This isn't first hand observation. But I am skeptical: if it is possible to store learned information in memory transfer, what then is the function of the enormously complex central nervous system? There would be no clear correlation between learning ability and the size of the central nervous system. This argues against it convincingly, I think. But, of course, it may be too early to judge the true validity of this research.

EVANS: To follow up a point we discussed earlier, many believe that your keen observations on animal behavior, particularly in the area of social behavior and mobility, have prompted a major reconsideration of methods of approach in the social sciences. This applies not only to psychology, but to political science, cultural anthropology, and sociology. You have brought

a greater focus on the effects of biological predisposi-
tions in man as factors with which to deal, as well as the
effects of the social environment. In a sense, you have
created the fields of behavioral anthropology, behavioral sociology, perhaps even behavioral political
science. Your focus on the effects of the environment
on the organism has contributed greatly to the field of
behavioral biology. Several concepts and questions
have come up as a result: one involves crowding and
personal space. We're all concerned about our crowded
cities and various hypotheses have been developed.
For example, some say that crowding may cause leadership patterns to shift from participatory to autocratic.
Does that make sense to you? If you begin with an essentially participatory or democratic type of leadership,
will crowding reduce it to a more autocratic type of
leadership?

LORENZ: This definitely happens in monkeys and
the mechanism is clearly established. I think it is justi-
fiable to deduce that the same process takes place in
man. In an uncrowded monkey population, particularly
among rhesus or baboons the ability to claim leadership
is largely dependent on the individual's capacity to
form alliances or friendships. Why not assume that the
simple friendships in man are instinctive and emotional? There's an innate basis in everything as emotional as friendship. Now the war leaders in the baboon
group studied by Washburn and DeVore (1961), were
very old, past their prime, but they maintained their
leadership by keeping together and defending each
other. Experiments have shown very similar patterns in
a normal rhesus colony. When you crowd them they
become irritable. If you crowd man, he becomes irritable. The most crowded place I know in the world is the
bus terminal on Forty-second Street in New York City,
and I know of no other place in the world where people
are more irritable. If you ask a man for the way, he

snaps at you—he is irritated by a lack of elbow room. If you crowd monkeys they get irritable and snap at each other. This snappishness breaks up friendships. The moment irritability and pettiness take over, aggressivity becomes stronger than bond behavior and old leaders cease to be friends. Naturally, the most violent, the strongest and most aggressive individual becomes the ruler. In this way, you get "one-man" government, as has been shown in a number of primate behavior studies. In a normal, uncrowded, kindly society, there is a minimum of aggression among alpha, beta, and gamma, among the president, vice-president, and the senate. In a crowded society, there is the greatest enmity, the greatest hostility, and the maximum of aggressive behavior patterns between the highest-ranking individuals. If you count aggressive behavior patterns per minute between alpha and beta, you get a minimum in the normal society and a maximum in the crowded society. The same phenomenon is found among lower mammals as well. For example, cats reveal elevated blood pressure and other symptoms of stress under crowded conditions.

EVANS: In the United States, people first move to the center of urban areas. This is usually followed by a flight to the suburbs. There is a pattern of movement— first to the crowd, then away from the crowd. Is this a pattern you can observe in animal groups as well?

LORENZ: I don't think so. That is cultural, on a higher level. I can't say that anything similar has ever been observed in animals.

EVANS: This discussion, of course, leads us to personal space. Recently, in American social psychology, we have become particularly interested in personal space. The whole idea of the territorial imperative was developed in more detail by your colleague Robert Ardrey. But how far can you generalize about the importance of personal space and the effects of crowding?

Isn't there a point at which you can jump too far with a concept like this? Is it really a sufficiently precise predictor of behavior in the final analysis, even at the animal level?

LORENZ: At the animal level, certainly. But man is a highly conditionable animal and cultural conditioning becomes second nature to the point where it affects body shape and individual attitudes. There's no saying to what extent you can train a man to fit into another environment. But I strongly doubt that you can condition him so he doesn't become nervous and neurotic by being crowded. I doubt that very strongly. In an area where people live in widely separated houses—miles from their nearest neighbors—you find the greatest human kindness. I remember an experience which has remained very fresh in my memory. While living in my Institute in Munich, I was saturated with human contacts. People always wanted to ask me questions and my friends came in all the time—even nice people can make you irritable. We had as our houseguests an American couple, conservation people who live in the wilds of Wisconsin. Just as we were sitting down to dinner the doorbell rang. I said, "Who the hell's that again?" If I had uttered the worst profanity I couldn't have shocked those two people more profoundly. Not to be overjoyed when the doorbell rings was completely incomprehensible to them. This incident made me realize how much I myself had become a victim of crowding.

EVANS: Professor Lorenz, of all your many noteworthy and unique contributions, which do you consider to be the most important?

LORENZ: As far as published books are concerned, I would say it is *The Evolution and Modification of Behavior*, which was actually my reply to Lehrman's (1953) critique of my work. I think this book puts in a nutshell the essence of my thinking.

EVANS: We've discussed a number of your other contributions. You were one of the founders of ethology and you are responsible for what I would call *psychological* ethology.

LORENZ: I can't claim credit for that part of ethology which investigated motor coordination or movement patterns of a species and the larger taxonomical groups characterized by such patterns. This was discovered by Whitman and Heinroth and it forms the basis on which ethology is built up. I might claim credit for the development of the concept of the releasing mechanisms. As long as the motor coordination or movement pattern was regarded as merely a chain of reflexes, the first reflex in the chain didn't stand out particularly. But when it was recognized that the primary pattern in an arrangement of the central nervous system consists of one mechanism-generating stimulus and another mechanism-inhibiting stimulus, my concept became crucial. Pavlov (1927) called this stimulus-selecting mechanism the detector. I might be credited with focusing on the releasing process, the selectivity of the reaction to a certain stimulus situation. This subsequently became the subject of the collaboration between Tinbergen and myself. Tinbergen began to investigate experimentally the innate releasing mechanism, which disinhibits motor patterns. The recognition of the duality of these two processes may be my most important discovery.

EVANS: Looking back over your life, which men and women do you feel had the greatest influence on you?

LORENZ: In forming my character a very great influence was exerted by a high-school teacher, a Benedictine monk. I thing it's remarkable and highly characteristic of the liberality of old Austria that I was taught about Darwin and natural selection by a monk. If your question is whom I most admire of men living or dead it is Charles Darwin, who, in a very pedestrian manner, made such great discoveries. I also admire a man against whom tradition—orthodox Christian tradition—fought such a tremendous battle, Thomas Huxley. As he once said, "Every truth starts life as a heresy and ends life as an orthodoxy." This is so true of Darwin's discovery. When Darwin was finally able to clarify his theory of evolution, he didn't feel like a victor or a great discoverer. "I feel like a murderer," he wrote in his diary.

EVANS: What criticisms of your work trouble you the most?

LORENZ: The most troubling aspect of criticism is finding something wrong with one's position. The mere defense of one's position doesn't necessarily require any personal involvement. However, criticisms that made me change my positions were those that troubled me the most and helped me the most at the same time. Or, to put it in another way, criticisms which troubled me are identical with the criticisms to which I reacted most completely. A good example is Daniel Lehrman's paper "Critique of Konrad Lorenz's Theory," where he expounded a more or less behavioristic attitude, saying that all the behavior I attributed to genetic programing could be learned. He cited the experiments of Z. Y. Kuo (1932), who believed that what teaches the chick to peck is the heartbeat moving passively by the chick's head. At the same time, his criticism more than slightly oversimplified my views. In that respect he was unjust. I answered him later in a paper which I prepared for the Congress on Instinct. I pointed out that in order to avoid the concept of innateness, Kuo postulated something like an innate schoolmarm, the heartbeat, teaching the chick how to peck. Of course, this "teacher" cannot teach the chick *at what* to peck. It is noteworthy that it took me about ten years to conclude that the innate schoolmarm, indeed, sums up the problem of all learning—if learning improves survival value, the learning apparatus must contain information about what ought to be learned and what ought not to be learned.

There must be a teacher who pats you on the shoulder and says, "That's right, do that again" or "No, no, no, don't do that, it causes a bellyache." My reactions to Lehrman's criticisms culminated in my paper "The Innate Basis of Learning" (1969) and in what I consider to be my most important paper, "The Evolution and Modification of Behavior" (1965). So the criticisms which troubled me most were, in the long run, the most constructive.

EVANS: One of the things that I observed from reading your work is that you have been rather concerned about overenthusiastic generalizations derived from your ethological studies. In particular, there were two books which have been widely read, Desmond Morris's *The Naked Ape* (1967) and Robert Ardrey's *The Territorial Imperative* (1966). They certainly contain broad generalizations of your work. Do these particular works bother you?

LORENZ: First, may I say that both Morris and Ardrey are very good friends of mine. Desmond Morris has always been one, and Robert Ardrey has become one. May I say, further, that Robert Ardrey is a very good ethologist in his own right; he has learned a lot. In his early books, particularly in *The Territorial Imperative*, the principles are slightly overgeneralized, a bit too daring. While reading it, I suffered all the agonies you suffer sitting next to a driver who takes a certain stretch of road much faster than you would dare do it yourself, but you're helpless to slow him down. In other words, Ardrey was sticking *my* neck out. I emphasize that this is not the case with Ardrey's later work. I'm fully in agreement with that.

EVANS: What about Morris?

LORENZ: I don't agree with some aspects of *The Naked Ape*, because it treats man as if his culture was a biologically irrelevant phenomenon. Nor do I agree with his view that every cumulative tradition is a side issue and something to be deplored, rather than admired, in the human species. If I give a name to a species, I choose a function by which the species survives—I call a woodpecker a woodpecker, because he lives by pecking wood. If I were forced to call the human species apes, I should at least show that they are the culture-apes, the cumulating-tradition apes, the ideal conception of all apes. That man is naked is irrelevant. He might just as well be furry.

EVANS: To conclude, Professor Lorenz, it would be interesting to hear what you're working on now and what you are planning to do in the future. I know that you're working on a new book. What is that all about? What research are you currently involved in?

LORENZ: I'm torn between epistemology, particularly the philosophy of values, and some very specific research which I'm still doing. At present, I am completing a book on the theory of knowledge which will be followed by a second volume on the human sense of values from a naturalistic point of view. But what I want to do in research work is more detailed studies of aggressive behavior in fish, of bond behavior, and of all of the aggression-inhibiting mechanisms in the higher animals. In other words, I want to go on studying the sociology of behavior.

VI

*Reintroducing Konrad Lorenz
to Psychology,
by Donald Campbell*

*Konrad Lorenz Responds
to Donald Campbell*

Four Papers by Konrad Lorenz

Overview | *This section includes an analytical review by Donald Campbell, currently President of the American Psychological Association, entitled "Reintroducing Konrad Lorenz to Psychology" and Professor Lorenz's reactions to it. This is followed by four of Professor Lorenz's papers which amplify Campbell's analysis. These are: "Evolution of Ritualization in the Biological and Cultural Spheres"; "The Fashionable Fallacy of Dispensing with Description"; "Kant's Doctrine of the A Priori in the Light of Contemporary Biology"; "The Enmity Between Generations and Its Probable Ethological Causes."*

Reintroducing Konrad Lorenz
to Psychology / Donald Campbell

The best-known image of Konrad Lorenz is that of the eminent scientist willing to go beyond the technicalities of his research in discussing a wide range of social concerns with the general public, the popular essayist of *King Solomon's Ring* (1952), *On Aggression* (1966), *Civilized Man's Eight Deadly Sins* (1973), and "The Enmity Between Generations" (1970) (reprinted in the section of this book to follow).

The Nobel Prize Award for Biology of 1973 presents another image of Lorenz: the cofounder along with Karl von Frisch and Nikolaas Tinbergen of an esoteric new scientific discipline, "ethology," or behavioral zoology, using detailed studies of innate animal behavior to describe evolutionary sequences and relationships among species. This side of Lorenz is best presented in the two volumes of his collected papers published by the Harvard University Press (1971, 1972), and is reflected in the fascinating "Evolution of Ritualization" (1966), reprinted here.

This introduction and the selected papers that follow present a third image, treating Lorenz as a psychologist of great breadth. The topics covered are cybernetic behaviorism, evolutionary epistemology, intergroup aggression, social evolution, and the political implications of evolutionary genetics. The psychologies involved include learning theory, psychology of knowledge, psychology of science, social psychology, and the psychology of individual differences. Inevitably this image overlaps with the Nobel Prize image, but it also presents some equally important achievements which have not yet received the attention they deserve. Inevitably there is also overlap with the popular essayist image. In this area I shall take the liberty of distinguishing some of Lorenz's emphases from my own because of his willingness to take strong stands on controversial issues and for the sake of my own colleagues who know my position on these issues better than they know my enthusiasm for Lorenz and may need help in reconciling the two. I hope that this discussion of our areas of disagreement will add to the validity of my introduction of Lorenz to psychologists.

In the William James Tradition

Thinking over what model of psychologist Lorenz is most like, I come up with the William James of *Principles of Psychology* (1890). This may seem a strange choice since the current membership in the William James fan club is dominated by phenomenologists and humanists. But James was a biological psychologist, enthusiastic about the implications of evolutionary theory for psychology, convinced of the purposiveness of human and animal behavior, and committed to seeking out explanations of that purposiveness compatible with a materialist orientation. He was a Darwinian natural selectionist adamantly opposed to Lamarckian or teleological explanations, while recognizing the teleonomic facts to be explained. He was interested in understanding conscious experience and relating it to biological and evolutionary perspectives, and in doing epistemology—theory of knowledge—in full competition and contact with philosophy. Like Lorenz, he tended to underplay cultural-environmental sources of human psychology in spite of being interested in social evolution as an extension and analogue of biological evolution (James, 1880). Both have been seriously concerned with the need to find a moral equivalent for war.

The distribution of attention is, of course, different. The most Lorenzian of James is confined to a few chapters, as in his discussions of instincts. Most Jamesian of Lorenz is not his most famous work but that represented in the selection reprinted here, "Kant's Doctrine of the A Priori" (1962), and in such essays as "Gestalt Perception as a Source of Scientific Knowledge" (1959), and "Do Animals Undergo Conscious Experience?" (1963), available in the Harvard volumes. Nonetheless, James serves to illustrate Lorenz's multifaceted relevance to a truly complete psychology better than does any other model I can think of.

Note that the biological grounding of James and Lorenz does not make them typical reductionists. Neither are they vitalists, although they are open to and indeed tend to accept the facts to which vitalists such as Bergson (1911), Driesch (1914), Uexküll (1926), and Polanyi (1969) point. But they accept these facts as puzzles needing explanation, and they seek out solutions compatible with physics, chemistry, and evolutionary biology. They both find in Darwin's concept of natural selection (1859) a key to such an explanation. Lorenz's handling of this problem is elegantly illustrated in "The Fashionable Fallacy of Dispensing with Description" (1973), reprinted here.

Cybernetic Behaviorism

Under this title I refer to the central core of Lorenz's contributions to the understanding of animal behavior, to the works that made the Max Planck Institute for Behavioral Physiology at Seewiesen-über-Starnberg a mecca for American psychologists from its founding in 1954 until Lorenz's retirement in 1973. (Under the auspices of the Austrian Academy of Sciences, he has since founded a new Institute for Comparative Behavior Research at Altenberg, near Vienna.)

The behaviorisms that are still dominant in psychology today (including the major mathematical models for learning) in my judgment are inadequate to the explanation of learned or innate adaptive behavior, or even such a coordinated act as reaching for a pencil. Cybernetics (Wiener, 1948; Ashby, 1952; 1956) provides a mechanistic model for purposive, goal-guided behavior which will, I believe, eventually be elaborated into an integrated psychological theory replacing current behaviorisms. When this cybernetic psychological theory is achieved, the work of Lorenz and the other ethologists will be one of the central pillars of the edifice.

Under this cybernetic model, for every adaptive act, the organism must have a sense-organ or perceptual criterion for its achievement (a multidimensional "homeostat," "reference signal," or "template" for the goal state). Where interaction with other animals or objects is involved, these criteria take on the character of "images," and a phenomenological dimension is added. Lorenz's concept of "releaser" belongs here. The organism must also have specific anatomical structures that monitor the many bodily states—blood-sugar level, serum salinity, etc.—that are involved in hunger, thirst, and other so-called drives, and it must have other sense organs signaling the probable satiation of the bodily deficit. Complex acts involve hierarchically organized sets of such purposive subunits. At each level there is an instigating-signal template, a build-up of responsiveness during periods of nonactivation, and a goal-completion template, which in turn may be one component of the releasing template for the next adaptive unit in the hierarchy. Where the releasing template or the completion template require external objects, there will be active search behavior at the perceptual and locomotor levels. Where learning is involved, there will be specific "pleasure" and "pain" sensory systems (Olds, 1958) activated jointly with certain of the intermediate goal-achievement templates.

This paraphrases Lorenz's many descriptions of specific instinctive systems in animals. A similar picture emerges when two orthodox behaviorists such as Miller (1959) and Sheffield (1950) study a supposedly singular drive-and-reinforcement system as hunger. Their rats run mazes to have taste buds titillated with nonnutritive saccharin, or for the joy of mouthing and swallowing food which never reaches their stomachs because of a by-pass operation, or to have a balloon blown up in their stomachs, no doubt producing that pleasant all-full feeling if not overdone. The behaviorist's concept of "drive reduction" has a hidden teleology, and must be replaced by a number of specific anatomical cybernetic units, as Lorenz has taught us. One of his very best essays on this topic is his recent "On the Innate Bases of Learning" (1969).

There is much of potential value for social psychologists in Lorenz's fascinating reconstruction of the evolution of instinctive interpersonal rituals in different species. Note how the courtship ritual in one species of birds seems to have evolved from the infant-feeding ritual, while in another from instinctive aggressive responses directed toward strange conspecifics. These studies are of Nobel Prize quality to evolutionary biologists because of their striking addition of behavioral evidence to studies of evolutionary sequence and speciation usually based on anatomy alone. For psychologists, who must eventually be concerned with the evolution of behavior, they have an additional value. "Evolution of Ritualization in the Biological and Cultural Spheres," reprinted here, is a charming introduction to this area, as is also Lorenz's justifiably popular *King Solomon's Ring* (1952).

Evolutionary Epistemology

By this phrase I refer to a field of study in which philosophers, biologists, and psychologists undertake to solve in a scientific spirit aspects of traditional problems in the philosophy of knowledge or epistemology. "Evolutionary epistemology" is a specific version of "descriptive epistemology," or, as Quine (1969) calls it, "epistemology naturalized."

Descriptive epistemology attempts to address the problems of knowledge—Do we know? How do we know as well as we do? Can we know for certain that our knowledge is accurate?—by using scientific knowledge such as the physics of the world to be known and the evolutionary biology and psychology of man the knower. There has always been a certain amount of such epistemology, but the purification of philosophy of the last century made it taboo. Philosophers have tended to react to such efforts as evidence of incompetence—a failure to understand what epistemology was all about. One understands their point of view especially easily with regard to the problem of induction or of justifying scientific knowledge. It is indeed circular reasoning to assume the validity of scientific knowledge in justifying the validity of the process generating that knowledge.

However, if one distinguishes the tasks of descriptive epistemology from traditional or analytic epistemology, a fascinating and useful field of scholarship emerges, one quite consistent with the major achievements of the skeptical empiricist tradition of Locke, Berkeley, Hume, Kant, and their modern successors. Their pessimistic conclusion is that we cannot logically justify our scientific beliefs, nor can we achieve certainty in any other way. The inductive "logic" or the procedures which we use in coming to scientific conclusions always leave open the possibility of our being wrong. These conclusions hold not only for scientific beliefs, but also for visual and tactile perception insofar as these generate in us beliefs about objects and events beyond the transient uninterpreted sensations themselves. Hume's "scandal of induction" was for a time neglected because of belief in the certain truth of Newton's physics. The modern overthrowing of that theory, plus careful examination of the historical grounds on which scientific theories are selected and rejected, has lead to a new preoccupation with this problem, either explicitly accepting Hume's logic and pessimism (Popper, 1959; 1963), or reinventing it as a novel observation (Kuhn, 1962; Toulmin, 1961; 1972).

In complete compatibility with this pessimistic solution of the logical problem of knowledge, a descriptive epistemology can ask how do we go about the admittedly imperfect knowing that we do? Given our disadvantaged epistemological predicament, how can we know as well as we seem to know? The classic epistemologists such as Hume and Kant provide conjectures on this, as do also the moderns such as Popper (1959; 1963), Polanyi (1958), Toulmin (1961; 1972), Kuhn

(1962), and others. What had been repressed in technical philosophy as a stupidity is now being practiced by an increasing brave minority within philosophy (see Campbell, 1974, for details).

Descriptive or evolutionary epistemology is an important new field. And it is by no means a monopoly of philosophers. In terms of the distinction which philosophers have usually made between philosophy and science, descriptive epistemology would have to be classified as a science. Philosophy supplies the ancient agenda of concerns, modern science supplies grounds for the solutions. Thus descriptive epistemology is a field in which physicists, biologists, psychologists, and sociologists should participate. When this discipline consolidates, Konrad Lorenz will be recognized as one of its founding fathers and major contributors. The physicist-philosopher Vollmer (1974) has already accorded Lorenz this status. One of Lorenz's most recent books, *Die Rückseite des Spiegels* (*The Other Side of the Mirror*) (1973), is entirely devoted to it. Reprinted in the present volume is his first such paper, "Kant's Doctrine of the A Priori in the Light of Contemporary Biology."

Our collegial friendship was formed in this area. When I published my first essay on the topic (1959), I was already aware of some of Lorenz's epistemological papers through an essay by Bertalanffy (1955) and a collection edited by Whyte (1951). Subsequently I had a translation made of the paper reprinted here and of "Gestalt Perception" (1959). The results were so uneven I spent months revising them, using a German-English dictionary at least once a sentence. So great was my investment, and the resulting neglect of my own writing, that I listed these accomplishments on my vita as "translation editor," where they made up two-thirds of my publications for 1962! I was greatly aided in the translations by intuitively sensing what Lorenz was trying to say. The major cement to our friendship was that we valued each other's contributions to an area in which at the time no one else seemed interested, but which to us was of the utmost fascination.

In writing "Kant's Doctrine of the A Priori in the Light of Contemporary Biology," the young Lorenz creatively solved a major epistemological puzzle. It turns out that at least twenty-two philosophers and eighteen biologists, physicists, or psychologists since Darwin have also made the suggestion that the a priori categories of perception and cognition might be products of biological evolution (Campbell, 1974), a recurrent heresy that has received so little attention that almost all have remained unaware of the other advocates. Of all of these, Lorenz's presentation is the best, fullest, and most subtle.

Epistemological relativism is a recurrent problem in the theory of knowledge, and Lorenz's mode of handling it is of particular value. Like his teacher Uexküll (1934), he recognizes that each animal (and each language, each culture, each historical period, each scientific paradigm) views reality from a different and limited perspective. Each perspective is based upon presuppositions which, however useful, are of unproven and limited validity. Such differences are marvelously presented in his speculations about the concepts of space and causality in the water shrew (in "Kant's Doctrine of the A Priori in the Light of Modern Biology"). He recognizes an analogous limited perspective to human knowing, even as reflected in modern physics. This he describes as epistemological relativism in our predicament as knowers.

Many who have achieved this sophistication go on to a philosophy which denies reality, or any other reality save that of our perceptions themselves, or any common reality reflected however imperfectly in different perspectives. Not so Lorenz. He combines his epistemological relativism with a hypothetical realism, a critical realism. His evolutionary theory leads him to find it necessary to posit a common physical space and causality which is imperfectly mapped by water shrew and man. Higher organisms often have more complete maps, combining the distinctions of their more primitive ancestors with more subtle discriminations. Advanced theories of physics may be able to encompass the perceptual categories of animals and naïve men yet still be partial and perspectively relative. This is still a minority view among philosophers of knowledge, but it is a steadily increasing one, even though in the history of ideas each new demonstration of epistemological relativity temporarily generates new converts to an ontological relativity.

He has also made contributions to other areas of descriptive epistemology. His essays "The Fashionable Fallacy of Dispensing with Description," reprinted here, and "Gestalt Perception as a Source of Scientific Knowledge" (1959) are prize contributions to the psychology of science. They provide a much-needed correction to those who mistakenly see quantified, atomized, and instrumented knowing as replacing ordinary perception in science (Campbell, 1966). The lighthearted charm of "Do Animals Undergo Conscious Experience?" (1963) should not be allowed to hide valuable contributions to the philosophers' problems of "other minds," and the "mind-body" relationship. Note that it challenges a common belief that it is the activity of the highest and evolutionarily most recent parts of the brain that corresponds to conscious experience. It is this conundrum of conscious perception that leads Lorenz to his paradoxical title, *The Other Side of the Mirror.*

Intergroup Aggression

On Aggression (1966) is Lorenz's best-known book among psychologists and social scientists, and the most vigorously attacked. In introducing Lorenz, I feel the need to discuss this work both because of its notoriety and because of my own concern with the problem of human intergroup hostility.

Lorenz's handling of animal aggression is a beautiful example of scientific problem-solving. For coral fish he fits together the separate puzzles of bright color patterns, fighting focused on members of their own species, stable living locations in the coral reefs, and the survival advantages of spacing. Similarly striking is his handling of pair bonding, nest defense, and aggression toward conspecifics in various species of geese, along with his identification of modified aggression gestures in their courtship rituals.

In these and many other examples the case is made that intraspecific aggression—aggression toward members of the same species—can be useful and adaptive, furthering species survival. Lorenz offers this fact as a corrective to Freud's explanation of aggression as the expression of a self-defeating death wish and of more general tendencies to see all expressions of hostility as evil, maladaptive, unnatural, and a product of abnormal environmental conditions; hence, his chapter entitled "What Aggression Is Good For," and the still more provocative title for the German edition of the whole book, *Das Sogennante Böse* (*The So-called Evil*). Such titles are a part of a conversation, a reaction to overextreme statements in other directions by the earlier participants. Considering the contents of the book as a whole, and the subsequent conversations it stimulated, a more accurate title with a reverse emphasis could have been used, e.g., "The Evil of Human

Aggression in Contrast with the Benignness of Animal Aggression in Stable Natural Environments." For Lorenz's overriding lesson is that human aggression as expressed in war, murder, and genocide is the paramount modern danger. Man desperately needs political innovations and popular understandings that will control such human aggressive tendencies. In this problem-solving and self-education, it will do harm rather than help to deny man's innate aggressiveness. Instead, we should try to understand aggression, and this includes understanding the past adaptiveness of tendencies which have gone awry and now threaten our very survival.

Many of my fellow peace-oriented liberals react with fear to the message "aggression is natural" because it implies to them "aggression is good," or they fear that it will imply this to the general public whom they are trying to educate about the dangers of traditional ethnocentric hostility toward outgroups. They fear that this message from an eminent scientist will serve to justify and vindicate these dangerous carry-overs from past social systems and/or stages in biological evolution. Lorenz and they agree on the danger and agree on the outmodedness of the aggressive traditions and instincts. Lorenz does not want to provide the semblance of scientific support for these traditions. Quite the contrary. Yet it unfortunately remains true in the present climate that labeling aggression as "natural" may well have the effect of labeling it "normal" and "good." Perhaps we should educate ourselves away from this oversimplified, overoptimistic morality, back toward that distrust of human nature found in our religious traditions.

My fellow liberals have another frightened reaction to the "aggression is innate" message because it is pessimistic, implying the difficulty or impossibility of preventing wars. The scientist who affirms such a message supports apathy and defeatism in regard to the problem of war, and perhaps jingoistic nationalism. So great are the practical political implications of an eminent scientist's authoritative pronouncements on this issue that he ought to refrain from the "aggression is innate" or "war is natural" conclusion unless the evidence is completely compelling, which it certainly is not at this time.

Does "natural" human aggressiveness lead to war, or is it human social organization that produces war? Lorenz refers to both biological inheritance and social evolution, and to both individual male territoriality and to tribal organization in regard to human warlikeness. For his popularizers, however, no such ambiguity is present. Instead, the message is clear: man's warlike behavior is due to the fact that he is a territorial animal. Lorenz, in the interview presented in this volume, now wishes he had made clearer the distinction between individual and organized group aggression. He has, in correspondence, expressed his agreement with the following statement:

The line of thought in both the 1965 paper and the present amendments must be sharply distinguished from the currently popular biological-evolutionary explanation of war. The concept of territoriality has added much to our understanding of aggression at the level of the individual fighting fish and gander (Lorenz, 1966). Realistic group conflict theory may be thought of as a theory of social group territoriality and social group aggression. But the relationship between these two levels of territoriality should be kept clear. Vertebrate territoriality as studied by the ethologists represents the behavioral syndrome of an individual male protecting a single female or harem and his offspring. Realistic group conflict theory is not the same theory and does not explain intergroup conflict as an expression of this territorial instinct in individual males. Rather, it is an analogous theory at a different level of organization. Realistic group conflict theory refers to organized groups involving many males and many families. In terms of the behavioral dispositions of individuals involved, the two levels of territoriality are in opposition rather than coterminous. Even though efforts to mobilize human ethnocentrism often make reference to protecting home and family, group-level territoriality has always required that the soldier abandon for extensive periods the protecting of his own wife, children, and home. Individual territoriality and aggression means *intra*group conflict, and is regularly suppressed in the service of *inter*group conflict. Proposition 4 of realistic group conflict theory (1965b, p. 288) states that *real threat causes ingroup solidarity.* In an early statement, Sumner says: "The exigencies of war with outsiders are what make peace inside, lest internal discord should weaken the we-group for war. These exigencies also make government and law in the ingroup, in order to prevent quarrels and enforce discipline" (1906, p. 12). It is the "internal discord" and the "quarrels within" that are the aggressive manifestations of instinctive territoriality, if any. This is the most recurrent proposition in the many sources of realistic group conflict theory. The Sherifs (1953) make a major point of it. And with the help of reviewers such as Coser (1956), Berkowitz (1962), and Rosenblatt (1964) one can readily assemble several dozen citations affirming it. It is also a major theme of the anthropological description of pyramidal-segmental societies (LeVine and Campbell, 1972). Thus it is not mammalian or primate territoriality which explains war in this theory. It is instead an analogous function at a larger organizational level, and one which requires the inhibition of the lower-level individual mammalian territoriality. It is this discontinuity which makes the social insects rather than the higher apes the closest functional analogue for complex human social organization. (Campbell, 1972, pp. 23–24.)

From this point of view, wars are fought on the basis of social indoctrination and organization, and require the inhibition of the "natural" territorial male aggressiveness. These social traditions and institutions of group hostility have been for some centuries thoroughly outmoded, dangerous, and evil, and are made suicidal with nuclear weapons.

In "Evolution of Ritualization" and "The Enmity Between Generations," both reprinted here, and in *Civilized Man's Eight Deadly Sins* (1973), Lorenz explains socially organized intergroup aggression as due to "pseudo-speciation," a term he borrows from E. H. Erikson (1966). Socially organized man's capacity for genocide is based on social devices which make those who speak a different language and belong to a different tribe seem unhuman, a different species from ourselves. This conceptualization is a valuable contribution to the social science theories of intergroup conflict, ethnocentrism, war, and genocide. Lorenz's views on the evil of killing conspecifics differentiated only by pseudo-speciation is essentially in agreement with Kelman's (1973) recent brilliant analysis.

Social Evolution and the Preservation of Tradition

Although professionally a zoologist, Lorenz has provided some wise observations and speculations on sociocultural evolution, sampled here in "The Enmity Between Generations and Its Probable Ethological Causes," and in "Evolution of Ritualization." The historical cumulation of customs, techniques, beliefs, and rules has probably taken place under the shaping of a "natural selection" or "selective retention" process analogous to biological evolution. Given a stable ecology or selective system, and given social systems capable of loyally reproducing the selected variants, such a process would result in wise and adapted customs, including "wise superstitions," the true advantages of which the public and its leaders might be unaware of, or rationalize in scientifically unsophisticated terms. One who holds this view—as, with qualification, I myself do (1965a)—is apt to arrive at a generalized respect for tradition. Just as belief in evolutionary theory produces in a biologist a puzzled awe for those bizarre forms of biological life whose adaptive advantage he does not yet understand, so too belief in social evolution should generate in the social scientist faced with an "incredible" traditional belief a tentative trust that underlying it was some adaptive truth he did not yet understand. While the wisdom of all evolutionary processes is wisdom about past environments, rather than present or future ones except as these remain similar to the past, it would probably improve the validity of social science if such a trusting attitude were more common. Certainly there is no justification for the commoner practice of invoking tradition only as an explanation of social malfunctions.

Biological evolution depends upon rigid mechanisms for loyally duplicating the cumulated selection of alternative genes. While this rigid retention and duplication is in opposition to mutational change, it is equally important. If either variation or retention is maximized, evolutionary adaptation is made impossible. One might expect evolutionary geneticists to favor increasing the mutation rate because this would increase the raw material for evolutionary innovation. On the contrary, they have uniformly opposed such increases, as produced by X-rays and nuclear reactions, on the grounds that these jeopardize the retention of already achieved adaptations. In their judgment, the balance between retention and variation is already tilted enough toward variation.

Similarly, one who believes that an historic sociocultural evolutionary process has produced adaptive systems whose functions we do not yet fully understand is apt to feel that precious treasures are in jeopardy when the social-custom retention mechanisms fail. There are grounds for concern if there is emerging a whole generation of young people who do not want to grow up to be like their parents, or if child-rearing patterns no longer lead a child to identify with its parents, or if parents are neglecting their disciplinary duties in reconciling children to self-restraint and to the existing social order, or if urban living and television are reducing stable group participation and social control. Lorenz addresses himself to these problems in "The Enmity Between Generations" and in *Civilized Man's Eight Deadly Sins* (1973). Such issues are now largely neglected, and Lorenz attempts a valuable mission in directing our attention to their dangers.

The popular acceptance of the scientific world view, with a consequent loss of credibility for supernatural sanctions, may have contributed to a possible disruption in the transmission of cultural wisdom. "The Enmity Between Generations" was published as a part of a collection of essays by eminent scientists arguing this possibility (Weiss, 1970; Polanyi, 1970; Eccles, 1970). Lorenz agrees: "The erroneous belief that only the rationally comprehensible or the scientifically provable belong to the fixed knowledge of mankind produces disastrous effects. It encourages 'scientifically enlightened' youth to throw overboard the enormous fund of knowledge and wisdom contained in the traditions of every old civilization and in the teachings of the great world religions (1973, p. 63)." But Lorenz's own emphasis on man's status as an animal may be particularly undermining to the authority of social tradition. The traditional emphasis upon man's difference from animals, his close-to-divine nature, may be a packaging of the truth that man is the carrier of a precious socially transmitted cultural civilization. Note that Monod (1971) in his chapter on "The Kingdom and the Darkness" finds himself in a similar bind, as too do Lorenz's enemies, the behaviorist psychologists.

I am in complete agreement on the importance of

the problems, and in considerable sympathy with
Lorenz's conclusions. But over-all these two essays
make me uncomfortable, and I end up not wanting to
be identified with them. As I sort through my mixed
feelings I come up with several points of disagreement.
The social evolutionist can assign a useful social role to
the elderly scold who automatically decries every deviation from a sentimentally idealized version of the
past. Nonetheless, it is distressing to see Lorenz losing
his broader social-evolutionist perspective and falling
into this one role. In these two essays he objects too
much and too automatically to all aspects of modernity,
and idealizes too much wild and archaic rural forms of
life adapted to no longer existing ecological niches, producing a contradictory set of criticisms. He objects to
industrialized mass production and mass-communication marketing of clothing, asserting that this produces
a passive, faddish uniformity of styles and leads to the
loss of traditional rural regional costumes. Yet the modern urban dweller has a much wider choice of styles,
and exercises enough choice to end up with a much
greater person-to-person diversity, individuality, and
freedom than did the archaic villager. What a tourist
sees as a valuable village-to-village variety in danger of
being lost through modern means of production and
distribution, was historically, for the individual within
any one village, an enforced homogeneity and oppres-
sive restriction of choice.

Furthermore, as Lorenz recognizes, both the ingroup uniformity and the meticulously maintained
group-to-group differences are a part of the pseudospeciation or ethnocentrism which Lorenz rightly decries.
While in these two essays he fails to list tribalism or nationalism as one of his deadly sins, considering these
essays jointly with *On Aggression*, I think he would
agree that the most seriously deadly sin is nationalism

which uses pseudospeciation to justify genocide. Indeed, he says as much in one paragraph of *Eight Deadly Sins:*

> Any clearly differentiated cultural group tends to consider itself a species apart, insofar as it does not accept the members of other, comparable units as of equal worth. In many native languages the term for one's own tribe is simply "man." To kill a member of a neighboring tribe therefore does not amount to real murder. This consequence of pseudospeciation is extremely dangerous: inhibition against killing a fellow human is largely overcome, while intraspecific aggression, elicited by conspecifics, and only by these, remains active. We hate the "enemy" with a hatred reserved only for fellow human beings and not even the most dangerous beast of prey; we can kill them [the enemy] with impunity since we do not feel that they are really human. Naturally it belongs to the well-tried technique of all warmongers to support this view. (1973, pp. 65–66.)

So strongly do I agree with this passage that I regret that it is used in this book merely to make the case for a similar pseudospeciation in the war between generations. The sin and danger of the latter seem to me trivial in comparison. While nuclear weapons are on his list of deadly sins, genocidal nationalism was already deadly sin number one even before the atom and hydrogen bombs.

Another point of disagreement: interest in the rigid retention mechanisms making possible social evolution also brings a sympathy, however grudging, for the fanatical conformity pressures and ostracism of deviants which well-indoctrinated group members exert even on seemingly functionless matters of style. A visible deviation from group norms operates like one of Lorenz's innate releasing mechanisms, triggering scolding retaliation and ostracism just as though something of fundamental importance was at stake. While I can understand the importance of such a mechanism, I hate to

his book on aggression

see it operating in Lorenz in these essays, in which he reacts to deviations in dress style and grooming by segments of the young like the proverbial bull to a red flag. This puzzles me particularly since he has himself conspicuously enjoyed deviating from the orthodox clean-shaven, suited-and-tied norm for scientists and businessmen.

More seriously, Lorenz's over-all message is that if things are left as they are, disaster looms ahead. Therefore, he should be, and in fact in places is, against those social traditional indoctrination procedures, conformity pressures, and ethnocentric group loyalties that are keeping things as they are. As he himself states, formerly wise traditions can become maladaptive if the selective system has changed, as, in fact, it has. He recognizes that he and the ethically concerned "hippies" agree on many of the sources of evil. Why can't he then regard their deviant uniforms as akin to the priest's collar, an outward public commitment to lead an unworldly altruistic life independent of the outmoded establishment culture which is leading us to disaster?

Still more serious are my reservations about his discussion of the "pseudodemocratic doctrine." As already shown, I share some of Lorenz's criticisms of behaviorism, but I find myself wholly identified with the environment-changing, learning-emphasizing, social-ameliorist "behaviorists" whom he scolds under the terms "pseudodemocratic doctrine" and "indoctrinability." Some specific quotations focus this concern:

It is an indisputable ethical truth that all men have an equal right to the same chances of development, but this truth is too easily converted to the untruth that all men are potentially equal. The behavioristic doctrine goes a step further in maintaining that all men would be equal if they could develop under the same external conditions, and indeed that they would become ideal people if only those conditions were ideal, therefore people cannot, or *must not,* possess any inherited properties, particularly those that determine their social behavior and their social requirements. (Lorenz, 1973, pp. 86–87.)

The fallacy of supposing that, given the proper conditioning, anything may be demanded of a person, anything made out of him, underlies many of the deadly sins committed by civilized mankind against nature, including the nature of man, and against humanity. If a universally accepted ideology, and the politics ensuing from it, are founded on a lie, this is bound to have disastrous effects. The pseudodemocratic doctrine here under discussion undoubtedly bears a considerable part of the blame for the moral and cultural collapse that threatens the Western world. (1973, pp. 87–88.)

The sins, evils, and collapse of the last paragraph go unspecified. I do not recognize them, and wonder anxiously what past social orders are being idealized? Hereditary monarchy and social castes justified by beliefs in hereditary genetic superiority? Special rights for a *Herrenvolk?*

Social ameliorist "behaviorists" like myself focus on environmental changes and learning because we see these as something a well-intentioned society can do something about, not because we deny all individual differences in ability. Free public education is one of our great goals and partial achievements. Think of what profound changes in society it would make if we took seriously that part of the equalitarian ideal which Lorenz endorses: "all men have an equal right to the same chances of development." It would produce the same sort of political goals that he seems to be decrying as equalitarian excesses. It would lead us to a "fair-start capitalism" or socialism in which one's chances for development were not biased by inherited wealth and privileged access to opportunities. Lorenz sees *horizontal* diversity of culture as an ideal. This is more threatened by special privileged economic imperialism than by democratic or socialistic equalitarianism. Instead, what he advocates seems to me to implicitly justify a *vertical* diversification of social class or caste, a hierarchy of subcultures accompanied by politically guaranteed special opportunities for those already at the top. But he is not explicit on what social order he is advocating as an alternative to that which he scolds.

The Political Implications of Evolutionary Genetics

Nicholas Pastore (1949) once did a study comparing the politics of psychologists who emphasized the influence of heredity with the politics of those emphasizing environmental determinants of intelligence. The correlation was strong—those emphasizing heredity were the more politically conservative. Lewis Terman, a socialist who emphasized heredity, was one of the few exceptions. I suspect that if zoologists were included in such a study they would tend both to emphasize heredity determinants of individual differences and to be more politically conservative, while sociologists would tend to be opposite on both counts. Much of this is simply the tendency to exaggerate the importance of one's own specialty, and there are, of course, exceptions. Karl Pearson (1887; 1897) combined enthusiastic Darwinian evolutionary biology with an enthusiastic pamphleteering socialism, Kropotkin (1902; 1924) with anarchism, and Haldane (1938) with openly expressed pro-communist sympathies. R. A. Fisher (1930) provided a detailed genetic theory of the decline of civilizations which could make one an advocate of socialism, or contraceptives, or both! In the private-property societies of ancient and modern civilizations, those genes associated with infertility increased the dowry and other social advantages provided to children, leading these genes to become associated with ability genes, eventually removing the latter from the population. But a general tendency for biologism to go with conservatism no doubt remains, and may be even stronger now than in the past. Today the advocacy of eugenicist social programs, such as restricting the procreational opportunities of incompetent and defective persons, appears only in right-wing political platforms. In the period 1880–1930 eugenics was often a part of liberal-democratic reform programs. Note that while Haldane (1938) scolds the Nazi eugenics policies, details the very small effects that could be expected, emphasizes the lack of adequate genetic knowledge upon which to base eugenics decisions, and raises the moral problem of who should decide, he still is far from completely ruling out all governmental eugenics policies.

A zoologist naturally tends to apply his biological perspectives to human affairs and to draw political implications. This is a tendency which the rest of us should encourage if it is done thoroughly and explicitly—we probably need detailed speculations on the effect of priestly celibacy in Ireland if the more intelligent were more often recruited into the priesthood. Speculations on the effect of contraceptives on future human sexual urges (e.g., Darwin, 1960) are in order. While I prefer environmentalist cultural-motivational explanations of the slight average Jewish-American superiority on intelligence tests (Klineberg, 1944), and am particularly fascinated by the heterocultural emancipation hypothesis of the ex-Norwegian-American peasant Thorstein Veblen (1919), I think we should have historical studies raising the question of whether or not in the European Diaspora the conditions of Jewish life were such that those persons most able in the skills required of high civilization also tended to have the most children who survived to adulthood. We also need speculations such as Herrnstein (1973) has produced about the possibility that increasing the equality of opportunity will eventually increase the genetic superiority of those in the professional and managerial roles over those in the more supervised occupations.

The present intellectual climate on the whole opposes such speculations, a tabooing so effective that we may lose some of the benefits that evolutionary genetics might contribute to social planning. This is the core of much of Lorenz's protests about "indoctrinability" and the "pseudodemocratic dogma." I see the roots of the opposition not in the populist behaviorism which he blames, but rather in the concerned intellectuals' reaction against specific political movements which have advocated doctrines of racial superiority with catastrophic results. On the U.S. political scene, black/white racist politics are such an ever-present danger that even though the Nazi threat is thirty years past, the need for political vigilance along these lines is still great. It is a regrettable cost if this vigilance suppresses a legitimate area of biological speculation and research. I do not see clearly how the dilemma can be resolved, but I sympathize with the biologist who feels that his scientific freedom of inquiry is being infringed upon.

On the other hand, I specifically disagree with many of the implications of the brief and casual comments on genetics that Lorenz makes in "The Enmity Between Generations," *Eight Deadly Sins*, and the interview presented in this book. He lists "genetic decay" as one of the deadly sins. Insofar as I can tell what he is talking about, I disagree. It is conceivable, even probable, that the widespread availability of eyeglasses has somewhat reduced an ancient tendency, operating as a selection pressure, for those with poorer eyesight to have fewer children. Nonetheless, our over-all species adequacy in the area of vision has been so greatly increased (including, for example, the ability of those over fifty to read) that our net adaptive adequacy, our survival value, has been greatly improved by the widespread use of optical aids. A comprehensive evolutionist, considering both biological and social evolution, should therefore favor the use of glasses even if they incur a genetic cost. One might make the similar case that artificial transportation devices, from the horse on, have reduced the selection pressure on innate components in speed of running. On this we have a hundred years of comparable Olympic records, in which top speeds show a steady increase instead of decrease, and no general advantage to the rural contestants over the urban, no doubt due to improved nutrition and training. But even if there were some evidence of a genetically based deterioration in running speed, this would be no cause for alarm, since speed of running is irrelevant to adaptive adequacy in modern man's ecological niche. Because of the slowness of evolutionary change, aesthetic preferences governing sexual selection and leadership choice might well perpetuate outmoded criteria of adaptive adequacy, but the consistent evolutionist should, it seems to me, decry these atavistic tastes rather than give them the status of approved moral and aesthetic standards.

Particularly frustrating in Lorenz's discussion of genetic decay is the combination of extreme conclusions—"There is no doubt that through the decay of genetically anchored social behavior we are threatened by the apocalypse in a particularly horrible form" (1973, p. 59)—with weak anecdotes of limited relevance. Instead of a case being made for his conclusions, we are given an instance in which one criminally insane person killed three more persons after three releases as cured. Does he believe that employing the death penalty or permanent incarceration in such cases would improve our genetic stock? Or that no murderers are ever safe for release? Or that psychiatry is adequate to make the required diagnoses? I find none of these beliefs justified. At very least, he should have specified his alternatives and argued their genetic impact. Clearly against permissiveness, he fails to make a case for punitiveness relevant to the grounds of his professed concerns.

Domestication is a genetic trend which he deplores. This seems to me misguided. Urbanization is the more appropriate term and modern man is undoubtedly better adapted to urban living and to a world-wide cosmopolitan culture than he ever was before in history. This adaptation no doubt includes genetic adaptation as well as cultural, and while hard to determine, is a legitimate issue for scientific inquiry. But to regret that this process is removing specific adaptations to specific regionally different ecological niches, as Lorenz seems to, is foolish when those ecological niches no longer exist. Genetic purity seems one of Lorenz's values, but modern studies of the genetics of natural populations in their natural environments find great heterozygosity rather than genetic uniformity or homozygosity. It is the systematic breeding of animals and plants in domestication that produces purity of genetic stock, which turns out to be a real liability both for control of lethal genes and for adaptability to environmental changes. From the point of view of genetic experience with animals and plants, insofar as I know, there are no dangers from hybridizing and no documented instances in which a valuable species-specific adaptation to a still relevant ecological niche was lost through racial mixing.

Konrad, I owe you and the reader an apology for spending so much space on issues that are a very small part of your total writings or of the four treasures being reprinted here. You will have recognized that my doing so is a sign that I too am influenced by what you call the dominance of the pseudodemocratic doctrine, and by what I recognize as the liberal intellectuals' well-grounded fears of racist politics. These very real social pressures make me unable to unself-consciously express my admiration for your great contributions to ethology, evolution of behavior, cybernetic behaviorism, descriptive epistemology, the dangers of group-organized aggression, and social evolution. Instead, I also feel the need to intrude myself in order to make clear where I stand on other controversial beliefs of yours. Were it not for the social pressures which we both agree are present (albeit with different explanations), I could have handled my disagreements by omission and could have produced a uniformly enthusiastic introduction. Such an introduction would have been fully as accurate as the present one—just distorted in the opposite direction.

As it is, however, I feel it necessary to make sure that my own reputation on the controversial issues is not confused by my expressions of great admiration for your work. So important to me is this selfish concern that, in addition to the discussion above, I feel the need to discuss an issue which you barely allude to toward the end of the interview—race differences in intelligence. This is an issue of crucial concern in U.S. psychology today, and one on which the pronouncements of psychologists are immediately picked up in racist politics. I feel that it is not enough for you to say that while races differ, these differences do not imply better or worse, since each is best adapted to some different ecological niche. Such a conclusion is patronizing and demeaning for races that now live in a common environment. It is also, I believe, wrong for the major components of past and current adaptations. In modern evolutionary theory, an understanding of race difference requires the specification of a difference in systematic selection pressures. For skin color, some of the selection pressures are now understood: in northern Europe, children are apt to absorb too little vitamin D from sunlight and in Africa they are apt to absorb too much. For sickle cell anemia, we can now specify the increased resistance to malaria for the heterozygous condition that led to a high gene frequency in central West Africa. Sixty centuries of cultural taboo explain the failure of the Chinese to have evolved the capacity to digest cows' milk. But for the traits of general adaptability to environmental novelty, no such differential selection pressure can be specified. As with speed of running, which Olympic records show to be widely distributed across races, it is my judgment that the evolutionary biologist's first expectation should be for a high selection pressure in favor of intelligence in the evolutionary background of all groups. Any speculations to the contrary should be accompanied by detailed examination of specified selection pressures operating in other directions.

The vocabulary skills which are the core of intelligence and achievement tests are so obviously learned that I cannot find them relevant to the issue of genetic differences where the groups in question have different opportunities to learn the vocabulary employed in the tests. Equality of opportunity is not even equal for brothers and sisters in the same family, and there are enough average opportunity differences to produce a dependable IQ difference favoring first-born children. Even so, studies comparing the IQ similarity of identical and fraternal twins may be relevant to the contribution of heredity when family environment is held relatively constant. Such determinations are, however, irrelevant to interpreting comparisons confounded by environmental differences, just as irrelevant as they would be to explaining the differences between English and French children on a French-language vocabulary test. I still find relevant and compelling Otto Klineberg's (1944) studies of the 1930's. The more similar the white/black educational environment, the smaller the difference. Since no available comparisons eliminate the environmental differences, the most plausible extrapolation is to no IQ difference at all if learning opportunities were to be equal.

My participation in the vigorous debates on race differences that are going on within U.S. psychology today has been limited but clearly on the side of the equalitarians. I have even called for a moratorium on further measurement of group differences unless accompanied by a meticulous measurement of each child's EIPQ (Environmental Intelligence Producing Quotient); that is, the vocabulary of his waking environment, the frequency of vocabulary rehearsal games, the intellectual stimulation and response to childish curiosity, the quality of toys, etc. (Campbell and Frey, 1970). The public political climate in America is such that environmentally produced differences, when publicized, are interpreted as racial and are used to justify sustained and increased differences in environmental opportunities. Unfortunately, Lorenz is wrong in judging equalitarianism to be dominant among the U.S. public. Fortunately, he is right about its dominance among U.S. intellectuals, although this dominance is currently eroding in spite of the harassment of the nonequalitarians.

One of the national experiences that is increasing the belief in hereditary social class and racial differences in ability is the poor showing of compensatory education programs. The programs never entirely remove the differences, and the effects fade rapidly. Frey and I have demonstrated that these are exactly the results that would be expected if IQ scores were entirely due to environmental opportunity differences, and are thus irrelevant to the heredity/environment argument (Campbell and Frey, 1970). Most of the evaluations of compensatory programs have involved quasi-experimental designs that underestimate the effects; indeed, make the programs look harmful if they are in fact ineffectual. I have spoken out vigorously on this bias

(Campbell and Erlebacher, 1970; Campbell, 1973). It is the few randomized experiments that produce the optimistic results. They never eliminate the gap entirely, but neither do they ever completely remove the gap in home and playground vocabulary.

I can imagine a political environment in which the discussion of genetic differences between races could be carried out in scholarly curiosity devoid of political passion. That environment would be one committed to equality of opportunity. In such an environment a person's race, or the average ability of his race, would have nothing to do with his opportunities. Instead, we have in America a structure in which a middle-class white of IQ 100 has innumerable advantages in life over a black of the same IQ. Some of these advantages still have quasi-legal status, others are imbedded in unofficial discriminations, opportunity structures, and subcultural differences. The few intellectuals who have publicly asserted a belief in race differences in intelligence have, illogically, it seems to me, tended to accompany this conclusion with policy recommendations (like special curriculums) that would increase the opportunity disadvantage and produce larger differences in the future. It would have been more logical had they recommended classifying children for such differential treatment on the basis of the tests they used to measure the average racial differences, for certainly they should believe that test scores are a better indicator of the relevant genes than skin color. In the U.S. it would be a moral gain to substitute segregation by IQ for segregation by race, and ability tracking within schools may approximate this. But such a system still does not live up to that equality of opportunity which both Lorenz and I endorse. Segregation by IQ adds additional opportunity differentials to the differentials already created by heredity and prior environment. We have at present no feasible proposals for educational systems that could truly equalize opportunity. Let us at least avoid policies that add to the differential.

Overview

In Konrad Lorenz's magnificent career he has made creative contributions to a wide variety of fields. In addition to those cited by the Nobel Prize committee, there are other works described here, as in cybernetic behaviorism and descriptive epistemology, which may in the long run be judged equally important. There are also his popular essays of later years which have become controversial best sellers, widely acclaimed and widely opposed. These have offered opinions which he knew in advance would be unpopular with many intellectuals, and on some issues succeeding so well that I have gone to great lengths to disassociate myself from them, producing a marked imbalance in this essay.

Rereading the first four and one-half sections of this introduction will help right the balance disturbed by the last one and one-half. So too will a reading of Lorenz's major works and the four essays reprinted here, as only one of them, "The Enmity Between Generations," goes into the controversial areas, and even it earns its place by its provocative broadening of perspectives.

Konrad Lorenz Responds to Donald Campbell

In his introductory essay (pages 88–118), Donald Campbell has expressed the hope that a discussion of areas of disagreement will add to the validity of his introduction of Lorenz to psychologists. Fortunately this discussion can be carried an important step further. Professor Lorenz responded in a personal letter which he has given us permission to reproduce in this volume.

Altenberg, 16 August, 1974

My Dear Donald,

As I have already said, I feel deeply grateful to you for writing "Reintroducing Konrad Lorenz to Psychology." As I did when I read your rendering of the first papers which you had translated, I felt that you had expressed that which I have been trying to say much more clearly than I ever could have done it. Also, you have beautifully analyzed the slight but important dis-

119

crepancy between my opinions and the interpretation given to them by some writers, for instance by Robert Ardrey in his much-too-simple interpretation of human territoriality. You are also exactly right in supposing that the belief in man's "close-to-divine nature may be a packaging of the truth that man is the carrier of a precious socially transmitted cultural civilization." This is exactly why I get furious at anybody who despises religious people or, worse, makes fun of their beliefs.

In relation to your deep understanding of 98 per cent of what I am trying to say, the few points on which I feel that you have misunderstood me hardly seem to count. However, I feel that on most of them a real consensus between us is possible and this feeling impels me to write what now follows:

1. (Page 105) I am certainly *not* "decrying any deviation from a sentimentally idealized version of the past!" I might just as well be decrying the fact that mutations do occur in a species. My point is that the interaction between factors preserving invariance on one side and factors effecting changes on the other side must maintain an equilibrium which corresponds exactly with the inconstancy of the environment in which the living system has to exist, *irrespective of whether this system be a species or a human culture.* I quite realize that the inconstancy of the human environment is rapidly increasing and that, therefore, the influence of rebellious youth must increase correspondingly while conservatism must be decreasing apace, if our culture is to remain viable. In my lecture in Stockholm three years ago, "The Enmity Between Generations," given before an audience consisting predominantly of hippified youngsters, I may have given the impression that I was on the conservative side rather than on theirs. Had I been speaking to an audience of conservative businessmen, I would indubitably have seemed to lean to the other side. I have become reconciled to the fact

that one becomes extremely unpopular with the conservative old as well as with the revolutionary young if one tells them that it is only *together,* in the balance of their antagonism, that they achieve the viability of any cultural system. If you want to have my opinion on the interaction between established civilization and those who feel that it needs to be thoroughly changed, read Theodore Roszak's book *The Making of a Counter Culture* (1969).

2. (Page 107) I do not react antagonistically to the uniform of revolutionary youth—aside from the fact that I strongly dislike uniforms of any kind. If, as an ethologist, I observe my own instinctive antagonistic response elicited by long manes and unwashed bare feet, a response which indeed is analogous to that of the proverbial bull, the result of this self-observation is quite another thing than the instinctive response itself. However, I do not agree with your opinion that this uniform is analogous to the dog collar of clergymen; I think it is comparable to the war paint of Indians. In fact, it was an amusing, if rather humiliating, self-observation that made me realize this. As you say, I myself usually deviate from the orthodox dress of scientists, but I do this for the sake of convenience and not as a signal directed at anybody else. When my young co-workers began to dress in a progressively hippified manner, I caught myself doing the opposite! One day, as I was putting on a collar and tie before going to one of our weekly colloquia in Seewiesen, I fell to puzzling as to why I was doing it. When I realized that I was actually war-painting in protest against the young people, I shamefacedly changed back into my old sloppy clothes. Also, I have to concede that the meaning of clothing has changed even for me: recently, on seeing a short-haired boy dressed nicely in collar and tie, I caught myself getting the impression that he must be rather a sissy. Incidentally, all this has already become obsolete: what was at

first the "war paint" of rebels has rather deplorably lost its edge by becoming generally accepted fashion.

3. (Page 105) I do indeed regard "industrialized mass production and mass-communication marketing" as a serious danger. Quite some time ago I had realized the deleterious ethical effects which the pseudodemocratic doctrine produces by relieving the human individual of all responsibility for his or her actions. This process abolishes most or all human values, as moral responsibility is not only a liability but a *prerogative of man* not granted to any beast. Slightly later I clearly understood the damage done to human ethics and morals by that which I have termed "technomorphic habits of thought" in "The Fashionable Fallacy of Dispensing with Description." I am rather ashamed that I failed to see the close interdependence of technocracy and pseudodemocracy until, quite lately, I read Theodore Roszak's (1969) great book. If I have always objected to extreme industrialization, it was because I always felt, in a vague and intuitive manner, what it is that Roszak makes so abundantly clear: all these processes are part and parcel of the technocratic trend to make men more malleable, more easy to manipulate, to deprive them more and more of the capacity to make their own decisions, in short, to take away their individuality. I do not agree with your statement that "the modern urban dweller has a much wider choice of styles, and exercises enough choice to end up with a much greater person-to-person heterogeneity, individuality, and freedom than did the archaic villager." I have lived in archaic villages most of the time, but also long enough in great modern cities, and I still disagree. The average city dweller may *seem* to have a lot of free choice, but really he is all too prone to follow the guidance of experts in the high art of manipulating customers. Technocracy is the regime of experts. It is, as Roszak has made very clear to me, a totalitarianism which remains

ideologically invisible because its techniques become progressively more and more subliminal. Technocracy could coerce, but "prefers to charm conformity from us by exploiting our deep-seated commitment to the scientific world view and by manipulating the securities and creature comforts of the industrial affluence which science has given us." Therefore, "it is not easy to question the thoroughly sensible, thoroughly well-intentioned but nevertheless reductive humanism with which the technocracy surrounds itself, without seeming to speak a dead and obsolete language." Nothing could express my feelings more exactly than do these words from Roszak's book.

All terms connoting *values* belong to this obsolete language. Technomorphic habits of thought have misled the majority of modern humanity into thinking that anything which cannot be defined in scientific language and verified by quantifying methods *does not possess any real existence.* Human freedom, dignity, and morals are regarded as mere illusions and this belief is most welcome to technocracy as, for obvious reasons, all emotions are undesirable from its point of view. The frictionless working of the technocratically organized society is dependent on the predictability of any individual's behavior. Hence the autonomy of the individuum must be abolished. Unpredictable emotions and individual decisions taken under their influence, all individual initiative, etc., constitute a danger to this kind of social system, as Aldous Huxley, that great prophet, has so clearly realized. Anyone really interested in the present predicament of humanity must regard it as a duty to read—or reread—*Brave New World* (1932) and *Brave New World Revisited* (1958) by Aldous Huxley, as well as Theodore Roszak's *The Making of a Counter Culture.*

There is only one important point on which I find myself strongly disagreeing with Roszak and I am sure you will find the same: Roszak equates science as such with a purely technomorphic analytical procedure. Although he is fighting on our side, he does not seem to realize that there are cognitive mechanisms other than rational thought and analytical quantifying procedures. Any "scientific world view," as he calls it, would be very unscientific indeed, in your and my opinion! In fact, it would be based on a lousy epistemology, being exactly that kind of pseudoscientific world view against which I have tried to argue in "The Fashionable Fallacy of Dispensing with Description."

4. (Pages 107–113) The slight change of position effected by the influence of Roszak urges me to qualify the statements on pseudodemocratic doctrine which you quote. The doctrine is only an outcome and maybe a tool of technocracy. The real evil, as I see it, is humanity's tendency to evolve culturally and perhaps genetically in the direction of the happy robot, which is best adapted to life in a maximally industrialized social system. Maybe all that I have said there ought not to stand in the chapter on indoctrinability, as Roszak is very probably right in saying that the progress of technocracy is "ideologically invisible," but, if so, this is exactly why it is so dangerous. We do not realize how quickly and easily we can be made into perfect fools by being surrounded by perfectly foolproof machinery, by being guided at every step by comfortably reliable signposts which make the faculty of orientation superfluous, let alone the faculty of coming to decisions. These then are the evils which you want me to specify. Again, this specification is the danger of "seeming to speak a dead and obsolete language."

You misunderstood me if you think that I am idealizing any past social order. Nothing is less congenial to me than historicism. Evolution and history are one-way processes, there is no static state which can be regarded as ideal. Nor do I see horizontal diversity of cultures as an ideal state, although it has been, in its time, a factor causing healthy selection. If you ask me what counter-measures I advocate, I am afraid I find myself in the typical position in which the medical man—which I am—so often finds himself: seeing with some clarity the causes of an illness without being able to suggest a remedy. Still you have got something with your sugges-tion of "horizontal diversification," at least as regards person-to-person relationships. In the natural coopera-tion of any two friends there regularly develops a divi-sion of labor in which, each relying on the particular faculties of the other, the two tend to become more dif-ferent from each other in a complementary way. Each regards and respects the other as his superior in respect to some special function that has to be performed in the services of their common undertaking. Whether it will ever be possible to produce a viable social system on the basis of this kind of "horizontal diversification," I do not know. In very small groups it does work, as long as none of its members pursues any goal other than that of the common undertaking. It is, then, perfectly feasi-ble to give any co-worker full power to decide, for the whole group, all those matters on which he or she is indeed the greatest authority. In my own department, I am proud to say, this horizontal delegation of authority has always worked to full satisfaction. However, it is quite another question whether it will ever be possible to institutionalize an analogous democratic system by rules and laws without the catalytic function of close personal friendship.

I now come to the most controversial point which you call frustrating, because you rightly feel that in this respect there is not a misunderstanding, but a real dif-ference of our opinions. You do not believe that my alarm cries concerning the dangers of genetic decay have a factual basis. Indeed I do not have any quantifia-ble verification to offer for their validity. However, consider this: selection is and always has been the main creative and developing agent, from the molecular stage at the very beginnings of life up to the process of gaining knowledge by falsification of hypotheses. The very moment elimination by falsification ceases, the great cognitive process of evolution or of cultural accumulation of tradition, or of scientific gaining of knowledge, not only stops dead, but immediately begins to become regressive. By the very achievements of his mind, man has eliminated all those selecting factors which have *made* that mind. It is only to be expected that humaneness will presently begin to decay, culturally and genetically, and it is not surprising at all that the symptoms of this decay become progressively more apparent on all sides. I may have changed my mind quite a bit concerning the relative importance of cultural and genetical dehumanization; the former proceeds faster by so much that one might regard the second as a rather unimportant *cura posterior*. This change of priority in my opinion was admittedly caused by Roszak, who has thoroughly frightened me with his convincing exposition of the dehumanizing effects of technocracy. However, the genetic "domestication" of civilized man is, I am convinced, progressing quite rapidly. Some cardinal symptoms which are present in most of our domestic animals are an increase in size and the hypertrophy of eating as well as of sexual activity. That all three of these symptoms have noticeably increased in man during the short span of my own life, is, to say the least, alarming. In my own family and among my friends I hardly know a single case in which the son is smaller than his father. Equally widespread is the quantitative increase of eating and sexual drive, accompanied in both cases by a loss of selectivity in releasing mechanisms. One has only to go to a beach where many urbanized people are bathing to note the rapidly increasing incidence of fat boys and young men or to look at a great modern illustrated paper in order to be confronted with both symptoms in a thoroughly alarming manner.

Of course I do not know for sure that these symptoms are genetic, they may well be cultural, at least in part, but that does not matter much. Cultural development is analogous to genetical evolution in so many areas that the causal distinctions become immaterial as regards the phenomenon here under discussion, except that cultural processes are not less, but more dangerous because of their incomparably greater speed. Moreover, the medical man is often forced to utter warnings, even if he is not quite sure of the facts. If two people in my home village who have just come back from their vacation in Portugal show symptoms of a light diarrhea, I have to act as if I *knew* they had cholera.

Like Theodore Roszak I am convinced that it is one of technocracy's most insidious stratagems to avoid all coercive methods and to rely on kind-seeming reinforcements alone. You yourself feel that I am being overhard on murderers and criminals in general. I do not advocate the death penalty, nor cruel punitive measures dictated by any idea of retribution or, worse, by any instinctive lust for revenge. A man who is a mass murderer is mentally ill by definition, because a mentally healthy person simply and predictably does not commit mass murder. Nevertheless, I do not think that a healthy philosophy of values can develop without a sense not only of what is good but also of what is evil. It is my chief reproach against the ideology of the pseudo-democratic doctrine that it tends to eradicate, throughout our whole culture, the sense of values on which alone the future of humanity depends. Public opinion ought not to relieve the delinquent of all responsibility by shifting it to the environment that effected his conditioning. It is my considered opinion that murder should be mildly discouraged, not encouraged and even glamorized, as it is today. Nobody can be more convinced than I am that the main cause of our present increase of criminality is to be sought in the widespread insufficiency of mother-child contact during early babyhood. However, another, if less important, cause lies in the undiscerning and unlimited permissiveness dictated by the pseudodemocratic doctrine.

I do not believe that the death penalty or incarceration are able to prevent our genetic stock from decay; in fact, there is nothing left in civilized society which could prevent retrograde evolution *except our nonrational sense of values,* which I still believe and hope can take a decisive hand in human evolution, both genetic and cultural. As regards genetics I still believe that the nonrational sense of values plays an important role in normal pair formation, in other words, in falling in love. If I have committed the retrospectively incredible stupidity of trying to tell this to the Nazi authorities—quite in vain, of course—the only way in which I can atone for it consists in pertinaciously preaching the same truth to another world, with which it is even less popular. Donald, there is such a thing as good and evil, there are decent guys and there are scoundrels and the difference between them is indubitably partly genetic. No living system can ever exist without elimination, however humanely it can be brought about and however much one tries not to make it appear as a punitive measure. Donald, even the falsification of a theory is a punitive measure. I know scientists to whom it is more painful than the drawing of a tooth. We *know* that evolution stops on its way upward and steps backward when creative selection ceases to operate. Man has eliminated all selective factors except his own nonrational sense of values. We must learn to rely on that.

Ever yours,
Konrad

Evolution of Ritualization in the Biological and Cultural Spheres* | Konrad Lorenz

I. Ethological Approach and Phylogenetic Ritualization

The young science of ethology can be simply defined as the biology of behavior. It is rather a paradox that the behavior of animals was not, from the beginning, investigated by zoologists and biologists, just as all other life processes were. Behavior study was begun by psychologists, and psychology is the daughter of philosophy, not of the natural sciences. The philosophical dispute between vitalistic and mechanistic psychologists did much to obscure the problems of "instinctive" behavior.

* In *Philosophical Transactions of the Royal Society of London*, 1966, 251 (Series B), 273–284.

Though a thoroughly scientific approach to these problems is clearly expressed in the writings of Charles Darwin, zoologists were slow to recognize behavior as a subject worthy of investigation. A special tribute is due to the ornithologists, whose intense pleasure and interest in just watching birds was instrumental in rediscovering the fact that biological approach and method can successfully be applied in the study of behavior, exactly as Darwin had done in his book, *The Expression of the Emotions in Man and Animals*. What, then, are these good old Darwinian procedures?

I would name the most obvious one first, as being most important. It is the unbiased observation of the organic system and the inventorizing of its component parts. In all natural sciences description has to precede systematization, and both together are the prerequisite for abstracting the natural laws prevailing in the operations of the whole.

Comparative anatomy and systematics, using a broad basis of induction gained by observation and description, brought order into the chaotic multiplicity of living species and prepared the way for the recognition of the common origin of all living creatures. Once this basic evolutionary fact was established, it was an unavoidable conclusion that a historical explanation is needed for practically every detail of structure and function observed in living creatures. Such historical explanation is indeed also a *causal* one: if we ask why man has auditory organs at the sides of his head, with auditory canals connecting them with the pharynx, one of the causal explanations of this state of affairs is that all this is so, because man is descended from water-breathing vertebrates which had gill openings in that part of their anatomy. Thus research into the phyletic history of an organ or function becomes an indispensable part of its scientific study. The application to behavior of the comparative method which reconstructs the phyletic history of organisms by studying the similarity and dissimilarity of their characters is indeed one of the most important procedures of ethological research.

Next to the comparative, the selectionist approach is, in my opinion, the most indispensable one for ethology; indeed, the two cannot be legitimately separated from each other. Finding out wherein lies the survival value of a structure or of a function is a prerequisite to understanding the factors causing its evolution. If we ask "what for?" about a cat's hooked retractile claws, and answer "to catch mice with," this is no profession of mystical teleology, but shorthand for a query concerned with causality, namely, "what is the function whose survival value exerted the selection pressure which produced cats with this kind of claw?" We call this type of inquiry "teleonomic," a term introduced by Colin Pittendrigh in the hope of setting off the corresponding concept against that of teleology as sharply as astronomy has been distinguished from astrology. Not only is the teleonomic approach essential for the deeper understanding of behavior, it may also be claimed that few zoologists have ever investigated the interaction of conflicting selection pressures with such subtlety as ethologists like Tinbergen and his pupils have done.

Last but not least I would mention, as essential for the ethological approach, a constant awareness of the organism's being a systemic whole, in the sense in which Otto Koehler defined this concept—an organized system in which each part stands in a mutual causal relationship with every other. This realization makes us cautious and circumspect in our experimenting, as we are very much aware that in any attempt to influence or isolate a single function experimentally, we must take into account the repercussions which our interference may have in all other parts of the system. One cannot do this without knowing something about the rest of the system; this is why ethological investigation has to begin with studying the intact organism in its natural biotope and getting to know it thoroughly before beginning experimentation.

Of course, the sequence of procedures just described is not exclusively characteristic of ethology. Indeed, there is no branch of biological science that does not proceed from observation and description, unbiased and free from preconceived hypothesis, to the phylogenetic and teleonomic approach before proceeding to experiment. But in many branches of the psychological and behavioral sciences it is today quite usual to devise, out of hand, some sort of experimental procedure, apply it to a highly complicated system about which next to nothing is known, and then record the results. Of course, information can be, and has been, gathered by this method; it is exactly the way in which a species, by random mutation and recombination, gathers "information" and adapts itself to its environment. However, we also know the very slow speed with which this procedure operates and we prefer to have results before the present interglacial period comes to an end. That is why ethology emphatically keeps to well-tried Darwinian procedures.

The historical origin of ethology may be ascribed to a discovery made by two zoologists, who were unbiased in the contemporary quarrels between different psychological schools and bent only on clearing up the taxonomic relations of the species of a comparatively small group of birds. The success of such endeavors, as every phylogenist knows, is dependent on the number of homologous characters that can be adduced to give a measure of genetic relationship between the forms investigated. In their search for more and ever more homologizeable characters, Charles Otis Whitman in the U.S. and Oskar Heinroth in Germany independently made the outstandingly important discovery that there are coordinated motor patterns of action which are just as characteristic of a species, a genus, a family, an order, and even of the higher taxonomic categories, as are any structural properties of the animal's anatomy. This fact alone justifies the conclusion that the coordination of these movements is performed in the genome of a species and that the concept of homology can be applied to them just as well as to morphological characters. Whitman, as early as 1898, made a statement which involves an essential part of ethology's present program: "Instincts and organs are to be studied from the common viewpoint of phyletic descent."

The study of the phylogenetic process of ritualization, with its cultural analogy, constitutes the main subject of our present conference, originated simultaneously with the comparative study of homologous motor patterns, for the simple reason that most of the motor coordinations used by the pioneers of ethology were themselves ritualized: both Whitman and Heinroth concentrated on the patterns of display and had good cause to do so, as I shall shortly explain.

It was Julian Huxley and Edmund Selous who first realized that a very special process of evolution had been at work in the production of threat, courtship, and other displays, which birds and other animals address to fellow members of their own species. They discovered that many of these movements serving communication are similar to and yet different from motor patterns developing an altogether different function in the everyday life of the species. For obvious reasons, into which I need not go here, the communicative movements have evolved from everyday functions. The process by which they do so was termed "ritualization" by Julian Huxley. It is of interest not only to the sociologist and the information theorist interested in communication, but also to the student of evolution in general. There are several reasons why ritualized movements lend themselves particularly well to comparative study: they are conspicuous, clear-cut, and easily recognizable: the process of ritualization is one of the fastest processes of evolution known in undomesticated animals, as can be concluded from their dissimilarity in comparatively closely related species. If one compares nonritualized instinctive movements such as locomotion, feeding, preening, nest-building, etc. within a taxonomic group of family or subfamily rank, like dabbling ducks, no appreciable differences appear between its members. In order to study the phylogeny of such types of motor pattern by the comparative method one must go much farther afield, studying their manifestations in different orders, or at least suborders. For this reason ritualized movements are of great help in ascertaining the phyletic relationship of closely allied species.

Another property of ritualized movements which makes them particularly valuable to comparative phylogenetics is a consequence of their functioning as signals. Any signal code is based on a convention between the sender and the receiver of the communication. The meaning of a word, for instance, is only intelligible to a person acquainted with this convention; on the basis of another convention, of another code, the word might have an altogether different connotation. If the historian finds, in two different and unrelated cultures, an ax or a plow of very similar construction, this similarity may be caused by the similarity of function and the investigator is not justified in assuming that the instrument of one culture has been derived, in some way, from that of the other. If, on the other hand, the comparative linguist finds that the words meaning "mother" in English, German, Latin, Greek, and Russian have a number of important structural properties in common, he concludes without hesitation that these words are derived historically from a common root. The chances of these similarities being coincidences are negligible, and no similarity of function can explain them. By the same reasoning, similarity caused by similar function, in the biologist's language convergent evolution, can be excluded in the comparative study of ritualized movements. All this contributes to make their study an extremely rewarding occupation for the comparative phylogenist; and as a considerable number of investigators, led by Whitman and Heinroth, seem to have realized this fact, we know more about their evolution than we do about that of any other kind of innate motor patterns.

The concept which we associate with the term "ritualization," like most biological concepts, can only be defined by what Bernhard Hassenstein has called an "injunctive" definition, that is to say, by the enumeration of a number of properties which constitute the essence of the concept only by summation. The properties of life, for instance, like metabolism, growth, propagation, etc., are all to be found in inorganic processes as well, but constitute life when realized in the same object. All injunctively defined concepts .lack a sharp borderline but merge by gradation into neighboring concepts.

The first and probably most important characteristic of ritualization has already been mentioned. A phylogenetically adapted motor pattern which originally served the species in dealing with some environmental necessities acquires a new function, that of communication. The primary function may persist, as in many fishes, birds, and mammals, in which locomotion has been ritualized so as to communicate, to the fellow members of the species, an animal's moving away. All these movements release the response to follow in conspecific animals. In many cases, however, the primary function recedes into the background or disappears altogether so that a complete change of function is achieved. Out of communication, two new, equally important, functions may arise, both of which, however differentiated the movement may become in their service, always retain a measure of communicative effect. The first of these new functions is the canalization of aggression in a manner permitting its discharge without damaging fellow members of the species, as is the case in the numerous forms of ritualized fighting found in fish, birds, and mammals; the second is the formation of a bond which keeps together two or more individuals. This is achieved by most so-called greeting ceremonies which an animal can perform only with a certain, individually known partner, whose presence, for this reason, becomes an indispensable need in the animal's life. It is quite erroneous to say that such ceremonies are "the expression of" a bond; indeed, they themselves constitute it.

The second characteristic of ritualized motor patterns is a change of form which the unritualized prototype underwent in the service of its new communicative function and which quite obviously was brought about by the selection pressure exerted by the survival value of communication. All those elements which, even in the unritualized primary movement, produce visual or auditory stimulation are strongly exaggerated, while those serving the original, mechanical function are greatly reduced or disappear altogether. This "mimic exaggeration" results in a ceremony which is, indeed, closely akin to a symbol and which produces that theatrical effect which first struck Sir Julian Huxley as he watched the now classical great crested grebes. A riot of form and color has evolved to enhance this effect. The beautiful forms and colors of a Siamese fighting fish's fins, the plumage of a bird of paradise, the peacock's tail, the amazing colors on both ends of a mandrill, one and all evolved under the selection pressure of the communicative function performed by some particular ritualized movement.

In the interest of greater unambiguity of the communication, the speed and amplitude of ritualized movements are strictly regulated, a phenomenon termed "typical intensity" by Desmond Morris, who was the first to draw attention to it. The same aim is served by frequent rhythmical repetition, which very often is in itself sufficient to recognize a behavior pattern as ritualized. Finally, a great number of elementary instinctive movements, which are independently variable in the unritualized prototype, are in many cases welded into a single obligatory sequence.

This important effect is achieved by evolving an altogether new motor pattern which copies, in ritual form, a whole series of primarily independent and independently variable movements. The so-called inciting ceremony of ducks furnishes a good example. In its primary form, it consists of behavior patterns motivated by at least three independent factors. The female duck runs aggressively toward an adversary, is then overcome by fear, and rushes back to the protection of her mate. The moment she has re-established contact with him, she regains courage and begins to threaten the antagonist again. In its primary form, which is to be observed in sheldrakes, the component parts mentioned vary in intensity and duration, the attitudes of the female when threatening are exclusively dependent and the positions of herself, her drake, and the "enemy." All angles between her body axis and the direction in which she stretches forward her neck in threatening are equally possible. There is one standard case, however, which occurs more frequently than others: very often, the duck, after running back to her drake for protection, stops in front of him without turning her body around, almost touching him with her breast, and now starts

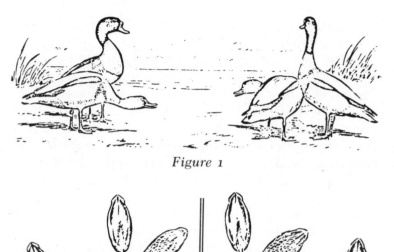

Figure 1

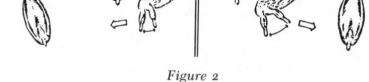

Figure 2

again to stretch her neck threateningly in the direction of her enemy. The spatial relationship between the female, her drake, and her enemy forces her to perform the threatening movement backward over her shoulder at an acute angle to her body axis. In many surface-feeding ducks, this special case of motor coordination has become fixated as one obligatory pattern. However, the head movement, directed backward over the shoulder, still contains the original orientation responses which, in the unritualized prototype, produce a motor pattern phenotypically identical with the one genotypically fixated in the surface-feeding ducks. The movements caused by the primary orienting responses are superimposed on the new pattern: if the enemy bird is standing directly in front of the inciting duck, her eyes remain fixated in his direction and the threatening movement backward over the shoulder is noticeably decreased; while it increases with the angle between the long axis of her body and the direction in which the enemy is standing. If he is situated directly behind her, the amplitude of the movement attains a maximum, the duck's bill almost touching her tail (figure 2). This superimposition of primary orientation responses and newly evolved fixed motor pattern often offers considerable difficulties to the motivation analysis of ritualized behavior.

A further important constitutive character of ritualization arises directly from the evolution of the new motor pattern: this acquires all the characteristics of an autonomous instinctive movement. It has its own releasing mechanism, its own spontaneity, and, therewith, its own appetitive behavior. Thus, by the process of ritualization, an entirely new instinct may be born which is, in principle, just as independent as any of the primary drives—hunger, sex, fear, and aggression—and may influence the behavior of a species just as strongly. If it did not, it would not be able either to oppose and master aggression, nor could it ever fulfill its other tasks of forming a bond of friendship literally "stronger than death." I have not the time to give you a convincing description of the amazing manner in which the triumph ceremony of geese achieves both these functions: suffice it to say that this ritual, derived from a redirected threat movement in the comparatively recent phylogeny of the subfamily Anserini, not only suppresses all aggression between the partners but holds them together with something of the death-defying fidelity which, in animal behavior, is familiar to us only in our faithful dogs.

As with most injunctively defined concepts, we use that of ritualization not only when all its constitutive properties are realized. If some intention movements— for instance, those of ducks about to take off—are rhythmically repeated, without being otherwise changed, in the service of communication, we can say that they are "slightly ritualized" although they possess none of the other properties just described. The essence of ritualized behavior, however, is represented by those cases in which it possesses all the properties I have discussed and achieves the full autonomy of an independent drive.

II. Ritualization in the Psychosocial Evolution of Human Culture

If Sir Julian Huxley, when first describing ritualization, used the term without inverted commas, he did so on purpose, to emphasize that it denoted a purely functional concept equally applicable to a phyletic and a cultural process. Professor Carstairs, a short time ago, said that he was "chary of analogies." I agree that an erroneous assumption of homology or, worse, of physiological identity can indeed be dangerously misleading. When I am lecturing about animals to scientists investigating human behavior, I usually begin with the caution that the central nervous system has an insidious way of performing analogous functions on different levels of integration in such a similar manner as to mislead even the sophisticated observer to assume physiological identity where it does not exist. However, I do not see that the statement of obvious analogies can lead us into any trap. Provided that an analogy concerns plainly comparable details sufficiently numerous to exclude the possibility of coincidence, we are fully justified in assuming that the two analogous structures or behavior patterns do indeed have the same function. Nothing except convergent evolution can account for their detailed similarity. If I were the first scientist to see a dead octopus and, on dissecting it, discovered an eye built like ours, with a cornea, a lens, an iris, focusing muscles, and a retina, I would be justified in assuming that this was a visual organ and in calling it an eye without further ado, even if I had no other proof of its function. "Eye" denotes a functional concept; cephalopods and vertebrates have no common ancestors with eyes of this type: their eyes are functionally analogous, not phylogenetically homologous.

An even better case can be made out for the application of our functional concept of ritualization to both the biological and the cultural spheres, because we need not rely on detailed formal analogy alone. We know from observation and ample experimental verification that rituals, whether phylogenetically or culturally evolved, do in fact perform the same functions of communication, of canalizing aggression, and of effecting the cohesion of pairs or groups. Before speaking of the obvious analogies between the processes of phylogenetic and cultural ritualization, I must say a few words about their differences. These differences concern the mechanisms underlying the two processes and the amounts of time required by each.

Conceptual thought and verbal speech, endowing man with the possibility of cultural tradition, changed man's evolution fundamentally by achieving something equivalent to the inheritance of acquired characters.

We have almost forgotten that the verb "inherit" had a juridical connotation long before it acquired a biological one. When a man invents, let us say, a bow and arrow, not only his progeny, but all his tribe and even all his culture will soon be in possession of these weapons just as securely as if they were organs grown on their bodies. Nor is the likelihood of their use being forgotten any greater than that of an organ of comparable survival value becoming vestigial. Thus, cultural development and tradition, within one or two generations, can achieve a process of ecological adaptation which, in normal phylogeny, would have required a period of an altogether different order of magnitude.

Though cultural rituals develop incomparably faster than phyletic ritualization their development is still less rapid than that of inventions. I do not think that the system of social norms and rites characteristic of a culture owes much to human insight and invention. It has been said that Moses prohibited the consumption of pork because he knew all about trichinosis. If he did, he trusted the devoutness of his followers rather than their insight, as he enunciated a religious law instead of giving lectures on parasitology. In general, the systems of social norms and rites characteristic of cultures rather give the impression that it was good old natural selection that molded their particular forms, but on a psychosocial instead of a genetic basis, using, as its raw material, randomly arising habits and customs instead of mutations and recombinations. I advance this speculation for all it may or may not be worth.

The role played by genetic inheritance in the evolution and maintenance of phylogenetically evolved rituals is, of course, taken over by tradition in cultural ritualization. In the process of tradition itself, however, there are some instinctive, in other words, phylogenetically programed, mechanisms at work. Primary among these is so-called creature habit. On deviating from an individually acquired but sufficiently deeply ingrained habit, man and beast alike experience anxiety. Margaret Altmann, during her studies of the social life of wapiti and American moose, followed the tracks of these animals for many months on her old horse, accompanied by an even older pack mule. When she had camped several times in one particular place, she found it impossible to ride past it without stopping: her mounts balked and were thrown into a panic when she forcibly tried to make them continue on their route. Being well

versed in the ways of animals, Margaret Altmann re-
sorted to a compromise—stopping, "symbolically" un-
packing, camping a few minutes, and repacking; after
this her mounts were quite satisfied and ready to march
on. This behavior, closely akin to human magical thinking as well as to human compulsive behavior, is caused
by a mechanism whose survival value is obvious. An
animal which has acquired a certain habit and has as-
certained that it leads to the desired goal without incurring danger is well advised to stick slavishly to all the
details of this procedure, because, not possessing any
insight into the causal connections of the whole, it cannot possibly know which details are essential to success
and safety, and which are not. Many human superstitions, like touching wood, etc., involve this principle:
one does not quite know what might happen if the custom were violated!

In addition to this compulsion to stick to habit, there
is a second mechanism which ensures that fidelity to an
acquired custom is handed down from one human generation to the next. Curiously enough, an analogous
process has recently been demonstrated in a bird. My
co-worker J. Nicolai has found that young bullfinches
learn their song from their father only. For a comparatively long time after fledging, young male bullfinches
stand in a peculiar, clearly sexual relationship to their
father. They crouch before him, performing the submissive gesture which, like that of many monkeys, is
derived from the female copulation posture, and they
are much more attached to him than to their mother.
During this period they learn their father's individual
song. Nicolai had a male bullfinch which had been
reared by canary birds and sang exactly like one. His
canarylike song was handed down in its pure form,
without admixture, through four generations bred in
aviaries in which plenty of normally singing bullfinches
were present. Nicolai also demonstrated experimentally

that a bullfinch can learn his song only from a "father figure" to which he takes the above described attitude.

In my view, the strong emotional value which human beings attribute to handed-down custom derives most of its motivational energy from a very similar relationship between the young generation and the elder. If the recipient of tradition does not feel, for at least one member of the older generation, that emotion of respect and love which, under normal conditions, a son feels for his father, the mechanism of passing on traditional norms and rites seems unable to function. In other words, something very like the psychoanalytical "situation of transference" is its indispensable prerequisite. If, on the other hand, this condition is fulfilled, traditional values gain strength from generation to generation. The farther the revered figure of the ancestor recedes into the past, the better it fulfills its function as the superego, the more inviolable become the standards of ritualized social behavior set by it. As the father figure, even if it takes the form of a personal immortal god, inspires not only fear, but also love, a new factor arises to motivate fidelity to culturally evolved social norms and rites. We not only feel a compulsory fear at their infraction, but we love them for their own sake, and for the sake of what they symbolize.

Habit formation, compulsive anxiety over infractions of accepted rules, reverence and love for traditional customs—these and whatever other mechanisms there may be to ensure the permanence of culturally ritualized social norms and rites, from generation to generation, perform an analogous function in culturally ritualized social norms and rites, to genetic inheritance in the evolution of phylogenetically ritualized forms of social behavior. Furthermore, all these mechanisms have themselves, of course, been phylogenetically evolved. Man, as Arnold Gehlen has aptly put it, is by nature a cultural creature. In other words, all his inherited norms of behavior have been selectively molded in phylogeny in such a way as to need being complemented by cultural tradition. The phylogenetically evolved part of our brain which endows us with the faculty of verbal speech would be quite unable to function, if the human individual were not brought into contact, during his ontogeny, with a culturally evolved language whose vocabulary he can learn. A man deprived of culture would not be a happy savage released from the bondage of civilization, but a wretched cripple comparable to someone with a damaged forebrain. It is necessary to keep in mind that even a partial loss of cultural tradition is very dangerous, and also that it can occur all too easily. While the phylogenetically evolved bases of social behavior will persist, for better or worse, under any changes, however rapid, imposed on human environment culturally evolved social norms and rites can be snuffed out like candles.

Having discussed the intrinsic difference of the mechanisms underlying the evolution of ritualization in the biological and the cultural sphere I now proceed to the amazing analogies in their results. These analogies concern all the constitutive properties of ritualization in general, of which I have already spoken.

I need say very little about the change of form which the primary, unritualized pattern of behavior undergoes in the service of its new functions of communication, of channeling aggression and of group cohesion (bonding). All the means ensuring unambiguity of communication are employed exactly as in phylogenetic ritualization. Mimic exaggeration, redundant repetition and typical intensity are clearly marked in most human ceremonies. In particular, "measured" speed, frequency, and amplitude are symptoms that mark human ceremonial behavior. The deans walk into the aula of the university with measured step; the Catholic priest's chanting during mass is strictly regulated in pitch and rhythm by liturgical rules. The riot of form and color accompanying human ceremonial, all its pomp and pageantry are developed, in cultural history, in the service of the same functions and along lines astonishingly parallel to those seen in phylogenetic ritualization. In both cases it is abundantly clear that the evolution of the stimulus-sending part of the communicatory system is adapted to the special requirements of the receiver: in other words, it is the receiving set which exerts the selective pressure responsible for the evolution of the sending mechanism.

I have, as I believe prudently, explained that rituals developing in cultural history attain their power of actively motivating human behavior in a way that is very different from that in which the instinctive motor patterns which evolved in phyletic ritualization achieve the character of independent, active drives. However different these two origins of the motivating forces are, their effect on social behavior is very similar. In both cases the rituals become sufficiently autonomous and stable to function as a sort of skeleton supporting the structure of society. This is true not only of the great, highly ritualized ceremonials, but even more so of inconspicuous everyday behavior patterns. The word polite is derived from the French verb *polire*, to smooth, to rub something until it shines, to give a finish. The omnipresence of this cultural polish is brought to our notice only when we observe, as an exception, human behavior in which it is entirely lacking. This sort of behavior is emphatically not supposed to be overtly performed in "polite society," like yawning and stretching uninhibitedly.

It is especially in the seemingly unimportant everyday cultural rituals which we call manners, that the triple function of all rituals, phyletic and cultural, can be best demonstrated: communication, control of aggression, and bond formation. Any human group which exceeds in size that which can be held together by the bonds of personal love and friendship depends on these three functions of cultural ritualization for its very existence. "Good" manners are by definition those characteristic of one's own group. As I said, we conform to them automatically and do not, as a rule, realize that they do indeed inhibit aggression and form a bond. Yet it is they that produce what sociologists call group cohesion, the sticking-together of a group. The function of good manners in permanently producing mutual conciliation between the members of a group can easily be demonstrated by observing what happens in their absence. I do not mean the effect produced by an active gross breach of manners, but by the mere absence of all the little polite looks and gestures by which one person, for example on entering a room, takes cognizance of another's presence. If a person considers himself offended by members of his group, and enters the room occupied by them without these little rituals, as if they were not there, his behavior elicits anger and hostility just as overt aggressive behavior does: such intentional suppression of the normal appeasing rituals is equivalent to overtly aggressive behavior.

Aggressivity elicited by any deviation from a group's characteristic manners and mannerisms forces all its members into a strict and uniform observance of these norms of social behavior. The nonconformist is discriminated against as an "outsider" and, in primitive groups, of which school classes or small military units serve as good examples, is cruelly mobbed or persecuted.

Culturally developed social norms and rites are characters of human groups of various size much in the same manner as inherited properties evolved in phylogeny are characters of subspecies, species, genera, and higher taxonomic units. Their history can be reconstructed by much the same methods of comparative study. Their divergence during historical development erects barriers between cultural units in the same sort of way as divergent evolution does between species: Erik Erikson has therefore aptly called this process pseudospeciation—leading to the production of cultural pseudospecies analogous to true biological species.

Though immeasurably faster than phylogenetic speciation, cultural pseudospeciation does need time. Its slight beginnings, the development of characteristic mannerisms of behavior in a group and discrimination against uninitiated outsiders, may be seen in any group of children, but to give stability and the quality of inviolability to a group's social norms and rites, its continued existence for at least a few generations seems to be necessary. For this reason, the smallest cultural pseudosubspecies I can think of is the school and it is surprising how old schools preserve their pseudo-subspecific characters throughout the years. The "old school tie," though often an object of ridicule nowadays, is something very real in a dual sense—as a bond as well as neckwear.

The important function of polite manners can be studied to great advantage in the social interactions between different cultures and subcultures. Many of the mannerisms enjoined by good manners are culturally ritualized exaggerations of submissive gestures, most of which probably have their roots in phylogenetically ritualized motor patterns conveying the same meaning. Local traditions of good manners in different subcultures demand a quantitatively different emphasis to be put on these expression movements. A good example is furnished by the attitude of listening politely, which consists in stretching the head forward and simultaneously tilting the head sideways, "lending an ear" to the person who is speaking. The motor pattern conveys readiness to listen attentively and even to obey. In the polite manners of some Asiatic cultures it has obviously undergone strong mimic exaggeration; in Austrians, particularly in well-bred ladies, it is one of the commonest gestures of politeness, while in other Central European countries it appears to be less emphasized. In parts of northern Germany it is reduced to a minimum, or even absent: instead, in these subcultures the correct expression of polite listening is to hold the head high and look the speaker straight in the face, just as a soldier is supposed to do when listening to orders. When I came from Vienna to Königsberg, two cities in which the difference in this motor pattern is, or was, particularly great, it took me some time to get over my misinterpretation of the polite listening gesture of East Prussian ladies: expecting a forward and sideways tilt of the chin, however small, from the lady to whom I was speaking, I could not help feeling that I had said something shocking when she sat rigidly upright looking me in the face.

Undoubtedly, little misunderstandings of this kind contribute considerably to intergroup dislike and hate. The man who, in the manner described, has misinterpreted the social signals of a member of another pseudosubspecies feels that he has been intentionally cheated. The mere inability to understand the expression movements and rituals of a strange culture creates distrust, suspicion, and fear in a way which can easily lead to overt aggression.

From the little peculiarities of speech and manner which cause the smallest possible subcultural groups to stick together, an uninterrupted gradation leads up to the highly elaborate, consciously performed and consciously symbolical social norms and rites which unite the largest social units of humanity in one nation, one culture, one religion, or one political ideology. Studying such systems and processes by the comparative method—in other words, investigating the laws of cultural pseudospeciation—would be perfectly possible, though it would be more complicated than the study of biological speciation, because of the frequent overlapping of group concepts, for instance of national and religious units.

As I have already said, the emotional appreciation of values gives motivational power to all ritualized norms of social behavior. Erik Erikson has recently shown that conditioning to the distinction of good and bad begins in early babyhood and continues all through human ontogeny. In principle, there is no difference between the rigidity with which we adhere to our early toilet training and our fidelity to the national or political norms and rites to which we become object-fixated in later life. The fixity of the transmitted rite and the tenacity with which we cling to it are essential to its proper function. At the same time, like the operation of even more rigid instinctive patterns of behavior, they need supervision by our rational, responsible morality.

It is right and legitimate that we should consider as "good" the manners which our parents taught us, that we should hold sacred the social norms and rites handed down to us by our cultural tradition. What we must guard against, with all the power of rational responsibility, is our natural inclination to regard the social rites and norms of other cultures as inferior. The dark side of pseudospeciation is that it makes us consider the members of pseudospecies other than our own as not truly or fully human. Many primitive tribes demonstrably do so, in whose language the word for their own tribe is synonymous with "man": from their viewpoint it is not, strictly speaking, cannibalism if they eat the fallen warriors of an enemy tribe. And some developed nations also have done the same, in proclaiming themselves as the chosen people or inherently superior, therefore justified in treating other races or nations by different moral or cultural standards.

The moral of the natural history of pseudospeciation

is that we must learn to tolerate other cultures, to shed our own cultural and national arrogance, and to realize that the social norms and rites of other cultures, to which their members keep faith as we do to our own, have the same right to be respected and to be regarded as sacred. Without the tolerance born out of this realization it is all too easy for one man to see the personification of evil in the god of his neighbor, and the sacred inviolability of rites and social norms, which is one of their most important properties, can lead to the most terrible of all wars, to religious or pseudoreligious (ideological) war—which is exactly what is threatening us today.

We must also learn to tolerate and indeed welcome changes in our own norms and rites, so long as they tend in the right direction—toward greater human fulfillment and fuller human integration.

The Fashionable Fallacy of Dispensing with Description * | Konrad Lorenz

To "explain" an event means to trace or "reduce" its regularities to more general laws of nature. If the event occurs within a system consisting of several different parts, a knowledge of their form and function is, in any science, indispensable to successful reduction. While physicists are interested in structure only as a means to this end, biologists regard a knowledge of structure as an end in itself. The current belief that only quantitative procedures are scientific and that the description of structure is superfluous is a deplorable fallacy, dictated by the "technomorphic" thought habits acquired by our culture when dealing preponderantly with inorganic matter.

* Lecture at the XXV International Congress of Physiological Sciences, Munich, July 25–31, 1971. *Naturwissenschaften* 60, 1–9 (1973). © by Springer-Verlag 1973.

Exclusive Esteem for Quantification

We live at a time when it has become fashionable to assess the so-called exactness and hence the value of any scientific result by the relative amount of mathematical operations used in obtaining it. In order to avoid misunderstandings, let me say that quantification and mathematics always have the last word in *verification*. However, as no less a man than Werner Heisenberg has pointed out, the laws of mathematics are not laws of nature, but the laws prevailing in *one* of the cognitive processes to which we owe our faculty of *understanding* nature—to a degree.

The current underestimation of *all other* cognitive mechanisms as sources of scientific knowledge has deleterious consequences. I shall come back to these later and turn now to what I consider to be the causes that impel present-day scientists to neglect some of Man's most indispensable cognitive faculties.

"Technomorphic" Thought Habits

Our culture has achieved mastery over the inorganic world to a degree never attained in the history of mankind and undreamt of a few generations ago. It owes its power to the high development of its analytical sciences, mainly to physics and chemistry, which, in their turn, derive their effectiveness from an equally highly developed science of analytical mathematics. On this basis, our culture has developed a technology which has changed and still is changing the ecology and the sociology of the human species at an ever-increasing rate. Though some of us begin to see the dangers of this development, the majority of mankind is still drunk with success and correspondingly arrogant, swelled with that pride which comes before a fall. The worst consequence of this has been pointed out by Hans Freyer: not only scientists of many different avocations, but people in general have acquired thought habits which were formed in dealing successfully with inorganic matter. Millions of laborers and technicians, throughout their lives, have had to deal exclusively with nonliving and man-made things; they have, in their day's work, rarely or never had to do with any living creature. Small wonder, if the majority of civilized men have quite forgotten how living things must be treated, even when exploiting them, and, therefore, with the greatest possible self-assurance, they apply their habitual methods in tackling problems in the world of living creatures, including man and human society.

Naturally, this has had devastating effects and has led some great humanists to believe that science as such exerts a dehumanizing influence on our culture. This is true only insofar as a science, biased in the way just described, has gained an inordinate influence on public thinking. What the great majority of men regard as "big" science is exactly of this kind and, as I shall try to show later, scientists of other branches, being true children of our time, are also inordinately influenced by the thought habits which are now fashionable.

Ethical Restrictions in Dealing
with Organic Systems

The exploitation of the inorganic world is largely exempt from ethical considerations—except that far-seeing economic ones might also be considered ethical. A coal mine may be exploited ruthlessly; it furnishes the same quantity whether one does it fast or slowly. The very idea that some kinds of procedure might be permissible and others might not does not enter the mind of people trained exclusively in dealing with the inorganic world. Men of that ilk are in the majority, they are ruling the world, hence the abysmal immorality of the present-day *Zeitgeist*. Whether it is eroding the soil it lives on, or exterminating the great whales, or poisoning its environment with insecticide or the minds of its own children by glamorizing crime and violence in its mass media, present-day humanity behaves consistently as if driven by the devil, whose exclusive aim it is to destroy all life on our planet. Satan could well achieve this aim even without resorting to nuclear weapons.

The *Zeitgeist* of present times seems unable to understand what life is and what life means. Living creatures, including superindividual communities, such as biocoenoses, or societies, or human cultures, are *systems,* built up through the interaction of many very unhomogeneous parts or "subsystems." Simpler and more complicated living systems are different from each other, not only quantitatively in the number of parts and in the number of kinds of different parts they embrace: they also differ essentially in quality. Whenever two hitherto independent subsystems become integrated into a functional unit, new systemic properties come into existence, and these make the organism different from his ancestors not only in degree, but in essence. This kind of integration is one of the most common and, at the same time, one of the most important steps in the evolution of a species as well as in the historical development of a culture.

Indispensability of Knowing Structure

In principle, causal insight into the workings of an organic system cannot be gained without a full understanding of the structures of all its parts, and of the way in which they interact. Furthermore, we must also know the phyletic history of the organism, otherwise we can never hope to understand why its structural and functional characteristics are what they are. Knowledge of phyletic history, in its turn, cannot be gained without understanding the process of adaptation and of the part which natural selection has played in it. None of these cognitive steps of elucidating the nature of living systems is dispensable and none of them *can be achieved by quantifying and analytic procedure alone.* In fact, the more complicated a system and the more highly integrated the interaction of its parts, the less directly accessible is it to these methods.

In discussing the differences between ethology and other behavioral sciences, Norbert Bischof has recently pointed out what severe limitations are imposed on the investigation of living systems and their behavior by neglecting other necessary cognitive acts, as is the case when using a physical science approach. As Bischof points out, physics, since the time of Galileo, has proceeded by the method of generalizing reduction. Physicists regard any real system which is being investigated at the moment (for instance, a planetary system, a pendulum, or a falling stone) as a special case of a more general systemic class (for instance, mass in a gravitational field). Then, they find the laws prevailing in each specific system (for instance, Kepler's laws, law of the pendulum), which in turn are derived from the laws which a more general system obeys (as, for instance, from Newton's laws). The structure and the behavior of the specific system investigated in any single case is studied only as a means to the end of attaining knowledge of the general law and is, indeed, forgotten once this goal is reached. For the validity of Newton's laws, the special properties of the solar system in which Isaac Newton found them are not essential. He would have found the same laws if he had investigated a quite different solar system with other sizes of celestial bodies, other orbits, and so on. The physicist, in trying to abstract *general* laws, is, in principle, bound to reduce to these general laws any special laws which he may find prevailing in some particular system. This reduction unavoidably will consist in showing how the *structure* of the system causes the general law to appear in the guise of a more special law characteristic of that system only. For instance, the physicist will demonstrate how the structure of a pendulum, which consists in the suspension of a mass, by a connection theoretically devoid of mass, from an axis theoretically free of friction, causes the general laws of gravity, inertia, etc. to appear in the form of the more special laws of the pendulum.

Of course, it is within the scope of theoretical physics to predict these laws deductively, but the experimental physicist has to resort to *real* pendulums in which the suspension possesses mass and in which the axis is never free from friction. The physicist must study and measure these factors and take them into account while digging his way downward, ever downward, toward the most general laws that can be reached. To him, the influence and, in fact, all these properties of the special real system are only obstacles to the procedure of generalizing induction. He is interested neither in the system nor in its structure per se.

This is exactly the attitude which the biologist must *not* take. Even if it were not for his duty to serve physiology and pathology in their aim to restore the health of systems which have gotten out of order, he would still have to be interested in living systems as such, and at all levels of integration and in all the more special and more general laws prevailing on all these levels. Of course, the analysis of the biologist, like that of the physicist, proceeds in a "downward" direction. In all our daily work, we act on the assumption that there is *one* set of mutually inclusive and noncontradictory laws of nature and that, should we ever arrive at the utopian goal of completely understanding nature, including the side of our own nature that can be objectively investigated, we should have explained the universe and everything that is in it, on the basis of all-embracing physico-chemical laws and of the *highly complex structures in which these laws are at work.* As investigators of behavior, we hope to arrive at its understanding on the basis of the physico-chemical processes taking place in the synapses, at the charged cell membranes, in stimulus conduction, and so on. In our method of proceeding we are, indeed, reductionists.

Ontological Reductionism or "Nothingelsebuttery"

However, we do not, on our "downward" progress, forget the immensely complicated structures in which these processes perform their wonderfully organized integrated systemic interactions. We do not push them aside as undesirable variables, we regard them as the subjects of our research no less than the most basic lawfulness at which we ultimately hope to arrive. Throwing aside structure in the grand manner permissible in physics would, in the investigation of living organisms, lead to the disastrous fallacy of ontological reductionism. An example may serve to illustrate the worldwide difference between methodological reduction, indispensable to natural science, and ontological reductionism. Science says: "Life processes are chemical and physical processes" or: "Human beings are animals belonging to the order of primates." Both statements are entirely correct. The reductionist says: "Life processes are nothing else but physico-chemical processes" and: "Human beings are nothing else but animals." Both statements are not only entirely false, but symptomatic of highly dangerous blindness to harmonies and to levels of integration, which means blindness to values. Julian Huxley has coined an English term for ontological reductionism: Nothingelsebuttery!

All truly biological lawfulness arises from the structure of living matter, beginning from that governing the events in the double helix up to that which prevails in human social behavior. For this reason, general laws, valid for all living creatures, can only be expected insofar as living systems have structural characters in common.

Behaviorism and Its Cognitive Restrictions

Yet there is in the behavioral sciences, in psychology, a tendency to apply to living systems the physicist's method of generalizing reduction. Many psychologists cherish the hope that they will be able to bypass the structure and the physiological functions of organisms, particularly those of their central nervous system, and yet succeed in finding the laws of behavior. Undoubtedly, B. F. Skinner is presently the most radical representative of this tendency to formulate general laws governing behavior without having recourse to the understanding of the physiological machinery which *makes* behavior. His "empty organism" doctrine has had a remarkable influence not only on American but also on German psychology. Studying the contingencies of reinforcement by means of purely operational approach, and evaluating by statistical methods the changes thus wrought (without giving a thought to that which is being changed) is still regarded by many not only as a legitimate but as the only legitimate way to study behavior.

The likelihood of finding by this method such behavioral laws as are equally valid for guinea pigs, pigeons, and men, is, of course, dependent on the existence, in all these creatures, of neural and sensory mechanisms which respond in the same way to the operations chosen for the experiment. Luckily for behaviorists, most phyla of animals which have evolved far enough to possess a centralized nervous system, have, indeed, independently of each other, "invented" a sensory-neural organization which enables them to learn by reward. This accounts for the fact that there are some lawfulnesses which hold true for the learning of all the organisms mentioned above. However important the experimental analysis of this one mechanism of learning by reinforcement may be, that which is completely disregarded by the behaviorist's procedure is still more important: it comprises *all the rest* of the organism; in fact, it comprises everything that makes a guinea pig a guinea pig, a pigeon a pigeon, and a man a man.

Motivations of the Behaviorist's Restrictions

I find it hard to put myself in the place of a scientist who is ready to forgo the use of most of the cognitive mechanisms which normal man uses as sources of knowledge; I find it still more difficult to imagine the motives that impel him to make this sacrifice. In order to maintain one's own belief that the organism is empty and that conditioning by reinforcement is the only organic process worth studying, it seems to be indispensable either to fetter the experimental organism, as I. P. Pavlov did, so that it can do nothing except show the expected response, or else to prevent oneself from observing the organism doing anything else by putting it into an opaque box. If the subject of investigation happens to be human, he or she is being literally dehumanized by being prevented from showing any response which a guinea pig or a pigeon might not show as well (in fact, the same experimental setup is often applicable to animal and human subjects). Worse, in that kind of experimentation, the experimenter himself is not permitted to be quite human, as he is strictly prevented from using most of the cognitive mechanisms with which nature endowed our species. I can think of only two reasons that can impel a man to make these truly ascetic and rather horrible sacrifices.

Aping Physics

One is an excessive admiration of physics. This may seem paradoxical, considering the behaviorist's singular lack of understanding for the physicist's or, for that matter, all scientists' manner of proceeding. However, it may be that it is just this misunderstanding which is responsible for the imitation of methods which the physicist applies in certain particular cases only. Whenever the atomic physicist resorts to the exclusive use of operationalistic approach and statistic evaluation of data, he does so because *all other cognitive processes are failing him.* He is working in a realm in which the human categories of thought, like causality or substantiality, and even the human forms of visualization, like space and time, *cease to be applicable.* The physicist keeps to his method because his object of investigation permits no other, not because he thinks it is the only one that is "scientific." Let a physicist be confronted with an object to which the common, everyday functions of cognition are applicable. Confront him with a system whose systemic properties depend on its structure and see how quick he is to use the same methods as a biologist. Ask him, for instance, to repair some electronic device which was made by somebody else and which has got out of order. He will certainly not apply an operational method and statistical evaluation of results, he will take the thing apart and see how it is wired, in other words he will resort to *description*. The behaviorist, however, with unshakable conviction, would deem this unscientific.

Wish for Power

The second reason I can think of is of an ideological nature: there are ideologies which do not *want* man to have structures. The very existence of phylogenetically evolved, hereditary systems of motivations, so-called instincts, in man make him less manageable, more resistant to manipulation. So it is wishful thinking on the part of the great manipulators that the empty organism doctrine should be true and that man should be nothing, indeed, but the creature of his conditioning. The weird picture which Aldous Huxley has drawn, in his novel *Brave New World*, of the ideally manageable citizen, could then be realized. The mutual wish to do so explains the otherwise surprising fact that the leaders of Western capitalism and those of Eastern communism are unanimous in accepting that which I call the pseudodemocratic doctrine.

Far-reaching Influences of Behaviorism

Psychology is, generally speaking, a daughter of philosophy and not of the natural sciences, and even psychologists who otherwise fully recognize most errors committed by behaviorists are still tempted to run into the blind alley of trying to by-pass the systemic organization of living creatures and to try to arrive at laws of behavior which are independent of systemic structure and valid for all organisms. The recognition of the fact that such laws simply do not exist seems to come very hard! Many psychologists and sociologists still are trying to unite the multiplicity of differently structured living systems into a continuum, in the hope of being able to formulate laws that are valid for all of this alleged unit. The same tendency is found in the study of motivation: some theorists have attempted to bring some spurious order into the host of independent motivations by postulating a "general drive" from which the others are supposed to be derived. Many other examples are mentioned by Bischof, such as Guthrie's attempt to reduce all life processes to a single principle of stimulation and movement, never paying attention either to the quality of the stimulation, nor to the form of the movement, and least of all to the adaptive value of their interaction. Another example is C. L. Hull's imposing system of postulates, strangely reminiscent of Newton's "Principia Mathematica," or, for another instance, T. C. Schneirla's attempt to explain all behavior on the principle of approach and avoidance, which hinges on the unfounded assumption that there is no qualitative difference between stimuli: strong stimuli are assumed to be always repellent, weaker ones to be attractive, intensity alone is regarded as the decisive parameter determining the organism's response. One of the most curious confessions of the belief in the complete unimportance of the living system and of the systemic properties arising from its particular structures, was uttered by E. C. Tolman, who wrote in 1938 (quoted from N. Bischof): "I believe that everything important in psychology . . . can be investigated in essence through the continued analysis . . . of the determiners of rat behavior at a choice point in a maze."

I have intentionally formulated as provocatively as possible the behavioristic fallacy of trying to find general laws governing behavior while completely neglecting the whole machinery which causes behavior; also I have drawn as lurid a picture as I could of the analogous errors committed by other behavioral scientists. Physiologists, of course, are well aware of systemic interactions and of the strategy indispensable to their investigation. Who should be in a better position to know these matters? So I do not believe that there exists any physiologist who is influenced by the behavioristic way of thinking. However, behaviorism is only *one symptom* of the fashionable fallacy of dispensing with description. The factors which have caused the majority of modern men to regard quantification as the most important cognitive process have had their influence on all of us. We are all tarred with the same brush, some less, but even I myself must confess to a slight feeling of inferiority when I realize that I have never in my life published a paper with a graph in it. I am impressed, against my better judgment, when any one of my coworkers deftly formulates a problem, for instance one of motivation analysis, in such a way that he or she can feed it to a computer.

Another circumstance which tends to make operationalistic approach and statistical evaluation of results appear preferable to descriptive studies of structures, lies in the simple fact that the latter take so much more time. Knowing any system well enough to be able to choose a point of experimental attack presupposes quite a lot of preliminary work. It is, therefore, so much more expedient to think of some nice simple operation within the scope of some automatic device which should be self-registering and contain a maximum of electronics. Thus an impressive amount of data can be gained with which even more impressive mathematical operations can be performed.

What I have just said is, of course, a rather bitter caricature, but the trend which I have sketched is indubitably present in all biological science of our days. Even those scientists who are quite aware of the nature of systems and of the strategy of approach thereby imposed upon us, tend to regard any experimental procedure as scientifically superior to any description. In my own field of ethology this has led to a rather grotesque situation: while experimental and analytical research has progressed, during the last decades, in a really satisfactory manner, the number of animal *species* which have been investigated has hardly increased at all. In other words, most of the experimental work is concerned with the same few kinds of animals which are relatively well known, all the while huge sectors of the animal kingdom remain *terra incognita* to the ethologist. Very little is known ethologically about arthropods, practically nothing about cephalopods. The preference for experimentation has simply strangled the indispensable growth of description. There is an immense amount of purely descriptive work still to be done.

The Dangers of Technomorphic Thinking

The necessity to know more species, especially those of the phyla just mentioned, is particularly urgent for those who want to study analogies, a task of the utmost importance in animal sociology. Structural analogy of form or behavior or both, found in two unrelated species, always indicates sameness of survival function. The more different the two species are in every other respect, the more reliable is this conclusion. Thus, the finding of analogies is the key to ascertaining, first, the existence of a definite survival function, then the solution of the problem wherein this survival value consists. One norm of social behavior which can, to the greatest advantage, be investigated by studying functional analogies, is that of monogamous pair bonding in many animals. Wolfgang Wickler has organized in my department a team of co-workers who, in concerted effort, are examining this phenomenon in as many and as different creatures as possible. Before asking the question about the physiological and behavioral mechanisms which keep a pair together, one naturally has to know in what species pair bonding is to be observed. Recently, we discovered a true individual monogamous pair bond in a species of shrimp, *Hymenocera*, and applied for a grant to the Deutsche Forschungsgemeinschaft to make it possible for a young research worker to thoroughly investigate pair bonding in these and other crustacea. The grant was approved, but not without the advisory board adding a little benign admonition: care should be taken, lest the investigation lapse into being merely descriptive, "daß die Untersuchung nicht ins Deskriptive *abgleitet*" (italics mine).

Approaching Living Systems: Darwin's Question

The worst of this widespread contempt for description is that it discourages people from even trying to analyze really complicated systems. Any intelligent man who is aware of the systemic nature of organisms will necessarily choose comparatively small subsystems. Please don't go away thinking that I consider this deplorable in itself: practically all important explanatory principles have been discovered that way. In fact, the only one I can think of at the moment which was discovered by nonexperimental observation and description is hereditary motor coordination, the discovery of which by C. O. Whitman and O. Heinroth gave rise to ethology as a branch of science. However, the drawback of the preference for experimental method is that it makes larger and more highly integrated living systems less attractive as potential objects of research, as obviously the direct approach by experimental and quantitative methods becomes the more difficult, the more complex and integrated an organic entity happens to be. Thus the main interest of biological and physiological science is directed away from highly integrated living systems, which means *away from man as a subject of research,* and this is one of the factors which make some humanists accuse present-day science as a whole of having a dehumanizing effect on our culture.

In fact, the trend of science here under discussion can well be the undoing of mankind. Medical science, that is, the endeavor to restore the health of organic systems which have gotten out of order, is necessarily based on causal physiological insight into the inner workings of these systems. Nobody in his right senses can doubt for a moment that humanity as a whole is a system which is very thoroughly out of order and that physiological insight is therefore a dire necessity if our species is to survive.

Taking an Inventory of Parts

Is it possible at all to approach a highly integrated living system, such as that of human society, by the methods of natural science, and, if so, what is the strategy of this approach? Let me make a few elementary remarks on these problems. Suppose that a couple of scientists who are not biased by the dangerous thought habits discussed in this lecture arrive from Mars—I think one has to search that far to find such people— and that they undertake to investigate a terrestrial system. For the sake of clarity, let us assume that it is a man-made system, for instance an automobile. The investigators would certainly begin their work by walking around the car and looking at it from all sides—which, as I shall explain, is already part of the only legitimate first step in approaching systems. Next they would probably ask themselves what the car is for, and they will have precious little chance to achieve an understanding of its working if they fail to grasp the fact that it is a *locomotor organ* of *Homo sapiens.* If a biologist asks the question "what for?" he is not professing a belief in any super- or extra-natural teleology, but confidence in Charles Darwin's theory of natural selection. Asking the question "what has a cat crooked, retractile claws for?" and answering it by saying "to catch mice with" is only shorthand for the statement that catching mice is the function, the survival value of which has *bred* cats with that kind of claws. Colin Pittendrigh has called this approach *teleonomic,* in order to divorce it from teleology as far as astronomy is divorced from astrology.

Relatively Independent Parts

Having grasped what the car is for, our extra-terrestrial scientists will not dream of beginning to *measure* anything yet. They will proceed to take the car apart and have a *look* at the parts. The task of understanding the interaction of the parts within a system is very similar to that of explaining them while teaching. If you try to explain the workings of a four-stroke engine to somebody who wants to get a driving license, you have to begin *somewhere,* at an arbitrarily chosen part of the system. You usually begin with the crankshaft turning and the connecting rod pulling down the piston which sucks mixture out of the carburetor, for no other reason than because you can illustrate the functions of these structures by histrionics, thus by-passing the need to represent the multitude of interactions in the linear sequence of spoken words which is so ill-fitted for that purpose. Goethe knew this when he said "Das Wort bemüht sich nur umsonst, Gestalten schöpf'risch aufzubau'n." In reality, your listener cannot possibly know, as yet, what a crankshaft, a carburetor, or a mixture is; all you can hope for is that, for each of these concepts, he keeps a conceptual vacuum provisionally open, to be filled in by explanation later. And this is exactly equivalent to the method of designing, as a first approach to the understanding of a system, a so-called flow-diagram with black boxes which, one hopes, will not remain entirely black forever. While you explain your four-stroke engine, you must remain conscious that your listener will not really understand how the piston sucks a combustible mixture out of the carburetor until he has also understood how the camshaft turns at half the speed of the crankshaft, how the cams open and shut the valves, how the ignition produces a spark when the mixture is compressed, etc. In other words, the function of any single part of the system can only be fully understood *simultaneously* with that of all other parts, or not at all. This fact was formulated nearly half a century ago with the utmost lucidity by my teacher Otto Koehler in Freiburg. In consequence of its full recognition, we must devise an obligatory strategy of research which, in an earlier paper, I have called "analysis on a broad front." This means that, having got some preliminary notion about what and how many parts of an entity are concerned in mutual interaction, one should try to advance one's knowledge of each of them at about the same pace as that about every other.

Strategy of Research Imposed by Systems

There are, however, exceptions to this rule, and in their recognition lies the subtlety of the method. There are contained in every living system certain elemental parts or subsystems which, while strongly influencing the structure and the function of the whole, are not appreciably influenced by it. Skeleton elements, at least in the adult organism, furnish a good example of this type of part which is relatively independent of the whole system. The discovery of any such "relatively independent part" always offers a welcome Archimedean point for further research. The comparatively small influence which the systemic entity exerts on such a part makes it permissible to isolate it, either in thought or experimentally, without incurring the reproach of neglecting a source of error. The discovery of such an element makes it possible to start digging deeply, "boring for oil," or, to use another simile, it is like finding, in a crossword puzzle, a very long word which is undoubtedly correct and stands in relationship to many others, so that a daring advance into unknown territory becomes feasible.

The discovery of such a relatively independent part is usually equivalent to the discovery of what is called a "new explanatory principle." If the discoverer himself is not trained in the art of thinking in terms of systems, in other words if he is not highly sophisticated in the technique of "analysis on a broad front," he almost invariably succumbs to the temptation of believing that the new principle all by itself is sufficient to explain "everything." The fallacy of *explanatory monism* is, in a manner of speaking, the prerogative of the discoverer's genius. If it is forgivable from this point of view, it is none the less one of the most serious obstacles to the further analysis of the system under investigation. If our extraterrestrial investigators of the autocar would, after having detached a nut and bolt from the object of their investigation, turn their backs on it and attempt, on the basis of these two elements, the *resynthesis* of the car, this endeavor would, in principle, be no less absurd than of explaining all behavior of all organisms as a bundle of "tropisms," as Jacques Loeb did, or as an accumulation of conditioned responses, as many American psychologists and anthropologists still do. The fallacy of explanatory monism often goes hand in hand with that of atomism, though it is by no means identical with it.

Atomism can be defined as the attempt to explain a function on the basis of more general laws of nature while disregarding for the moment the role which structure plays in the special expression which these general laws find in the case investigated. Atomism is in many cases bad research strategy, but it is by no means as detrimental a fallacy as explanatory monism. Atomism does not preclude the assumption of many parts, highly different from each other, taking part in the interaction within the systemic entity, nor does it restrict explanation to a single elementary process. The atomist is always ready to open himself to reality, to check his construction by observation, on all levels of organic integration. Unlike the reductionist and the explanatory monopolist, he has no ontological bias. Even if, in the extreme case, the atomistic approach culminates in the temerity of trying to *invent* all those structures which it does not deign to investigate and describe, this arrogant endeavor is not doomed to failure: there are many cases in the history of biocybernetics in which purely atomistic forms of reasoning have succeeded in elucidating systemic interactions, for instance, the self-regulating cycle of negative feedback, long before biology became fully aware of the all-important role which homeostasis plays in all living systems.

Pathology as a Source of Knowledge

The first task in tackling the analysis of a complicated living system undeniably consists in gaining a preliminary survey knowledge of the number and kind

of subsystems interacting in it. Intuitive Gestalt perception and daring guesses inspired by it are invariably the
first steps to the formation of a hypothesis which then is
susceptible to experimental verification. This is true,
even for those successful creators of theories who dislike Gestalt perception and deny the part which it takes
in their own work. Gestalt perception is nothing miraculous, even if it is the function of a very wonderful
built-in computer in our central nervous system. Like
other comparable computers, it needs a lot of redundant
input in order to compensate for the "noisiness" of its
channels, so as to be able to discriminate between the
essential and the accidental information. Hence it is
only the patient observer, the expert, who is vouchsafed
the benefit of what is wrongly called inspired guess or
intuition, which is despised as unscientific by hard-
nosed scientists and which is really the function of one
of our most indispensable cognitive mechanisms. The
older medical men among you will know it as "the clinical eye."

However high our opinion of the powers of Gestalt
perception, and however important a function we
ascribe to the functions of gaining a survey knowledge
of the system to be analyzed, it is clear that these are
only the preliminary steps in the endeavor to gain a real
understanding of any system. You remember that the
extraterrestrial scientists of my parable only stood
around that car for a limited time, ascertaining its teleonomy by asking the question "what for?" and then
proceeded to pull it apart.

Both procedures—a) ascertaining teleonomy and b)
pulling apart—meet with difficulties when we approach
the one living system the understanding of which is the
ultimate aim of all science: the system of human society. Whenever the biologist or the ethologist asks the
question "what for?" in respect to a bodily structure or

to a behavior pattern, he does so because he is confident of receiving an acceptable answer. In fact, the more bizarre the structure or the behavior pattern, the surer he is of getting such an answer. If, however, we ask the selfsame question concerning some typical and recurring human behavior patterns, we draw a blank: what is the survival value which commercial competition, or the war in Vietnam, or changing fashions, or a sit-in of university students, or a parade on the Red Square in Moscow have for the survival of the human species? What indeed? We are forced reluctantly to the conclusion that humanity very often does things which, far from helping its survival, are indubitably detrimental to it.

Quite a number of patterns of human behavior, and quite particularly of human social behavior, are clearly *pathological*. The statement that this is so does not, however, help us much in solving the problems which arise as a consequence. It is, in fact, quite difficult even to give a workable definition of what is "normal" and what is "pathological." My late friend Bernhard Hellmann, when confronted with some weird or bizarre behavior of a captive animal, the survival value of which was not at once apparent, used to ask quizzically: "Is this how the constructor meant it?" The "constructor" being, of course, the factors of evolution which cause structures and functions to achieve survival value. I could give no better definition of the normal than to say it was "meant thus by the constructor"! Of course, in our own species matters are complicated by the swift change of ecology wrought by our technology. Thus, a behavior pattern which has been demonstrably "selected for" by the factors of evolution may be devastatingly detrimental to survival under the present conditions of human life. At the same time, there may be an equal number of behavior patterns which owe their nonadaptedness to other and more typically "pathological" factors such as neuroses and other mental disturbances.

At a superficial glance, one might despair of ever gaining any understanding of human society as a living system. Not only is it the most complicated of all existing systems and for this reason the most difficult to analyze, but the teleonomic question which, as I said, is the first step in approaching any system, meets with ambiguous answers. The otherwise reliable teleonomic lawfulness of the system is disturbed in an irregular and unpredictable manner by pathological phenomena. One might indeed despair, were it not for the fact that *the pathological disturbance of a system, far from being an obstacle to its analysis, is indeed very often the key to it.*

I need not tell you, as physiologists, how often it has happened in the history of our science that a subsystem which at the time had not even been suspected to exist, called the investigator's attention to its existence by the illness caused by its malfunction, nor need I tell you how physiology gains knowledge by intentionally eliminating some particular functional unit. I am not well-versed in history of science, but I think that the investigation of the endocrine glands was really one of the first paradigms of how medical men began to think in terms of systems. You all know the story of the Swiss surgeon, E. T. Kocher, who first suspected that the thyroid gland had to do with Basedow's disease and tried to cure it by thyroidectomy. His first patient died of tetany because he had removed the parathyroids as well, and later subjects died more slowly of what Kocher called "cachexia thyreopriva." But that rang a bell. Kocher saw the similarity of symptoms between this medically induced illness and myxoedema! Basedow's disease was due, not to a qualitatively changed function of the thyroid, but to a simple excess of it!

My late friend Ronald Hargreaves, whom I consider to have been one of the most inspired psychiatrists, once wrote to me that he had disciplined himself to ask, whenever he was confronted by some unexplained mental trouble, two simultaneous questions: a) what is the primal survival value of the function here miscarrying? and b) is the malfunction due to an excess or to a deficiency? The great number of cases in which a convincing answer is, indeed, possible to Hargreaves' double question seems to indicate that the sensory-neural system underlying human behavior, and the innumerable independent motivations it produces, act very much like endocrine glands. Small wonder, as the endogenous impulses activating innate motor patterns and similar elementary parts of behavior seem to be closely akin to neurohormones, and the self-regulating balance between antagonistic factors seems to be one of the most important among these principles.

Language as a Source of Knowledge

The first task in attempting the analysis of a system is, as I said, to assess the number and kind of its component parts. This, in respect to the system of human society, is indeed a tall order. However, in our initial survey we may accept help from an unexpected side, from *language*. Colloquial, naturally grown language reflects in the most subtle way subconscious psychological facts. So, in our preliminary search for the subsystems of human motivation, which in their balanced antagonisms *cause* men and women to behave as they do, we may refer to a definition of the subsystem which Paul Weiss once gave. Although he gave it as an aphorism and on the spur of the moment, it is most pertinent here: "A subsystem is anything unitary enough to deserve a name." We may indeed provisionally assume that grown language has developed names only for such things which are indeed real and which are unitary enough to deserve a name!

So you may take it, as a rough rule of thumb but still as an invaluable help in our first approach to the most ambitious undertaking of science, that any *word* which a language has developed for a qualitatively definite human motivation does indeed correspond to one that really exists. There are many such words—love, friendship, hate, jealousy, envy, lust, fear, rage—but still their number is *finite*. In fact, I cannot think of any more at the moment. We may also assume that the question whether any of these motivations be "good" or "bad" is quite as much beside the point as to ask whether the thyroid gland be good or bad. On the other hand, it does make sense to ask, in respect to any disturbance of social behavior, whether there be an excess or a deficiency of one of these motivations. If one of them is regarded as unconditionally "good," like fidelity, friendship, or honesty, one may take it that there is a general deficiency of it in our society and in the tradition which gave its name to it.

Nobody in his right senses can doubt that humanity is a system which at present is thoroughly out of balance, in fact, threatened with destruction. No scientist can doubt that re-establishment of the lost equilibrium is only possible on the base of causal insight into the mechanisms of the normal regulative functions, as well as into the nature of their disturbance. It is my personal but well-considered opinion that this necessary insight can only be achieved by the kind of approach I have just sketched. It will never be achieved without asking Bernhard Hellmann's question "Is this how the constructor meant it to be?" nor without asking Ronald Hargreaves' double question concerning the special survival function of the disturbed function. No insight into the system of human social behavior will be reached without considering the medical aspect; that is, without exploiting as a source of knowledge the pathological disturbances of social behavior.

An immense amount of *purely descriptive work*—for instance, plain writing of case histories—will have to be accomplished *before* quantification and quantitative verification can be brought to bear. I beg you not to go away thinking that I despise quantification because the quantifiers despise description. I don't. I fully appreciate the fact that quantification has the last word in verifying scientific truth. But I am convinced that approaching the urgent problems of humanity by quantifying methods *alone* is just plain stupid.

Ethical Aspects

Permit me now to return to the ethical aspect of the fashionable fallacy of dispensing with description. As I have said, it was the very success which physics and chemistry, based on analytical mathematics, had in mastering man's inorganic environment, which imbued man with the arrogant belief that he knew all the answers. Much worse, man came to believe he knew as well *all the right questions* to ask. It is the success of this kind of approach in dealing with nonorganized, simply structured matter that has blinded humanity to the nature of integrated, highly structured living systems. As proud as Lucifer, humanity has dealt with organic systems by employing methods which are legitimate and moral only in respect to inorganic matter, and has worked havoc with them. Proud as Lucifer is *not* a figure of speech, it is meant literally. The way in which humanity is coming near to destroying its biotope, and therewith itself, is truly satanic. Humanity is just beginning to learn its lesson the hard way and, curiously enough, scientists—at least the great bulk of them—seem to be lagging behind in the realization of the fact that the current contempt for description is implicated in the process of disintegration.

Blindness to the existence of systems is the immediate consequence of concentrating on quantification alone, and with the blindness to systems comes the blindness to harmonies and, ipso facto, to values as such. The organ with which we are endowed to perceive aesthetic values is identical with the one which enables us to perceive ethical values. This perceptiveness is closely linked with Gestalt perception—and Gestalt perception requires a certain amount of training. For the European, Arab music is a chaotic kind of moaning, because the European ear is not trained to perceive the lawfulness of the oriental whole-tone scale. The man whose eye is not trained to perceive the harmony of nature, the beauty of the well-balanced biosphere, is absolutely blind to it and does not feel the least compunction in "developing" the last beautiful spots still left on our earth, bulldozing down trees, covering everything with concrete and building luxury hotels. Nor does the harmony-blind man feel any compunction in perpetrating the most incredible cruelties on his domestic animals. "Intensive" ways of animal husbandry—methods of fattening calves or keeping hens in laying-batteries—are alarming symptoms of dehumanization. A robust mind might tolerate the idea of tormenting a few millions of hens or calves, finding an excuse in nature's own cruelty, as everybody can witness who has seen a water shrew eating a frog or some other equally horrid "normal" happening. However, the really frightening thing is that, as Paul Leyhausen has aptly formulated it, the battery consumer is the unavoidable counterpart of the battery hen. Just look at one of the modern mass-dwellings of modern cities, if you doubt this. It is commercial competition which forces the farmer willy-nilly into perpetrating progressively more atrocious cruelties on his animals. If his neighbor puts four hens in a battery cage to his own three, he *must* follow suit or go bankrupt.

Commercial competition! One of the most disastrous consequences of regarding the whole universe, nonliving and living, as nothing but homogeneous, quantifiable material lies in the fact that this kind of philosophy leads to the ultimate outrage of attempting to quantify the unquantifiable: human emotions. As a very witty reduction to the absurd, my wife used to answer my very silly question, how much she loved me, by saying: "eight." However, the fulfillment of human desires is apt to *cost money* and their intensity thus becomes, in a way, quantifiable by comparing expenses. Money thus becomes a measure for all human instinctual yearnings for power, status, possessions, love, and what not. It is forgotten that money is primarily a means to an end and not an end or goal in itself, and this further adds to the general disqualification of qualities.

The most infernal (again, this is not meant as a swear word but in the literal sense) consequence of modern man's supercilious blindness to harmonies is that it renders him incapable of discovering new systemic entities. When our reductionist fails to understand the workings of a system, he is far more likely to look at it more closely than he is to step back a bit and to look at it in a wider context. He never even suspects that there may be entities of a higher, perhaps of a very high order.

My friend William H. Thorpe has given, in his book *Science, Man and Morals,* a truly inspired definition of religiosity: it consists in man's consciousness of being an infinitesimally small part, but as a reasonable being, also a *responsible member* of a systemic entity immeasurably greater and of immeasurably higher value than he is himself.

We do know, and the best of us are most deeply

aware of the fact, that each of us, as an individual, represents a part and is a responsible member of quite a number of superindividual systems, some of them integrated into higher and more comprehensive ones—there is our family, our country, our team of co-workers, there is science and there is humanity—but we do not know·what is the *ultimate* and all-enclosing system to which we all are responsible. It is the road to ruin to shut our eyes to the existence of systems and to think that we know all the questions which we ought to ask. Pardon me for closing on a more than hackneyed quotation: "There are more things in heaven and earth, Horatio, than are dreamt of in your quantifying, cheese-paring philosophy!"

Kant's Doctrine of the A Priori in the Light of Contemporary Biology* / Konrad Lorenz

For Kant, the categories of space, time, causality, etc. are givens established a priori, determining the form of all of our experience, and indeed making experience possible. For Kant, the validity of these primary principles of reason is absolute. This validity is fundamentally independent of the laws of the real nature which lies behind appearances. This validity is not to be thought of as arising from these laws. The a priori cate-

* In L. von Bertalanffy & A. Rapoport (Eds.), *General Systems, Yearbook of the Society for General Systems Research*, Vol. VII. Society for General Systems Research (205 N. Forest Ave., Ann Arbor, Michigan), 787 United Nations Plaza, New York. 1962, pp. 23–35. Translated from: Kant's Lehre vom apriorischen im Lichte gegenwärtiger Biologie. *Blätter für Deutsche Philosophie*, 1941, 15, 94–125. This rough translation has been prepared by Charlotte Ghurye and edited by Donald T. Campbell with the assistance of Professor Lorenz and William A. Reupke. Ghurye, Lorenz, and Reupke have not had opportunity to see the translation in its present form. While the translation is still very uneven, there is one naiveté of wording which represents a

gories and forms of intuition cannot be related to the laws inherent in the "thing-in-itself" by abstraction or any other means. The only thing we can assert about the thing-in-itself, according to Kant, is the reality of its existence. The relationship which exists between it and the form in which it affects our senses and appears in our world of experience is, for Kant, alogical (to somewhat overstate it). For Kant, the thing-in-itself is on principle unknowable, because the form of its appearance is determined by the purely ideal forms and categories of intuition, so that its appearance has no connection with its essence. This is the viewpoint of Kantian "transcendental" or "critical" idealism, restated in a condensed version.

Kant's orientation has been transformed very liberally by various natural philosophers. In particular, the ever more urgent questionings of the theory of evolution have led to conceptions of the a priori which are perhaps not so far removed from those of Kant himself as from those of the Kantian philosopher tied to the exact terms of Kant's definition of his concepts.

The biologist convinced of the fact of the great creative events of evolution asks of Kant these questions: Is not human reason with all its categories and forms of intuition something that has organically evolved in a continuous cause-effect relationship with the laws of the immediate nature, just as has the human brain? Would not the laws of reason necessary for a priori thought be entirely different if they had undergone an entirely different historical mode of origin, and if con-

---

deliberate avoiding of some more sophisticated usages. The hyphenated phrase "thing-in-itself" has been used as a translation for the Kantian phrases "Ding an sich," "An sich Seienden," "An sich Bestehenden," "An sich der Dinge," "An sich existierenden Natur," etc. This has seemed preferable here to the usual usages of leaving the phrase untranslated, or of translating it into the Greek "noumena." To preserve some Kantian distinctions even at the expense of awkward renditions, these equivalents have been used: Wahrnehmung = perception; Anschauung = intuition; Realität = reality; Wirklichkeit = actuality; Gegenstand = object; Ding = thing.

sequently we had been equipped with an entirely different kind of central nervous system? Is it at all probable that the laws of our cognitive apparatus should be disconnected with those of real external world? Can an organ that has evolved in the process of a continuous coping with the laws of nature have remained so uninfluenced that the theory of appearances can be pursued independently of the existence of the thing-in-itself, as if the two were totally independent of each other? In answering these questions the biologist takes a sharply circumscribed point of view. The exposition of this point of view is the subject of the present paper. We are not just concerned with special discussions of space, time, and causality. The latter are for our study simply examples of the Kantian theory of the a priori, and are treated incidentally to our comparison of the views of the a priori taken by transcendental idealism and by the biologist.

It is the duty of the natural scientist to attempt a natural explanation before he contents himself with drawing upon factors extraneous to nature. This is an important duty for the psychologist who has to cope with the fact that something like Kant's a priori forms of thought do exist. One familiar with the innate modes of reaction of subhuman organisms can readily hypothesize that the a priori is due to hereditary differentiations of the central nervous system which have become characteristic of the species, producing hereditary dispositions to think in certain forms. One must realize that this conception of the "a priori" as an organ means the destruction of the concept: something that has evolved in evolutionary adaptation to the laws of the natural external world has evolved a posteriori in a certain sense, even if in a way entirely different from that of abstraction or deduction from previous experience. The functional similarities which have led many researchers to Lamarckian views about the origin of hereditary modes of reaction from previous "species experience" today are recognized as completely misleading.

The essential character of the natural sciences of today signifies such an abandonment of transcendental idealism that a rift has developed between the scientist and the Kantian philosopher. The rift is caused by the fundamental change of the concepts of the thing-in-itself and the transcendental, a change which results from the redefinition of the concept of the a priori. If the "a priori" apparatus of possible experience with all its forms of intuition and categories is not something immutably determined by factors extraneous to nature but rather something that mirrors the natural laws in contact with which it has evolved in the closest reciprocal interaction, then the boundaries of the transcendental begin to shift. Many aspects of the thing-in-itself which completely escape being experienced by our present-day apparatus of thought and perception may lie within the boundaries of possible experience in the near future, geologically speaking. Many of those aspects which today are within the sphere of the imminent may have still been beyond these boundaries in the recent past of mankind. It is obvious that the question of the extent to which the absolutely existent can be experienced by one *particular* organism has not the slightest influence on the fundamental question. However, such consideration alters something in the definition which we have to make of the thing-in-itself behind the phenomena. For Kant (who in all his speculations took into consideration only mature civilized man, representing an immutable system created by God) no obstacle presented itself to defining the thing-in-itself as basically uncognizable. In his static way of looking at it, he could include the limit of possible experience in the definition of the thing-in-itself. This limit would be the same for man and amoeba—infinitely far from the thing-in-itself. In view of the indubitable fact of evolution this is no longer tenable. Even if we recognize that the absolutely existent will never be completely knowable (even for the highest imaginable living beings there will be a limit set by the necessity of categorical forms of thought), the boundary separating the experienceable from the transcendental must vary for each individual type of organism. The location of the boundary has to be investigated separately for each type of organism. It would mean an unjustifiable anthropomorphism to include the purely accidental present-day location of this boundary for the human species in the definition of the thing-in-itself. If, in spite of the indubitable evolutionary modifiability of our apparatus of experience, one nevertheless wanted to continue to define the thing-in-itself as that which is uncognizable for this very apparatus, the definition of the absolute would thereby be held to be relative, obviously an absurdity. Rather, every natural science urgently needs a concept of the absolutely real which is as little anthropomorphic and as independent as possible of the accidental, present-day location of the limits of the humanly experienceable. The absolutely actual can in no way be a matter of the degree to which it is reflected in the brain of a human, or any other temporary form. On the other hand, it is the object of a most important branch of comparative science to investigate the type of this reflection, and to find out the extent to which it is in the form of crudely simplifying symbols which are only superficially analogous or to what extent it reproduces details, i.e., how far its exactness goes. By this investigation of prehuman forms of knowledge we hope to gain clues to the mode of functioning and historical origin of our own knowledge, and in this manner to push ahead the critique of knowledge further than was possible without such comparisons.

I assert that nearly all natural scientists of today, at least all biologists, consciously or unconsciously assume in their daily work a real relationship between the thing-in-itself and the phenomena of our subjective experience, but a relationship that is by no means a "purely" ideal one in the Kantian sense. I even would like to assert that Kant himself assumed this in all the results of his own empirical research. In our opinion, the real relationship between the thing-in-itself and the specific a priori form of its appearance has been determined by the fact that the form of appearance has developed as an adaptation to the laws of the thing-in-itself in the coping negotiation with these continuously present laws during the evolutionary history of mankind, lasting hundreds of millennia. This adaptation has provided our thought with an innate structuralization which corresponds to a considerable degree to the reality of the external world. "Adaptation" is a word already loaded with meaning and easily misunderstood. It should not, in the present condition, denote more than that our forms of intuition and categories "fit" to that which really exists in the manner in which our foot fits the floor or the fin of the fish suits the water. The a priori which determines the forms of appearance of the real things of our world is, in short, an organ, or, more precisely, the functioning of an organ. We come closer to understanding the a priori if we confront it with the questions asked of everything organic: "What for?" "Where from?" "Why?" These questions are, first, How does it preserve the species? second, What is its genealogical origin? third, What natural causes make it possible? We are convinced that the a priori is based on central nervous systems which are entirely as real as the things of the external world whose phenomenal form they determine for us. This central nervous apparatus does not prescribe the laws of nature any more than the hoof of the horse prescribes the form of the ground. Just as the hoof of the horse, this central nervous apparatus stumbles over unforeseen changes in its task. But just as the hoof of the horse is adapted to the ground of the steppe which it copes with, so our central nervous apparatus for organizing the image of the world is adapted to the real world with which man has to cope. Just like any organ, this apparatus has attained its expedient species-preserving form through this coping of real with the real during its genealogical evolution, lasting many eons.

Our view of the origin of the "a priori" (an origin which in a certain sense is "a posteriori") answers very fittingly Kant's question as to whether the forms of perception of space and time, which we do not derive from experience (as Kant, contrary to Hume, emphasizes quite correctly) but which are a priori in our representation "were not mere chimeras of the brain made by us to which no object corresponds, at least not adequately." * If we conceive our intellect as the function of an organ (and there is no valid argument against this) our obvious answer to the question why its form of function is adapted to the real world is simply the following: our categories and forms of perception, fixed prior to individual experience, are adapted to the external world for exactly the same reasons as the hoof of the horse is already adapted to the ground of the steppe before the horse is born and the fin of the fish is adapted to the water before the fish hatches. No sensible person believes that in any of these cases the form of the organ "prescribes" its properties to the object. To everyone it is self-evident that water possesses its properties independently of whether the fins of the fish are biologically adapted to these properties or not. Quite evidently some properties of the thing-in-itself which is at the bottom of the phenomenon "water" have led to the specific form of adaptation of the fins which have

---

* *Prolegomena,* First Part, Note III. The present translators have used here the translation of Kant provided by P. G. Lucas, Manchester University Press, 1953.

been evolved independently of one another by fishes, reptiles, birds, mammals, cephalopods, snails, crayfish, arrow worms, etc. It is obviously the properties of water that have prescribed to these different organisms the corresponding form and function of their organ of locomotion. But when reckoning in regard to structure and mode of function of his own brain the transcendental philosopher assumes something fundamentally different. In paragraph 11 of the *Prolegomena* Kant says: "If anyone were to have the slightest doubt that both [the forms of intuition of space and time] are not determinations of the thing-in-itself but mere determinations of their relation to sensibility, I should like to know how it could be found possible to know a priori and thus prior to all acquaintance with things, namely before they are given to us, what their intuition must be like, which is the case here with space and time." * This question clarifies two very important facts. First, it shows that Kant, no more than Hume, thought of the possibility of a formal adaptation between thought and reality other than through abstracting from previous experience. Second, it shows that he assumed the impossibility of any different form of origin. Furthermore, it shows the great and fundamentally new discovery of Kant, i.e., that human thought and perception have certain functional structures prior to every individual experience.

Most certainly Hume was wrong when he wanted to derive all that is a priori from that which the senses supply to experience, just as wrong as Wundt or Helmholtz who simply explain it as an abstraction from preceding experience. Adaptation of the a priori to the real world has no more originated from "experience" than has adaptation of the fin of the fish to the properties of water. Just as the form of the fin is given a priori, prior

---

* Translation of P. G. Lucas, Manchester University Press, 1953.

to any individual coping of the young fish with the water, and just as it is this form that makes possible this coping; so it is also the case with our forms of perception and categories in their relationship to our coping with the real external world by means of experience. For animals there are specific limitations to the forms of experience which are possible. We believe we can demonstrate the closest functional and probably genetic relationship between these animal a prioris and our human a priori.

Contrary to Hume, we believe, as did Kant, in the possibility of "pure" science of the innate forms of human thought independent of all experience. This "pure" science, however, would be able to convey only a very one-sided understanding of the a priori forms of thought because it neglects the organic nature of these structures and does not pose the basic biological question concerning their species-preserving meaning. Bluntly speaking, it is just as if someone wanted to write a "pure" theory on the characteristics of a modern photographic camera, a Leica for example, without taking into consideration that this is an apparatus for photographing the external world, and without consulting the pictures the camera produces which enable one to understand its function and the essential meaning of its existence. As far as the produced pictures (just as experiences) are concerned, the Leica is entirely a priori. It exists prior to and independently of every picture; indeed, it determines the form of the pictures, nay, makes them possible in the first place. Now I assert: to separate "pure Leicology" from the theory of the pictures it produces is just as meaningless as to separate the theory of the a priori from the theory of the external world, of phenomenology from the theory of the thing-in-itself. All the lawfulnesses of our intellect which we find to be there a priori are not freaks of nature. We live off them! And we can get insight into their essential meaning only if we take into consideration their function. Just as the Leica could not originate without the activity of photography, carried out long before the Leica was constructed, just as the completed Leica with all its incredibly well-conceived and "fitting" constructional details has not dropped from the heavens, so neither has our infinitely more wonderful "pure reason." This, too, has arrived at its relative perfection from out of its activity, from its negotiation with the thing-in-itself.

Although for the transcendental idealist the relationship between the thing-in-itself and its appearance is extraneous to nature and alogical, it is entirely real for us. It is certain that not only does the thing-in-itself "affect" our receptors, but also vice versa, our effectors on their part "affect" absolute reality. The word "actuality" comes from the verb "to act." ["*Wirklichkeit*" *kommt von wirken!*] What appears in our world is by no means only our experience one-sidedly influenced by real external things as they work on us as through the lenses of the ideal possibilities of experience. What we witness as experience is always a coping of the real in us with the real outside of us. Therefore the relationship between the events in and outside of us is not alogical and does not basically prohibit drawing conclusions about the lawfulness of the external world from the lawfulness of the internal events. Rather, this relationship is the one which exists between image and object, between a simplified model and the real thing. It is the relationship of an analogy of greater or less remoteness. The degree of this analogy is fundamentally open to comparative investigation. That is, it is possible to make statements as to whether agreement between appearance and actuality is more exact or less exact, in comparing one human being to another, or one living organism to another.

On these premises also depends the self-evident fact that there are more and less correct judgments about the external world! The relationship between the world of phenomena and thing-in-itself is thus not fixed once and for all by ideal laws of form which are extraneous to nature and in principle inaccessible to investigation. Neither do the judgments made on the basis of these "necessities of thought" have an independent and absolute validity. Rather, all our forms of intuition and categories are thoroughly natural. Like every other organ, they are evolutionarily developed receptacles for the reception and retroactive utilization of those lawful consequences of the thing-in-itself with which we have to cope if we want to remain alive and preserve our species. The special form of these organic receptacles has to the properties of the thing-in-itself a relationship grown entirely out of real natural connections. The organic receptacles are adapted to these properties in a manner that has a practical biological sufficiency, but which is by no means absolute nor even so precise that one could say their form equals that of the thing-in-itself. Even if we as natural scientists are in a certain sense naïve realists, we still do not take the appearance for the thing-in-itself, nor the experienced reality for the absolutely existent! Thus we are not surprised to find the laws of "pure reason" entangled in the most serious contradictions not only with one another, but also with the empirical facts whenever research demands greater precision. This happens particularly where physics and chemistry enter the nuclear phase. There not only does the intuition-form of space-perception break down, but also the categories of causality, of substantiality, and, in a certain sense, of quantity (even though quantity otherwise appears to have the most unconditional validity except for the intuition-form of time-perception). "Necessary for thought" in no way means "absolutely valid" in view of these empirical facts, highly essential in nuclear physics, quantum mechanics, and wave theory.

The realization that all laws of "pure reason" are based on highly physical or mechanical structures of the human central nervous system which have developed through many eons like any other organ, on the one hand shakes our confidence in the laws of pure reason and on the other hand substantially raises our confidence in them. Kant's statement that the laws of pure reason have absolute validity, nay, that every imaginable rational being, even if it were an angel, must obey the same laws of thought, appears as an anthropocentric presumption. Surely the "keyboard" provided by the forms of intuition and categories—Kant himself calls it that—is something definitely located on the physicostructural side of the psychophysical unity of the human organism. The forms of intuition and categories relate to the "freedom" of the mind (if there is such a thing), as physical structures are usually related to the possible degrees of freedom of the psychic, namely by both supporting and restraining at the same time. But surely these clumsy categorical boxes into which we have to pack our external world "in order to be able to spell them as experiences" (Kant) can claim no autonomous and absolute validity whatsoever. This is certain for us the moment we conceive them as evolutionary adaptations—and I would indeed like to know what scientific argument could be brought against this conception. At the same time, however, the nature of their adaptation shows that the categorical forms of intuition and categories have proved themselves as working hypotheses in the coping of our species with the absolute reality of the environment (in spite of their validity being only approximate and relative). Thus is clarified the paradoxical fact that the laws of "pure reason" which break down at every step in modern theoretical science, nonetheless have stood (and still stand) the test in the practical biological matters of the struggle for the preservation of the species.

The dots produced by the coarse screens used in the reproductions of photographs in our daily papers are satisfactory representations when looked at superficially, but cannot stand closer inspection with a magnifying glass. So, too, the reproductions of the world by our forms of intuition and categories break down as soon as they are required to give a somewhat closer representation of their objects, as is the case in wave mechanics and nuclear physics. All the knowledge an individual can wrest from the empirical reality of the "physical world-picture" is essentially only a working hypothesis. And, as far as their species-preserving function goes, all those innate structures of the mind which we call "a priori" are likewise only working hypotheses. Nothing is absolute except that which hides in and behind the phenomena. Nothing that our brain can think has absolute, a priori validity in the true sense of the word, not even mathematics with all its laws. The laws of mathematics are but an organ for the quantification of external things, and, what is more, an organ exceedingly important for man's life, without which he never could play his role in dominating the earth, and which thus has amply proved itself biologically, as have all the other "necessary" structures of thought. Of course, "pure" mathematics is not only possible, it is, as a theory of the internal laws of this miraculous organ of quantification, of an importance that can hardly be overestimated. But this does not justify us in making it absolute. Counting and mathematical number affect reality in approximately the same manner as do a dredging machine and its shovels. Regarded statistically, in a large number of individual cases each shovel dredges up roughly the same amount, but actually not even two can ever have exactly the same content. The pure mathematical equation is a tautology: I state that if my dredging machine brings in such and such a number of shovels, then such and such a number are brought in. Two shovels of my machine are absolutely equal to each other because strictly speaking it is the same shovel each time, namely the number one. But only the empty sentence always has this validity. Two shovels filled with something or other are never equal to each other, the number one applied to a real object will never find its equal in the whole universe. It is true that two plus two equals four, but two apples, rams, or atoms plus two more never equal four others because no equal apples, rams, or atoms exist! In this sense we arrive at the paradoxical fact that the equation two plus two equals four in its application to real units, such as apples or atoms, has a much smaller degree of approximation to reality than the equation two million plus two million equal four million because the individual dissimilarities of the counted units level out statistically in the case of a large number. Regarded as a working hypothesis or as a functional organ, the form of thought of numerical quantification is and remains one of the most miraculous apparatuses that nature has ever created; it evokes the admiration of the biologist, particularly by the incredible breadth of its sphere of application even if one does not consider its sphere of validity absolute.

It would be entirely conceivable to imagine a rational being that does not quantify by means of the mathematical number (that does not use 1, 2, 3, 4, 5, the number of individuals approximately equal among themselves, such as rams, atoms, or milestones, to mark the quantity at hand) but grasps these immediately in some other way. Instead of quantifying water by the number of the filled liter vessels, one could, for example, conclude from the tension of a rubber balloon of a certain size how much water it contains. It can very well be purely coincidental, in other words brought about by purely historical causes, that our brain happens to be able to quantify extensive quantities more readily than intensive ones. It is by no means a necessity of thought and it would be entirely conceivable that the ability to quantify intensively according to the method indicated by the example of measuring the tension in the rubber balloon could be developed up to the point where it would become equally valuable and replace numerical mathematics. Indeed, the ability to estimate quantities immediately, present in man and in a number of animals, is probably due to such an intensive process of quantification. A mind quantifying in a purely intensive manner would carry out some operations more simply and immediately than our mathematics of the "dredging-scoop" variety. For example, it might be able to calculate curves immediately, which is possible in our extensive mathematics only by means of the detour of integral and differential calculus, a detour which tides us over the limitations of the numerical steps, but still clings to them conceptually. An intellect quantifying purely by intensity would not be able to grasp that two times two equals four. Since it would have no understanding for the number one, for our empty numerical box, it would also not comprehend our postulate of the equality of two such boxes and would reply to our arrangement of an equation that it is incorrect because no equal boxes, rams, or atoms exist. And in regard to its system, it would be just as correct in its statement as we would be in ours. Certainly an intensive quantification system would perform many operations more poorly, that is, in a more involved manner, than does numerical mathematics. The fact that the latter has developed so much further than the ability of intensive quantitative estimation speaks for its being the more "practical" one. But even so it is and remains only an organ, an evolutionarily acquired "innate working hypothesis" which basically is only approximately adapted to the data of the thing-in-itself.

If a biologist attempts to grasp the relationship of hereditary structure to the regulated plasticity of all that is organic, he arrives at a universal law holding both for physical and intellectual structures and as valid for the plastic protoplasm and the skeletal elements of a protozoan as for the categorical forms of thought and the creative plasticity of the human mind. From its simplest beginnings in the domain of the protozoa, solid structure is just as much a condition for any higher evolution as is organic plasticity. In this sense, solid structure is just as indispensable and as consistent a property of living matter as is its plastic freedom. However, every solid structure, although indispensable as a support for the organic system, carries with it an undesired side effect: it makes for rigidness, and takes away a certain degree of freedom from the system. Every enlistment of a mechanical structure means in some sense to bind oneself. Von Uexküll has said aptly: "The amoeba is less of a machine than the horse," thinking mainly about physical properties. Nietzsche has expressed poetically the same relationship between structure and plasticity in human thought: "A thought—now still hot liquid lava; but all lava builds a castle around itself. Every thought finally crushes itself with 'laws.' " This simile of a structure crystallizing out of the liquid state goes much deeper than Nietzsche sensed: It is not entirely impossible that all that becomes solid, in the intellectual-psychic as well as in the physical, is bound to be a transition from the liquid state of certain plasma parts to the solid state.

But Nietzsche's simile and Uexküll's statement overlook something. The horse is a higher animal than the amoeba not despite, but, to a large extent, because of its being richer in solid differentiated structures. Organisms with as few structures as possible must remain amoebae, whether they like it or not, for without any solid structure all higher organization is inconceivable. One could symbolize organisms with a maximum of highly differentiated fixed structures as lobsters, stiffly armored creatures which could move only in certain joints with precisely allowed degrees of freedom, or as railroad cars which could only move along a prescribed track having very few switching points. For every living being, increasing mental and physical differentiation is always a compromise between these two extremes, neither one representing the highest realization of the possibilities of organic creation. Always and everywhere differentiation to a higher level of mechanical structure has the dangerous tendency to fetter the mind, whose servant it was just a moment ago, and to prevent its further evolution. The hard exoskeleton of the arthropods is such an obstruction in evolution, as is also the fixed instinctual movements of many higher organisms and the industrial machinery of man.

Indeed, every system of thought that commits itself to a nonplastic "absolute" has this same fettering effect. The moment such a system is finished, when it has disciples who believe in its perfection, it is already "false." Only in the state of becoming is the philosopher a human being in the most proper meaning of the word. I am reminded of the beautiful definition of man which we owe to the pragmatist and which probably is given in its clearest formulation in Gehlen's book *Der Mensch*. Man is defined as the permanently unfinished being, permanently unadapted and poor in structure, but continuously open to the world, continuously in the state of becoming.

When the human thinker, be it even the greatest, has finished his system, he has in a fundamental way taken on something of the properties of the lobster or the railroad car. However ingeniously his disciples may manipulate the prescribed and permitted degrees of freedom of his lobster-armor, his system will only be a blessing for the progress of human thought and knowledge when he finds followers who break it apart and, using new, not "built in," degrees of freedom, turn its pieces into a new construction. If, however, a system of thought is so well joined together that for a long time no one appears who has the power and the courage to burst it asunder, it can obstruct progress for centuries: "There lies the stone, one has to let it be, and everyone limps on his crutch of faith to devil's stone, to devil's bridge!" (Goethe, *Faust*).

And just as a system of thought created by the individual human being enslaves its creator, so also do the evolutionarily developed supraindividual forms of thought of the a priori: They, too, are held to be absolute! The machine whose species-preserving meaning was originally in quantifying real external things, the machine that was created for "counting rams," suddenly pretends to be absolute and buzzes with an admirable absence of internal friction and contradiction, but only as long as it runs empty, counting its own shovels. If one lets a dredging machine, an engine, a band saw, a theory, or an a priori function of thought run empty in this way, then its function proceeds ipso facto without noticeable friction, heat, or noise; for the parts in such a system do not, of course, contradict one another and so fit together intelligibly and in a well-tuned manner. When empty they are indeed "absolute," but absolutely empty. Only when the system is expected to work, that is, to achieve something in relation to the external world in which the real and species-preserving meaning of its whole existence does indeed consist, then the thing starts to groan and crack. When the shovels of the dredging machine dig into the soil, the teeth of the band saw dig into the wood, or the assumptions of the theory dig into the material of empirical facts which is to be classified; then develop the undesirable side noises that come from the inevitable imperfection of every naturally developed system: *and no other systems exist for the natural scientist.* But these noises are just what does indeed represent the coping of the system with the real external world. In this sense they are the door through which the thing-in-itself peeps into our world of phenomena, the door through which the road to further knowledge continues to lead. They, and not the unresisting empty humming of the apparatus, are "reality." They, indeed, are what we have to place under the magnifying glass if we want to get to know the imperfections of our apparatus of thought and experience and if we want to gain knowledge beyond these imperfections. The side noises have to be considered methodically if the machine is to be improved. The fundamentals of pure reason are just as imperfect and down to earth as the band saw, but also just as real.

Our working hypothesis should read as follows: everything is a working hypothesis. This holds true not only for the natural laws which we gain through individual abstraction a posteriori from the facts of our experience, but also for the laws of pure reason. The faculty of understanding does not in itself constitute an explanation of phenomena, but the fact that it projects phenomena for us in a practically usable form onto the projection screen of our experiencing is due to its formulation of working hypotheses; developed in evolution and tested through millions of years! Santayana says: "Faith in the intellect is the only faith that has justified itself by the fruit it has borne. But the one who clings forever to the form of faith is a Don Quixote, rattling with outmoded armor. I am a decided materialist with regard to natural philosophy, but I do not claim to know what matter is. I am waiting for the men of science to tell me that."

Our view that all human thought is only a working

hypothesis must not be interpreted as lowering the value of the knowledge secured by mankind. It is true that this knowledge is only a working hypothesis for us, it is true that we are ready at any moment to throw overboard our favorite theories when new facts demand this. But even if nothing is "absolutely true," every new piece of knowledge, every new truth, is nevertheless a step forward in a very definite, definable direction: the absolutely existent is apprehended from a new, up to this point unknown, aspect; it is covered in a new characteristic. For us that working hypothesis is true which paves the way for the next step in knowledge or which at least does not obstruct the way. Human science must act like a scaffolding for reaching the greatest possible height, without its absolute extent being foreseeable at the start of the construction. At the moment when such a construction is committed to a permanently set supporting pillar, the latter fits only a building of a certain form and size. Once these are reached and the building is to continue, the supporting pillar has to be demolished and rebuilt, a process which can become the more dangerous for the entire structure, the more deeply that which is to be rebuilt is set in its foundation. Since it is a constituent property of all true science that its structure should continue to grow into the boundless, all that is mechanically systematic, all that corresponds to solid structures and scaffoldings must always be something provisional, alterable at any time. The tendency to secure one's own building for the future by declaring it absolute leads to the opposite of the intended success: just that "truth" which is dogmatically believed in sooner or later leads to a revolution in which the actual truth content and value of the old theory are all too easily demolished and forgotten along with the obsolete obstructions to progress. The heavy cultural losses which may accompany revolutions are special cases of this phenomenon. The character of all truths as working hypotheses must always be kept in mind, in order to prevent the necessity of demolishing the established structure, and in order to preserve for the "established" truths that eternal value which they potentially deserve.

Our conception that a priori forms of thought and intuition have to be understood just as any other organic adaptation carries with it the fact that they are for us "inherited working hypotheses," so to speak, whose truth content is related to the absolutely existent in the same manner as that of ordinary working hypotheses which have proven themselves just as splendidly adequate in coping with the external world. This conception, it is true, destroys our faith in the absolute truth of any a priori thesis necessary for thought. On the other hand it gives the conviction that something actual "adequately corresponds" to every phenomenon in our world. Even the smallest detail of the world of phenomena "mirrored" for us by the innate working hypothesis of our forms of intuition and thought is in fact preformed to the phenomenon it reproduces, having a relationship corresponding to the one existing between organic structures and the external world in general (e.g., the analogy of the fin of the fish and the hoof of the horse). It is true that the a priori is only a box whose form unpretentiously fits that of the actuality to be portrayed. This box, however, is accessible to our investigation even if we cannot comprehend the thing-in-itself except by means of the box. But access to the laws of the box, i.e., of the instrument, makes the thing-in-itself relatively comprehensible.

Now what we are planning to do with patient empirical research work is an investigation of the "a priori," of the "innate" working hypotheses present in subhuman organisms. This includes species that achieve a correspondence to the properties of the thing-in-itself less detailed than that of man. With all their incredible accuracy of aim, the innate schematisms of animals are still much more simple, of coarser screen, than those of man, so that the boundaries of their achievement still fall within the measurable domain of our own receptive apparatus. Let us take as analogy the domain that can be resolved with the lens of a microscope: the fineness of the smallest structure of the object still visible with it is dependent upon the relationship between angle of aperture and focal length, the so-called "numerical aperture." The first diffraction spectrum which is thrown by the structural grating must still fall into the front lens in order that the grating is seen as such. If this is no longer the case, one does not see the structure; rather, the object appears with a smooth surface and, strangely enough, brown.

Now let us suppose I had only one microscope. Then I would say structures are only "conceivable" up to that fineness, finer ones do not exist. Moreover, though I would have to admit that there are brown objects, I would have no reason to assume that this color has the slightest relationship to the visible structures! However, if one also knew of less strongly resolving lens which register "brown" for structures which are still visible as structures by our instruments, then one would be very skeptical toward our instrument's registering brown (unless one had become a megalomaniac and pronounced one's own receptive apparatus absolute, just for the reason that it was one's own property). If one is more modest, however, one will draw the right conclusion from the comparison of the limits of achievement and the fact that the various instruments register brown. The conclusion is that even the most powerful lenses have limits as to the fineness of structure resolved, just as do simpler apparatuses. In a methodically similar way one can learn much from the functional limitations which the various apparatuses for organizing the image of the universe all have. The lesson so learned provides an important critical perspective for judging the limits of achievement of the highest existing apparatus, which today cannot be investigated from the observation tower of a still higher one.

Looking at it from a psychological viewpoint, it is self-evident that our neural apparatus for organizing the image of the world is basically like a photoprint screen which cannot reproduce any finer points of the thing-in-itself than those corresponding to the numerically finite elements of the screen. Just as the grain of the photographic negative permits no unlimited enlargement, so also there are limitations in the image of the universe traced out by our sense organs and cognitive apparatus. These too permit no unlimited "enlargement," no unlimited view of details, however self-evident and real the image may appear at superficial inspection. Where the physical image of the universe formed by man has advanced to the atomic level, there emerge inaccuracies in the coordination between the a priori "necessities of thought" and the empirically real. It is as though the "measure of all things" was simply too coarse and too approximate for these finer spheres of measurement, and would only agree in general and at a statistical-probabilistic level with that which is to be comprehended of the thing-in-itself. This is increasingly true for atomic physics, whose entirely impalpable ideas can no longer be experienced directly. For we can only "spell out as experience" in a directly experienceable manner (to apply Kant's own expression to this physiological fact) that which can be written on the crudely simplifying "keyboard" of our central nervous system. But in different organisms, this keyboard can be differentiated in a more simple or more complex manner. To represent it by the analogy of the photoprint screen, the best possible picture that can be reproduced by an apparatus of a given degree of fineness corresponds to those representations encountered in cross-stitch embroideries which build round-contoured animals and flowers from small rectangular elements. The property of "being composed of squares" in no way belongs to the represented thing-in-itself, but is due to a peculiarity of the picture apparatus, a peculiarity which can be regarded as a technically unavoidable limitation. Similar limitations accompany each apparatus for organizing the image of the world, if only because of its being composed of cellular elements (as is the case for vision). Now if one examines methodically what the cross-stitch representation permits to be stated about the form of the thing-in-itself, the conclusion is that the accuracy the statement is dependent upon the relationship between the size of the picture and the grain of the screen. If one square is out of line with a straight-line contour in the embroidery, one knows that behind it lies an actual projection of the represented thing, but one is not sure whether it exactly fills the whole square of the screen or only the smallest part of it. This question can be decided only with the help of the next finest screen. But behind every detail which even the crudest screen reproduces there certainly lies something real, simply because otherwise the respective screen unit would not have registered. But no tool is at our disposal to determine what lies behind the registering of the finest existent screen unit, whether much or little of the contour of that which is to be reproduced protrudes into its domain. The fundamental indiscernibility of the last detail of the thing-in-itself remains. We are only convinced that all details which our apparatus does reproduce correspond to actual attributes of the thing-in-itself. One becomes more and more firmly convinced of this entirely real and lawful correlation between the Real and the Apparent, the more one concerns oneself with the comparison of apparatuses for organizing the image of the world of animals as different from one another as possible. The continuity of the thing-in-itself, most convincingly emerging from such comparisons, is completely incompatible with the supposition of an alogical extrinsically determined relationship between the thing-in-itself and its appearances.

Such comparative research brings us closer to the actual world lying behind the phenomena, providing we succeed in showing that the different a priori formations of possible reaction (and thus of possible experience) of the different species make experienceable the same lawfulness of real existents and lead to its control in a species-preserving way. Such different adaptations to one and the same lawfulness strengthen our belief in its reality in the same manner as a judge's belief in the actuality of an event is strengthened by several mutually independent witnesses giving descriptions of it that are in general agreement, though not identical. Organisms that are on a much lower mental level than man struggle quite evidently with the same data that are made experienceable in our world by the forms of perception of space and time and by the category of causality; but they do it by means of quite different and much simpler achievements, which are accessible to scientific analysis. Even if the a priori human forms of perception and thought remain inaccessible to causal analysis for the time being, we as natural scientists must nevertheless desist from explaining the existence of the a priori (or, in general, of pure reason) by a principle extraneous to nature. We must instead regard any such explanatory attempt as a completely arbitrary and dogmatic division between the rationally comprehensible and the unknowable, a division which has done as serious damage in obstructing research, as have the prohibitions of the vitalists.

The method to be used can be explained, by analogy to the microscope, as a science of apparatuses. Basically, we can comprehend only the lower precursors of our own forms of perception and thought. Only where laws represented through these primitive organs can be identified with those represented on our own apparatus can we clarify properties of the human a priori, using the more primitive as a starting point. In this way we can draw conclusions about the continuity of the world lying behind phenomena. Such an enterprise succeeds quite well compared with the theory of the a priori forms of perception of space and the category of causality. A large number of animals do not comprehend the "spatial" structurization of the world in the same way we do. We can, however, have an approximate idea what the "spatial" looks like in the world picture of such organisms because in addition to our spatial apprehension we also possess the ability to master spatial problems in their manner. Most reptiles, birds, and lower mammals do not master problems of space as we do through a simultaneous clear survey over the data. Instead, spatial problems are learned by rote. For example, a water shrew, when placed into new surroundings, gradually learns by rote all possible paths by slow crawling about, constantly guided by sniffing and feeling with the whiskers in such a manner as perhaps a child learns piano pieces by rote. In the laborious piecemeal sequence of the limb movements, first short stretches become "known movements," followed by a smoother linking of these parts. And these movements, smoothing and steadying themselves by becoming kinesthetically ingrained, extend farther and farther, and finally flow together into an inseparable whole which, running off fast and smoothly, has no longer any similarity with the original search movements. These sequences of movement, so laboriously acquired, and run off so extraordinarily fast and smoothly, do not take the "shortest way." On the contrary, chance determines what spatial pattern such a path learning takes. It even happens that the winding path intersects itself, without the animal necessarily noticing how the end of the path can be brought closer by cutting off the superfluous piece.*

For an animal, like the water shrew, that masters its living space almost exclusively by path learning, the thesis is by no means valid that the straight line is the shortest connection between two points. If it wanted to steer in a straight line (which lies basically within its abilities) it would constantly have to approach its goal sniffing, feeling with its whiskers and using its eyes, which are not very efficient. In this process it would use up more time and energy than by going the path it

* Rats and other mammals that are on a higher mental level than the water shrew notice such possibilities of a shortcut immediately. I experienced a highly interesting case with a graylag goose in which the possibility of a shortcut in path learning was undoubtedly noticed, but not made use of. When a gosling, this bird had acquired a path learning which led through the door of our house and up two flights of a wide staircase to my room, where the goose used to spend the night. In the morning it used to make its exit by flying through the window. When learning the path, the young graylag goose ran first of all toward a large window in the yet strange staircase, past the lowest step. Many birds, when disquieted, strive for the light, and so this goose, too, decided to leave the window and come to the landing to which I had wanted to lead it only after it had quieted down a little. This detour to the window remained once and for all an indispensable part of the path learning which the graylag goose had to go through on its way to the place where it used to sleep. This very steep detour to the window and back gave a very mechanical effect, almost like a habitually performed ceremony, because its original motivation (anxiety and therefore shying away from the darkness) was no longer present. In the course of this goose's path learning, which took almost two years, the detour became gradually leveled off, that is, the line originally going almost as far as the window and back had now sloped down to an acute angle by which the goose deflected its course toward the window and mounted the lowest step at the extremity facing the window. This leveling off of the unnecessary would probably have led to attaining the actually shortest way in two more years and had nothing to do with insight. But a goose is, properly speaking, basically capable of finding such a simple solution by insight; though habit prevails over insight or prevents it. One evening the following happened. I had forgotten to let the goose into the house, and when I finally remembered, it was standing impatiently on the doorstep and rushed past me and—to my great surprise—for the first time took the shortest way up the stairs. But already on the third step it stopped, stretched its neck, uttered the warning cry, turned around, walked the three steps down again, made the detour to the window hastily and "formally" and then mounted the stairs calmly in the usual way. Here obviously the possibility of a solution by insight was blocked only by the existence of that learned by training!

knows by rote. If two points which on this path lie quite far apart are spatially close together, the animal knows it not. Even a human being can behave in this way, for example, in a strange city. It is true, however, that under such circumstances we humans succeed sooner or later in getting a spatial survey which opens up the possibility of a straight-line shortcut for us. The sewer rat, which is on a much higher mental level than the shrew, likewise soon finds shortcuts. The graylag goose could, as we have seen, achieve the same thing, but does not do it for religious reasons, as it were; it is prevented by that peculiar inhibition which also ties primitive people so much to habit. The biological meaning of this rigid clinging to "tradition" is easily understandable: it will always be advisable for an organism that does not have at its disposal a spatial-temporal-causal survey over a certain situation to persist rigidly in the behavior that has proved successful and free of danger. So-called magical thought, by no means present only in primitive people, is closely related to this phenomenon. One need only think of the well-known "knock on wood." The motive that "after all, one cannot tell what is going to happen if one omits doing it" is very clear.

For the true kinesthetic creature, such as the water shrew, it is literally impossible as far as its thinking is concerned to find a shortcut. Perhaps it learns one when forced by external circumstances, but again only by learning by rote, this time a new path. Otherwise there is an impenetrable wall for the water shrew between two loops of its path, even when they almost or actually touch. How many such new possibilities of solution, in principle equally simple, we humans may overlook with equal blindness in the struggle with our daily problems! This thought obtrudes itself with compelling force upon anyone who in his direct daily associations with animals has come to know their many human characteristics and at the same time the fixed limits to their achievement. Nothing can be more apt to make the scientist doubt his own godlike character and to inculcate in him a very beneficial modesty.

From a psychological viewpoint, the water shrew's command of space is a sequence of conditioned reflexes and kinesthetically ingrained movements. It reacts to the known steering marks of its path with conditioned reflexes which are less a steering than a control to ascertain that it is still on the right path, for the kinesthetic movement known by rote is so precise and exact that the process takes place almost without optical or tactile steering, as in the case of a good piano player who need hardly look at the score or the keys. This sequence formation of conditioned reflexes and known movements is by no means only a spatial but also a spatial-temporal formation. It can be produced only in one direction. To run the course backward requires completely different trainings. To run the paths learned by rote the wrong way is just as impossible as to recite the alphabet in the wrong sequence. If one interrupts the animal running along its trained path, taking away a hurdle that has to be jumped, it becomes disoriented and tries to reconnect the chain of the ingrained links at an earlier place. Therefore it runs back and searches until it becomes reoriented in the signs of its path and tries again. Just like a little girl who has been interrupted in reciting a poem.

A relationship very similar to the one we found between the disposition toward learning paths by rote and the human form of perception of space exists between the disposition toward developing conditioned reflexes (associations), and the human category of causality. The organism learns that a certain stimulus, for example, the appearance of the keeper, always precedes a biologically relevant event, let us say, feeding; it "associates" these two events and treats the first as the signal for the

occurrence of the second one by starting preparatory reactions upon the onset of the first stimulus (e.g., the
salivation reflex investigated by Pavlov). This connection of an experience with the regularly following *post
hoc* is totally unrelated to causal thought. It should be
remembered that, for example, urination, a completely
unconscious process, can be trained to conditioned reflexes! The reason why *post hoc* was still equated with
and mistaken for *propter hoc* is that the disposition for
association and causal thought actually achieves the
same thing biologically; they are, so to speak, organs for
negotiating the same real datum.

This datum is without any doubt the natural lawfulness contained in the first main thesis of physics.
The "conditioned reflex" arises when a certain outer
stimulus, which is meaningless for the organism as
such, is followed several times by another, biologically
meaningful one, that is, one releasing a reaction. The
animal from now on behaves "as if" the first stimulus
were a sure signal preceding the biologically significant
event that is to be expected. This behavior obviously
has a species-preserving meaning only if in the frame-
work of the real a connection between the first, the
"conditioned," and the second, the "unconditioned"
stimulus, exists. A lawful temporal sequence of different events regularly occurs in nature only where a
certain quantity of energy appears sequentially in different phenomenal forms through transformation of
force. Thus connection in itself means "causal connection." The conditioned reflex "advocates the hypothesis" that two stimuli, occurring several times in a certain sequence, are phenomenal forms of the same
quantity of energy. Were this supposition false and the
repeated sequence conditioning the association of the
stimuli only a purely accidental one, a probably never
returning *post hoc,* then the development of the conditioned reaction would be a dysteleological failure of

achievement on the part of a disposition which is generally and probabilistically meaningful, in the sense of being species-preserving.

Since we are today ignorant of its physiological foundations, we can examine the category of causality only through critical epistemology. In its biological function, it is an organ for comprehending the same natural lawfulness aimed at by the disposition to acquire conditioned reflexes. We cannot define the concept of cause and effect in any other way than by determining that the effect receives energy from the cause in some form or other. The essence of *propter hoc* which alone differentiates it qualitatively from a *uniform post hoc* lies in the fact that cause and effect are successive links in the infinite chain of phenomenal forms that energy assumes in the course of its everlasting existence.

In the case of the category of causality, the attempt to explain it as a secondary abstraction from preceding experience (in Wundt's sense) is instructive. If one attempts this, one always arrives at the definition of a "regular *post hoc*," but never at that highly specific quality which lies a priori in every sensible use of "why" and "because" even by a little child. One cannot expect a child to have the ability to comprehend abstractly a fact which was not stated in an objective, i.e., purely physical, form until 1842, by J. R. Mayer. Joule, in a lecture given in 1847 * declared in a surprisingly simple manner that it is "absurd" to assume living force could be destroyed without in some way restoring something equivalent. The great physicist thus quite naïvely takes the point of view of critical epistemology. In terms of the history of ideas, it would be a highly interesting question whether in his discovery of the equivalent of heat he started with the a priori "unthinkableness" of the destruction and creation of energy, as it would ap-

* *On Matter, Living Force and Heat.* London, 1884, p. 265.

pear, judging by his above remark. It does not fit into our concept of cause and effect that the a priori category of causality is actually based upon nothing but the inevitable sequence of two events and that it can happen that the event occurring later in time does not draw its energy from the preceding one, but that both are mutually independent side chains of a branching chain of causality. The case can arise that an event regularly has two effects, of which one occurs faster than the other, thus always preceding it in experience. Thus lightning follows electrical discharge more quickly than thunder. Nevertheless, the optical phenomenon is by no means the cause of the acoustic one! Perhaps one may object here that this consideration is splitting hairs, and for many naïve people lightning still is the cause for thunder. But the hairsplitting frees us from a primitive conception and moves us one step closer to the real connection of things. Mankind today lives by the function of the innate category of causality.

We shall now examine methodologically the functionally analogous achievements of animals from the higher observation tower of human form of perception of space and category of causality; first, the disposition to kinesthetic learning by rote of paths, and then the disposition to blind association of sequential events. Is it "true" what the water shrew "knows" about the spatial? In the water shrew's case, learning creates an *ordo et connectio idearum,* also visible in our image of the universe: namely, the condition that places and locomotive parts are strung like a row of pearls. The water shrew's orderly scheme is entirely correct—as far as it reaches! In our perception the string of pearls is visible, too; the sequence of the links is true. Only for us there exist (and are true) an immense number of further data which the shrew lacks: for example, the possibility to short-cut the loops of a path. Also from a pragmatic point of view, our perception is true to a higher degree than is the animal's image of the universe.

Something very similar results when we compare the disposition to association with our causal thought: here, too, the lower, more primitive rendering by the animal gives a connection between the events which exist also for our form of thought: the temporal relationship between cause and effect. The deeper actuality, essential to our causal thought, that energy is received from the cause by the effect is not given to purely associative thought. Here, too, then the lower form of thought corresponds a priori and adequately to the reality of a higher order, but again only as far as it reaches. Here, too, human form of thought is more true from the pragmatist's point of view; think of all it achieves that cannot be achieved by pure association! As I have said, we all live by the work of this important organ, almost as by the work of our hands.

With all the emphasis on these differences in the degree of correspondence between image of the universe and actuality we must not forget for one moment that something real is reflected even in the most primitive "screens" of the apparatuses for organizing the image of the universe. It is important to emphasize this because we humans likewise use such apparatuses even though they may be very different. Progress in science always has a certain tendency to de-anthropomorphize our image of the universe, as Bertalanffy has correctly pointed out. From the palpable and sensible phenomenon of light, the impalpable, un-visualizable concept of wave phenomena has developed. The self-evident comprehension of causality is replaced by considerations of probability and arithmetic calculations, etc. One can actually say that among our forms of perception and categories there are "more anthropomorphic" ones and "less anthropomorphic" ones; or some that are more specialized and others that are more general. Doubtless a rational being lacking the sense of vision could comprehend the wave theory of light, while not comprehending specifically human perceptual experience. Looking beyond specifically human structures, as is done to the highest degree in mathematical science, must not lead to the view that the less anthropomorphic representations approach a higher degree of actuality, that is, that they approach the thing-in-itself more closely than does naïve perception. The more primitive reproduction has just as real a relationship to the absolutely existent as does the higher one. Thus the animal's apparatus for organizing the image of the universe reproduces only one detail, and in a purely associative manner, from the actuality of the transformation of energy, namely, that a certain event precedes another one in time. But one can in no way assert that the statement "a cause precedes an effect" is less true than the statement that an effect arises from the preceding phenomenon through transformation of energy. The advance from the more simple to the more differentiated lies in the fact that additional, new definitions are added to those already existing. If in such an advance from a more primitive reproduction of the universe to a higher one certain data which are represented in the first are neglected in the second, then it is only a question of change in point of view, and not a matter of a closer approach to the absolutely existent. The most primitive reactions of the protozoa reflect an aspect of the world to which all organisms must similarly relate, just as much as do the calculations of a Homo sapiens who studies theoretical physics. But we can no more ascertain how much exists in absolute actuality in addition to the facts and relationships rendered in our image of the universe than the water shrew can ascertain that it could short-cut many detours in its crooked path learning.

With regard to the absolute validity of our "necessities of thought" we are accordingly modest: we believe only that in some details they correspond more to the actually existent than do those of the water shrew. Above all, we are conscious of the fact that we surely are just as blind in regard to as many additional things as that animal is; that we too are lacking the receptive organs for infinitely much that is actual. The forms of perception and categories are not the mind, but rather are tools the mind uses. They are innate structures that on the one hand support, but on the other hand make for rigidity. Kant's great conception of the idea of freedom, namely that the thinking being is responsible to the totality of the universe, suffers from the ailment of being chained to the rigidly mechanical laws of pure reason. The a priori and the preformed ways of thought are just the ones that are by no means specifically human as such. Specifically human, however, is the conscious drive not to get stuck, not to become a vehicle running on rails, but rather to maintain a youthful openness to the world, and to come closer to actuality through a constant reciprocal interaction with it.

Being biologists, we are modest regarding man's position in the totality of nature, but more demanding in regard to what the future may yet bring us in the way of knowledge. To declare man absolute, to assert that any imaginable rational being, even angels, would have to be limited to the laws of thought of Homo sapiens, appears to us to be incomprehensible arrogance. For the lost illusion of a unique lawfulness for man, we exchange the conviction that in his openness to the world he is basically capable of outgrowing his science and the a priori formulations of his thought, and of creating and realizing basically new things that have never existed before. To the extent he remains inspired by the will not to let every new thought be choked by the cover of the laws crystallizing around it, in the fashion of Nietzsche's drops of lava, this development will not so soon encounter any essential obstacle. In this lies our concept of freedom; it is the greatness, and, at least on our planet, the provisional uniqueness of our human brain that, in spite of all its gigantic differentiation and structurization, it is an organ whose function possesses a proteuslike changeability, a lavalike capacity to rise against the functional restrictions imposed on it by its own structure, to the point where it achieves a flexibility even greater than that of protoplasm lacking solid structures.

What would Kant say about all this? Would he feel that our naturalistic interpretation of human reason (for him, supernaturally given) is desecration of the most sacred? (This it is in the eyes of most neo-Kantians.) Or would he, in view of his own occasional approaches to evolutionary thought, have accepted our conception that organic nature is not something amoral and god-forsaken, but is basically "sacred" in its creative evolutionary achievements, especially in those highest achievements, human reason, and human morals? We are inclined to believe this, because we believe that science could never destroy a deity, but only the earthen feet of a man-made idol. The person who reproaches us with lacking respect for the greatness of our philosopher we counter by quoting Kant himself: "If one starts with an idea founded but not realized and bequeathed to us by another, by continual thinking one can hope to progress further than did the ingenious man to whom one owed the spark of this light." The discovery of the a priori is that spark we owe to Kant and it is surely not arrogance on our part to criticize the interpretation of the discovery by means of new facts (as we did in criticizing Kant with regard to the origin of the forms of perception and categories). This critique does not lower the value of the discovery any more than it lowers that of the discoverer. To anyone following the erroneous principle *omni naturalia sunt turpia* who persists in seeing a desecration in our attempt to look at human reason naturalistically we counter by again quoting Kant himself: "When we speak of the totality of nature, we must inevitably conclude that there is divine regulation. But in each phase of nature (since none are at first given simply in our sensory world) we have the obligation to search for underlying causes, insofar as possible, and to pursue the causal chain, so long as it hangs together, according to laws that are known to us."

The Enmity Between Generations
and Its Probable Ethological
Causes* / Konrad Lorenz

I. The Darwinian Approach and
the Question of Adaptation

"Ethology" is simply the application to the field of behavioral study of all those methods of approach which, since the days of Charles Darwin, have been regarded as obligatory in all other branches of biological research. In other words, ethology regards behavior as a *system* which owes its existence and its special form to a series of historical events which have taken place in the course of phylogeny. The purely causal question, *why* a living system happens to be structured as it is and not otherwise, cannot be answered except

* Some parts of this paper were read at several meetings of the Frensham Group (initiated and sponsored by Oscar van Leer; cf. Foreword by Paul A. Weiss, p. 905). *Studium Generale*, 23 (1970), pp. 963–997.

by investigating the history of its evolution, in other words its *phylogeny.*

Investigating behavior, including human behavior, from the phylogenetical viewpoint has brought ethology into the center of an ideological controversy which is still going on. The doctrine that human behavior is entirely determined by processes of conditioning which are brought about by environmental influence, originated from an immoderate generalization and simplification of the findings of I. P. Pavlov. It became the basic theory of American behaviorism, yet it would imply injustice and even slander to call it the "behavioristic" doctrine, because many intelligent scientists who consider themselves "behaviorists" have never believed in it. I therefore suggest the term "pseudo-democratic" doctrine. This is justified by the fact that the doctrine derives its worldwide distribution as well as its moral weight from the rather insidious distortion of a democratic truth: it is a truth and indubitably a moral postulate that all men should have equal opportunities to develop. But an untrue dogma is easily derived from that truth (if only by those who reject logic, as Philip Wylie has pointed out): that all men are potentially equal. The doctrine carries the premise one step further by asserting that man is born as a *tabula rasa* and that all his behavior is determined by conditioning.

Ethology has run foul of this doctrine by demonstrating irrefutably that all behavior, exactly like all bodily structure, can develop in the ontogeny of the individual only along the lines and within the possibilities of species-specific programs which have been mapped out in the course of phylogeny and laid down in the code of the genome. "Biology," says Philip Wylie, "has proven that men are not equal, identical, similar or anything of the sort, from the instant of conception. Common sense ought to have made all that evident to Java man. It didn't and still doesn't, since common sense is what men most passionately wish to evade." This passion has the character of truly religious zeal. The pseudo-democratic doctrine has indeed become a world religion. Like many religions, it is the simplification of a truth, as such, easy to understand, and it is welcome to those who are interested in manipulating great masses of people. It would indeed be of equal advantage to capitalistic producers and to super-Stalinistic rulers, if men, by proper conditioning, could be molded into absolutely uniform and absolutely obedient consumers or communistic citizens. This explains the otherwise surprising fact that the pseudo-democratic doctrine rules supreme in America as well as in the Soviet Union and in China!

Like all devout supporters of a religion, the doctrinaires of the pseudo-democratic doctrine do not stop at anything when it comes to silencing the heretic. The approach to human behavior as to a phylogenetically evolved system has been rejected for a large number of pseudo-rational reasons and branded as immoral in a large number of ways, of which the book *Man and Aggression* edited by M. F. Ashley Montagu offers a rich choice of examples, one of which is sufficient to demonstrate the near-religious bias. "There is," says Ashley Montagu, "not the slightest evidence or ground for assuming that the alleged 'phylogenetically adapted instinctive' behavior of other animals is in any way relevant to the discussion of the motive-forces of human behavior. The fact is that, with the exception of the instinctoid reactions of infants to sudden withdrawals of support and to sudden loud noises, the human being is entirely instinctless." More modern representatives of the pseudo-democratic doctrine take another and more subtle attitude. While conceding that ethology is, in principle, correct in trying to separate phylogenetically evolved and ontogenetically acquired programs of behavior, they contend that ethologists attribute an exaggerated importance to this distinction, in other words, that the question "innate or acquired?" is no more than a quibble. It isn't, and I shall come back to this point at the end of this paper.

For the moment it suffices to say that most of the properties which we encounter in the structure as well as in the behavior of organisms owe their specific form to that oldest and most efficient of cognitive processes which we call *adaptation*. The fact of adaptedness entails a question characteristic of biology and unknown to chemistry and physics, the question "what for?" When we ask, "what are the cat's crooked retractile claws for?" and answer, "to catch mice with," we are not looking for the ultimate teleological meaning of the cat's claws, we are only using an abridged way of expressing a truly scientific *causal* question which, fully stated, should read: "what is the function whose survival value exerted the selection pressure *causing* cats to evolve that particular form of claws?"

A lifetime spent in asking this question (which I shall refer to henceforward as Charles Darwin's question) with reference to a great many morphological structures and behavior patterns, results in great support for Darwin's theories, for the simple reason that so very, very often a clear-cut and convincing answer can be found. In fact, we have grown so accustomed to receiving such an answer that we find it hard to believe that there *are* any highly complex and differentiated patterns or structures which do *not* owe their specific form to the selection pressure exerted by their function. The more bizarre they appear on their face value, the surer one may be of discovering such a function.

II. Creative Integration and the
Method of Approaching Systems

Before expounding the methods obligatory in the approach of complex systems, a few words must be said about the way in which unprecedented systemic properties spring into existence when two pre-existent but independent systems are linked together; if, for instance, two systems of electric circuit, one running over a coil, the other obstructed by a condenser, are linked together, the new system will possess the property of oscillation which is not to be found, on principle, in any of the two subsystems in their unconnected state. This kind of event obviously has happened and is happening whenever phylogenesis makes a step forward. The term "evolution" as well as the German word "Entwicklung," implies etymologically that something *preformed* is merely being unfolded in the process. None of our Western languages possesses a verb for the coming-into-existence of something entirely new, because, at the time of their origin, the only process of development known was that of ontogeny for which these terms are indeed etymologically adequate. Sensing its inadequacy for the creative events of phylogeny, some philosophers used the term "emergence" which is still worse as it implies that something which was invisible to a literally superficial view, becomes visible by surfacing. In my paper "Innate Bases of Learning" in which I discussed these matters in detail, I suggested the use, in a new sense, of the term "fulguration" which had been introduced by medieval mystics to describe acts of creation, implying, of course, that it was God's own lightning that caused something new to spring into existence. For the scientist, lightning is an electric spark like any other, and if he notices an unexpected spark within a system, the first thing it brings to mind is a short circuit. This makes the term fulguration strangely appropriate. That which constitutes a step forward in the sequence of creative phylogenetic events regularly consists in the coming-into-existence of a new systemic property which is caused by a new causal relationship springing up, within the living system, between two of its existing subsystems, integrating them into a new one of higher order. As we refuse to believe in miracles, we are convinced that it is always a structural change that brings about such a new integration and causes new laws of nature, which had not previously existed, to come into existence.

The new lawfulness arising out of new structures never abolishes the laws of nature prevailing within the living system previous to the new event of integration. Even the systemic properties of the newly united subsystems need not be entirely lost. This is true of every step taken by evolution, even of its greatest, an initial step from the inorganic to the organic. It is quite particularly true of what we, in admitted pride, are apt to consider the second greatest step, the one leading from the anthropoid to Man. The processes of life are still physical and chemical processes, though, by virtue of the complicated structure of chain molecules, they are something very particular besides. It would be plain nonsense to assert that they are "nothing else but" chemical and physical processes. An analogous relationship exists between man and his pre-human ancestors: man certainly is an animal but it is simply not true that he is nothing but an animal.

III. Cumulative Tradition as an Example

The fulguration of those properties which are essentially of man and which do not exist, at least not together and not to any appreciable degree, in any other animal, furnishes an excellent example of the way in which new systemic properties come into existence with new connections of pre-existing systems. Exploratory behavior leading to a considerable degree of objective knowledge of objects exists in many animals and so does the true tradition of individually acquired knowledge. In Man alone are they brought together into an integrated system.

Self-exploration, which had been dawning in the anthropoids, must have progressed by leaps and bounds as our forefathers proceeded from tool-using to tool-making. The working hand, as a part of one's own body, together with the manipulated object in the same visual field could not fail to draw attention to the fact that oneself as subject is also an object, and one extremely worthy of consideration! By the consciousness of his own self, by "reflection," a new objectivity was forced upon man's attitude to the objects of his environment. Originally, and for the majority of all animals, one object possesses entirely different meanings depending upon the different psychological and physiological states in which the organism happens to be at the moment. A potential prey animal has entirely different "valences" for a hungry lion and for a satiated one. Once we have realized that we are ourselves "real things," participating in an interaction with the other "things" in our environment, we have automatically gained a higher and altogether new level of objectivity transcending by far that which had hitherto been possible by virtue of the abstracting function of Gestalt perception and by the effects of exploratory play. Not being hungry, we might be totally disinterested in a food object and pass it by as the sated lion does, but knowing ourselves as we do, we are able to take our own momentary state into consideration and abstract from it, rightly foreseeing that the object in question may and will become highly interesting in a short while.

It is only together with and on the basis of all the other objective functions which already pre-existed in higher animals, that true reflection could come into being. Self-exploration could never have happened except on the basis of a pre-existing, highly developed exploratory behavior. The comprehension of a concept could never have been achieved had it not been for the observation of one's own prehensile hand taking hold of and interacting with environmental objects.

Tradition existed before that. Rats can pass on the knowledge concerning the deadly effects of a poison over many generations without any individual having to repeat the personal experience leading to that knowledge. Jackdaws can hand down to the inexperienced young their knowledge of dangerous predators, and monkeys have been known to pass on the tradition of certain acquired motor skills, for instance, that of washing sweet potatoes in seawater. However, all these processes of the handing down of acquired knowledge are dependent on the presence of their object. Without it, the rat cannot tell its young what poison not to eat, nor can the jackdaw teach its progeny which predator to avoid, nor the monkey demonstrate its skill. Even so, we cannot quite explain why traditional knowledge does not tend to accumulate in any species of social animal beyond the degree to which we actually find it developed. Thus, right up to the fulguration of cumulative tradition in man, the genome remained the only mechanism capable of an accumulating, long-time storage of knowledge.

With the coming-together of conceptual thought and tradition, unprecedented systemic properties sprang into existence. The continuity of tradition made it possible for concepts to become associated with the free symbol of the spoken word. The growth of syntactic language was thus rendered possible, and, in turn, opened a new avenue to an accumulation of traditional knowledge, ever increasing with the number of generations following one another. The new system is that which is generally called culture, and its unique systemic property consists in its being able, like the genome, to store practically unlimited quantities of information and at the same time being able, unlike the genome, to acquire knowledge worth storing within minutes instead of millennia. If a man learns how to make, or invents a bow and arrow, not only his progeny but all his culture will henceforward possess these tools, nor is the likelihood of their ever being forgotten any greater than that of a bodily organ of equal survival value ever becoming rudimentary. The new systemic property is neither more nor less than the famous inheritance of acquired characters and its biological consequences are hard to exaggerate. It was the selection pressure of accumulating tradition which caused man's telencephalon to grow to its present size. It is bodily structures, such as the forebrain and the various speech areas in the dominant hemisphere which make man *by nature* a creature of culture. Without cultural tradition, these structures would be as devoid of function as the wings of an ostrich, only more so. Yet all these tremendous changes, which certainly do make man something very different indeed from that which we would describe as "just an animal," were wrought by the rather simple integration of two sub-systems of behavior, neither of which is exclusively characteristic of our species.

Our knowledge of the way in which, during phylogeny, systems of higher integration came into being by a series of unique and unpredictable historic events has far-reaching consequences in two entirely unrelated respects.

IV. The Axiomatic Scale of Organismic Values

The first concerns our philosophy of values. We cannot help feeling that organic systems are the more valuable the more highly integrated they are, in fact, our accustomed way of calling some animals higher and some lower is the immediate outcome of this inescapable value judgment. Its axiomatic nature is easily demonstrated by the following thought-experiment. Visualize yourself confronted with the task of killing, one after the other, a cabbage, a fly, a fish, a lizard, a guinea pig, a cat, a dog, a monkey and a baby chimpanzee. In the unlikely case that you should experience no greater inhibitions in killing the chimpanzee than in destroying the cabbage or the fly, my advice to you is to commit suicide at your earliest possible convenience, because you are a weird monstrosity and a public danger.

The scale of values extending between lower and higher organisms is quite independent of that other one which stretches between all the degrees of less and more successful adaptation to environment. The chances of disadaptation and illness are roughly the same on all levels of creative integration; if anything, the higher creatures seem to be more vulnerable than the lower. A man or, for that matter, a whole culture may be in direct danger of disintegration and yet be of higher value than another which is in the best possible state of health and superlatively viable. We are apt to become aware of the independence of the two parameters of value judgment when we come to consider our own moral responsibility. Obedience to the moral law within us, as Immanuel Kant has called it, may often exact a behavior which is far from healthy, and not too rarely human beings are faced with the alternative of either behaving immorally or making the great sacrifice of martyrdom—which may as well be entirely in vain.

V. *Methods Obligatory in the Approach to Integrated Systems*

The second all-important consequence which is forced upon us by the realization of the "stratified" structure of organic systems concerns the strategy of their analysis. For obvious reasons, the first step to the understanding of a system which consists of a whole hierarchy of subsystems, integrated into each other level by level, must be to gain some provisional survey knowledge of those subsystems which, on the highest level of integration, are immediately subordinate to the whole. To begin with this first task is the more obligatory, the more complicated and the more highly integrated the system under investigation actually is. In other words, the chances of gaining insight into the makeup of a system by atomistic and operationalist methods decreases in proportion to its complication and its level of integration. We must be successful in quite a few inspired guesses in order to arrive even at that pre-hypothetical stage of vague suspicion which allows us to shift our observations sufficiently to arrive at a workable hypothesis as to what are the greatest and most widely embracing subsystems to approach. In this task, plain observation and the free play of our own Gestalt perception are the most promising methods. I wish to assert seriously and emphatically that in our first tentative approach to the understanding of complicated living systems, the "visionary" approach of the poet—which consists simply in letting Gestalt-perception rule supreme—gets us much farther than any pseudo-scientific measuring of arbitrarily chosen parameters. I do not mean that a man who is "nothing else but" a poet has a better chance of understanding integrated systems than a scientist has. What I want to express is that a scientist, with all the scientist's methodological and factual knowledge at his disposal, has no chance of ever understanding a complex living system, such as that underlying human social behavior, unless he utilizes his Gestalt perception to the utmost, giving it an absolutely free rein while at the same time feeding into its ample hold as many pertinent observational data as he can get hold of. There are people who seem to be able to do just that. One of them is Erik Erikson who, in my opinion, knows more about the deepest roots of human behavior than anybody else I could name.

VI. Pathological Disturbance as a Source of Knowledge

Even so, Gestalt perception would not lead us far enough in the understanding of really complex systems like that of human behavior, to make it possible to begin applying the quantitative methods of verification, were it not for help from a rather unexpected side.

There are cases in which Charles Darwin's question "what for" fails to get an answer. In captive animals and quite particularly in civilized men we find regularly recurring behavior patterns which are not only devoid of value but even demonstrably detrimental to the survival of the individual as well as of the species. If one asks Darwin's question with regard to a military parade, a voodoo ceremony in Haiti, a sit-in of students at a Vienna university or modern war, one finds oneself unable to obtain an answer—at least as long as one applies the question in the simple and unsophisticated way in which, as biologists, we are accustomed to put it.

When confronted with such a puzzling and disturbing behavior pattern, my late friend Bernhard Hellmann used to ask another question: "Is this as the constructor intended it to be?" Though this question was asked half jestingly, it implies a deep realization of the existence of a borderline which, though extremely difficult to define, plays an all-important role in biological and particularly in medical thought: the borderline between the normal and the pathological, between health and illness.

When, in respect to some crazy pattern of human behavior, we fail to get an answer to Charles Darwin's question "what for?" as well as to Bernhard Hellmann's question "is this how the constructor meant it to be?," we need not lose confidence in the normal biological approach, though we have to resort to additional questions belonging to a different way of approach, to that of the medical man. In one of his last letters to me, my late friend Ronald Hargreaves, psychiatrist at Leeds, wrote that he had schooled himself to ask in approaching any mental disorder, two simultaneous questions. The first is: what is the normal survival function of the process here disturbed? The second is: what is the nature of the disturbance, and, in particular, is there an excess or a deficiency of the function in question?

At first sight it might seem that the unpredictable pathological disturbance of a system which is superlatively complicated and therefore most difficult to understand in any case, would add yet another and unsurmountable obstruction to the endeavor of its analysis. However, physiologists have known for a long time that this is not so. So far from being an additional obstacle to the analysis of a system, its pathological disturbance is, as often as not, the key to its analysis. In fact, the history of physiology has recorded a great number of cases in which the very existence of an important physiological mechanism or system was not even suspected until an illness caused by its disturbance drew the scientists' attention to it. The history of the discovery of endocrine glands and of the progress of their analysis offers an excellent paradigm of the method obligatory in approaching systems. When E. T. Kocher, in the attempt to cure hyperthyroidism, had removed the thyroid gland, he found that he had provoked what he termed "cachexia thyropriva." From this he deduced correctly that the function of the thyroid gland stood in a relation of balanced antagonism with that of other endocrine glands and that Basedow's disease, or hyperthyroidism, consisted in the disturbance of this equilibrium in favor of an excess of thyroid function.

The rationale of this approach is most strictly applicable to the majority of the disturbances nowadays observable in the social behavior of human beings. Indeed, very many of them consist in the loss of equilibrium between two or more behavioral systems, the word "system" being used in the sense of the excellent definition Paul Weiss has given in his paper "Determinism Stratified": a system is everything unitary enough to deserve a name. Ronald Hargreaves' double question ought to make everybody realize how inane it is to attribute the adjectives "good" or "bad" to any mechanism of behavior, such as love, aggression, indoctrination, ritualization, enthusiasm and so on. Like any endocrine gland, every one of these mechanisms is indispensable and, again like a gland, every one, by its excess function, can lead to a destructive disequilibration. There is no human vice which is anything else than the excess of a function which, in itself, is indispensable for the survival of the species.

I shall now proceed to illustrate the application of Ronald Hargreaves' double question to certain phenomena which are obviously threatening our culture and which, in my opinion, can be attributed to the disequilibration of two important behavioral systems. The first is the mechanism which ensures what Sigmund Freud described as the balanced economy of pleasure and displeasure. The second is the rather complicated system whose function it is to transmit traditional knowledge from one generation to the next while, at the same time making sure that obsolete items of tradition can be discarded and new ones acquired.

VII. The Disequilibration of Pleasure-Displeasure Economy

I begin with the description of some symptoms which I believe to be caused by the disturbance of pleasure-displeasure equilibrium. Perhaps the most telling of these symptoms is the *urge for instant gratification*. In a considerable percentage of present-day humanity, and not only among the younger generation, there is a demonstrable decrease in the ability and willingness to strive for aims that can only be achieved in the future. Any goal that cannot be attained *at once* ceases to appear worth striving for. Even large business concerns refuse to look more than a very few years into the future. In science the unwillingness to undertake long-term programs has led to a deplorable neglect of *descriptive* branches in which a patient and protracted gathering of knowledge is necessary.

Although it is not clear which is cause and which is effect, there is certainly a close connection between the current loss of patience and a general *inability to endure any kind of pain or displeasure*. The enormous consumption of anodynes and tranquilizers bears witness to this intolerance. Once I observed my nephew swallowing an enormous spoonful of Pyramidon powder and commiseratingly asked him whether he had got a bad headache. No, he said, but he was somewhat afraid that he might get one. Kurt Hahn tells a story about a pupil coming to school carrying with him a package of tablets which his parents had given him and which were guaranteed to be an unfailing cure against any onset of homesickness.

A third queer symptom, closely allied to the two already mentioned, is a general *unwillingness to move.* Any exertion of striated musculature has become unfashionable, to the point of changing the facial expression of large numbers of people: a tired, languishing, bored look, occasionally slightly overlaid by an expression of reproach and sulkiness is observable in all-too-many young people. Between the twenty-year-olds of, say, 1920 and those of 1969, there is a very considerable behavioral difference in the quantity of locomotion performed for its own sake. In the Vienna Woods, which were teeming with young people in 1920, one rarely meets walkers, and if one does, they are over 60. Amongst young people who consider themselves very sporting there may be a certain willingness to perform muscular labor, but only for its own sake, and not in pursuance of any other goal. This would be considered as "work." Therefore, athletic young people can be seen queuing-up for 40 minutes at a ski lift instead of walking uphill for 20.

Technological production caters for the growing unwillingness to perform muscular work: a prosperous citizen cannot be expected to walk upstairs or to turn a crank to open a window or the sliding roof of his smart car; to press a button is the utmost he will condescend to do.

It was Kurt Hahn who called attention to the disquieting fact that this type of physical laziness is very often correlated with an accompanying *sluggishness of emotion.* A weakness of ability to feel *compassion* is, according to the great expert, a frequent concomitant of the typical laziness of blasé adolescents. I do not think I need mention examples; every daily paper is full of instances in which people have been tortured, killed or raped in well-frequented streets of big cities in the presence of hosts of inhumans who refused to "get involved" by assisting the victim. Inability to feel compassion also plays an important part in the acts of open hostility against weak old people of which adolescents often are guilty.

Now let us ask, in respect to the phenomena just described, the first of the two questions proposed by Ronald Hargreaves. What is the normal function which is miscarrying in each of these cases and what is the nature of its miscarriage? I think we can give a fairly probable tentative answer to these questions, and what is more, the same applies to all four of the phenomena mentioned.

All organisms capable of true conditioning possess a built-in mechanism whose function it is to mete out reward and punishment, reward for behavior achieving survival value for the individual or the species, or both, and punishment for all that is contrary to these interests. "Reward" and "punishment" are terms here used only as shorthand for the functions of *reinforcing or extinguishing* the preceding behavior. Pleasure and displeasure are the equally real subjective experiences which accompany these learning processes.

Many otherwise profound theories of learning have overlooked a fact which is of supreme importance to our consideration, namely that this highly integrated computing mechanism must possess in its program phylogenetically acquired information, in fact, *knowledge of what is good and what is bad for the organism.* This mechanism "knows" all the values of reference which all the homeostatic cycles within the organism are supposed to keep constant, it administers the punishment of making us feel lousy if anything is out of order in any of these regulating cycles, for instance, if we have too little or too much oxygen, glucose or whatever else in our blood, if we are too hot or too cold etc. It rewards us by making us feel good whenever our behavior has contributed to correct these values, as we do when we ingest the right kind of food etc. It puts a premium on performing any of the typical species-preserving activities in the biologically "right" manner.

This great teaching mechanism, the "innate schoolmarm," as I have jestingly called it, could theoretically work with reward (or reinforcement) alone, or with punishment (or extinguishing) alone. We have introspective knowledge, however, that it uses *both* principles and there are objective criteria supporting the assumption that the same is true of animals. Perhaps it is just a case of assurance being made doubly sure, a procedure of which there are many examples in evolution. Another tentative answer, which I thought sufficient until quite recently, lies in the fact that it is difficult to make organisms behave in a very *specific* manner by the exclusive use of repellent stimuli. It is very hard to *drive* a bird into a cage, as one would have to use a large number of stimuli impinging from all spatial directions with the exception of that of the cage door to do so. Thus it would seem preferable to put some reward into the cage and thus entice the creature to enter it. We find that evolution has learned that trick and "applies" extinguishing procedures, if the biological aim is just to keep an animal away from noxious environmental influences, but "uses" the allurement of reinforcement in cases in which the organism is requested to do something more specific.

A further difference between reinforcing and extinguishing processes lies in the manner in which external stimulation is evaluated. In appetitive behavior, in which the organism is endeavoring to reach the source of stimulation, any increase in the quantity of incoming stimuli acts as a reinforcement while, in avoidance behavior, any decrease in stimulation reinforces the preceding mode of behavior.

These considerations are quite correct, as far as they go, yet they do not contain the real answer to the question why the conditioning apparatus of high animals is constructed on the basis of two opposing principles. The antagonistic effect of two independently variable motivations is necessary to uphold an *economic* equilibrium between certain biological advantages gained and the expenses incurred in gaining them. By virtue of conditioning, the organism is made capable of going straight for the achievement of some goal which has survival value and which offers a *future* reward, in spite of the fact that it has to begin its activity in the teeth of a *present* stimulus situation acting as a strongly extinguishing deterrent.

It is this element of *foresight* that constitutes the most important function of conditioning. It enables the organism to pay a price for something to be gained later, the price consisting of the expenditure of energy, of incurring certain risks and other disadvantages. The balance of pleasure and displeasure, all the phenomena which Sigmund Freud called "Lust-Ökonomie," represent the subjective side of that kind of deal.

If this negotiation is to yield, to the organism or its species, a net gain in terms of survival value, the price paid must be in proportion to the gross gain which it purchases. It would be bad strategy for a wolf to go hunting, regardless of the cold, on a particularly bad winter's night; he simply could not afford to pay for one meal with a frozen toe or two. However, circumstances may arise, for instance a dire famine, in which our wolf would indeed be well advised to go hunting regardless of costs and risks, playing a single, last chance.

This example serves to illustrate that there is no constant relationship between the values of the goal achieved and the price paid for its achievement. Exactly as in commercial economy, the price which is to be considered as adequate in a given situation is determined by the laws of supply and demand. The varying strength of the motivations causing appetitive behavior is to a great extent determined by the *needs* of the organism or the species—very often, indeed, in a most direct manner by the tissue needs of the individual. The effectiveness which the achievement of the goal develops *as a reinforcement* of the preceding behavior, varies in proportion to the strength of this motivation. The readiness to tolerate punishment, which is unavoidable in the conquering of obstacles, does exactly the same. It is an immensely complicated and finely adjusted system of adaptively variable reinforcing and extinguishing mechanisms which achieve a balanced equilibrium in the organism's economy.

I believe that we can unhesitatingly answer Ronald Hargreaves' first question concerning the survival function of the disturbed mechanism by saying that the symptoms hitherto discussed, the inability to wait, the inability to bear displeasure, the unwillingness to move and the weakness of compassionate emotion, are all caused by a disturbance of the mechanism achieving the balanced equilibrium of pleasure-displeasure economy.

I proceed to Hargreaves' second question: what is the nature of the disturbance? In order to make my tentative answer intelligible, I must say a few more words about the physiological as well as about the historical properties of this balancing mechanism.

Like many other neuro-sensory functions, the mechanism under discussion is subject to habituation or "sensory adaptation." This term, though generally accepted by sensory physiologists, is not a happy choice, because the effect of the phenomenon need not necessarily be adaptive in the sense of survival. The *waning* of the response to an often-repeated stimulus—or combination of stimuli—is advantageous only on the premise of the statistical probability that an ever-recurrent stimulus is not likely to denote something really important. Whatever it signals is likely to be rather "cheap" economically. In some respects, habituation may be similar to fatigue and it may even have evolved phylogenetically from certain forms of fatigue. Its function, however, is entirely different. Also, habituation is not localized in the peripheral sense organ, but, as Margret Schleidt has shown experimentally, in the central nervous system itself. Habituation is not always specific to one particular stimulus, but often to a highly complicated combination of stimuli. It is only the threshold of this particular stimulation that is raised, or in other words, it is only the response to this that decreases, while all other responses to all other stimulus situations, even very similar ones, remain unaltered.

The second physiological property, also common to very many neural functions, is that of *inertia*. Any time-lag in a regulative cycle leads to the effects of rebound and oscillation. If a deviation from the "Soll-Wert" occurs in any homeostatic cycle, the restitution of this value is hardly ever reached in a direct damped curve, but in most cases *overshoots* the reference value and finally reaches it by way of one or several oscillations above and below the value. This overshooting of the mark set by the regulating system constitutes what is generally called a rebound or a contrast. Among other more complicated causes, contrast is one of the factors which makes activities appear in bursts or bouts, instead of "dribbling" constantly. In the constant presence of food, for example, an animal does not eat constantly and very slowly, but eats its fill and then stops for a considerable time. This is because the regulating cycles of food uptake overshoot the mark both ways: first the animal continues eating by virtue of inertia, slightly longer than it ought to, then, having slightly overeaten, it remains refractory to the constantly present food, because the stimulation emanating from the latter, by "creeping in," elicits a response again slightly later than would exactly correspond to the threshold of the reference value.

Lastly, in order to understand the function of the pleasure-displeasure-equilibrating apparatus, it is necessary to consider the circumstances under which it originated historically. At the time of its probable origin humanity eked out a precarious existence. Hence it bears all the marks of a selection pressure working in the direction of the utmost economy. At the dawn of humanity, men could not afford to pay too high a price for anything. They *had* to be extremely reluctant to make any expenditure of any kind of energy, of risk, or of possessions. Any possible gain had to be greedily seized upon. Laziness, gluttony and some other present-day vices were virtues then. To shun everything disagreeable, like cold, danger, muscular exertion and so on, was the wisest thing they could do. Life was hard enough to exclude all danger of becoming too "soft." These were the circumstances to which our mechanism balancing pleasure and displeasure has been adapted in evolution. They must be kept in mind in order to understand its present miscarriage.

For obvious reasons, our apparatus of pleasure-displeasure economy is prone to disfunction under the conditions of modern civilization. Man has been all too successful in evading and circumventing all stimulus situations causing displeasure, and all too clever in devising more and more rewarding "supernormal" enticements. The inevitable consequence of this has been an ever increasing sensitization to all stimulation eliciting sensations of displeasure, accompanied by a corresponding waning of the responses to formerly pleasurable stimulus situations. It is an old, hackneyed truth that there is no joy, however great, which does not become stale with constant repetition, yet modern humanity seems to have forgotten it. Furthermore, in all his alleged wisdom, man does not seem to understand that the highest levels of happiness which are accessible to him at all, can only be reached by exploiting the phenomenon of contrast. There is no path to the peaks of bliss except through the valley of sorrows, and modern man is so pampered and coddled that he shrinks from paying even the moderate toll of discomfiture and toil which nature has set as a price for all earthly joy. It is as simple as that!

To expend any joy down to the point of full exhaustion, is outright bad pleasure-economy, and still worse is to push that point of heightened threshold still higher by finding supranormal stimulation. Such a procedure is comparable to driving a cart with a permanently tired horse which, by continuous flogging, cannot be made to go faster than a rested animal would go without the whip. Besides being unhealthy for the horse, this precludes a maximum performance which can occasionally be attained by whipping the well-rested horse. One might think that the stupidest human being on earth should see through that error, yet people don't. There are many sides to civilized life in which intelligent people commit faults analogous to that of a silly mother who thinks she can increase the food-intake of a weak child by feeding it exclusively on delicacies. In regard to the economy of pleasure, this is just as stupid as what has frequently enough happened in commercial economy. The whaling industry, for instance, has exhausted the whale population to the point of leaving hardly anything worth exploiting, and *keeps* it exhausted, because the exploiters lack the intelligence and foresight, as well as the financial reserves necessary for the only sensible strategy of letting the whale population recover to the extent at which it would furnish a maximum yield. This is a perfect commercial model of what happens in human pleasure-economy.

The inability to wait, to hold back for the period necessary to let the threshold of pleasurable stimulation recover its normal values, has, of course, pernicious consequences for the *rhythm* in which consummatory activities are repeated. As I have already explained, the apparatus which balances the price to be paid against the advantage to be gained, is also responsible for the important function of making activities appear in bursts or bouts, instead of "dribbling" continuously. This, however, is exactly what happens as the consequence of the disturbance here under discussion. The subject afflicted by it is unable to put up, even for a short period, with the slightest deprivation. Like my young nephew, he may even be so afraid of the mildest pang of any want that he has to anticipate it even before he feels it. The normal rhythm of eating with enjoyment, after having got really hungry, the enjoyment of any consummation after having strenuously striven for it, the joy in achieving success after toiling for it in near-despair, in short, the whole glorious amplitude of the waves of human emotions, all that makes life worth living, is damped down to a hardly perceptible oscillation between hardly perceptible tiny displeasures and pleasures. The result is an inmeasurable *boredom.*

If you have eyes to see, you will perceive this boredom in a truly frightening multitude of young faces. Have you ever watched young people courting, kissing, petting and all-but-copulating in public? You need not be a Peeping Tom to do it, you cannot help observing if you walk in the evening through Hyde Park or ride on the Underground in London. In these unfortunates, the fire of love and the thrill of sex are toned down to the intensity of emotion to be observed in a pampered baby half-disgustedly sucking an unwanted lollipop. The bored juvenile is in a particular hell of his own, he must be an object of sincere pity and we must not be deterred from our commiseration by the fact that he hates us more than anything in the world.

The causes of this hostility consist only partly in the disturbance of the pleasure principle of which I have spoken hitherto. To a greater extent they lie in a disfunction of the mechanism which transmits cultural norms of social behavior from one generation to the next. Of this I shall speak anon, but first I must discuss the arousal of hate by the effects already mentioned.

"Going soft" is a rapidly progressive process, therefore the younger generation is automatically more severely afflicted by it than the older. Parents are therefore easily tempted to play the role of the "Spartan father" and to sermonize on the merits of a hard, frugal life. This of course is the worst thing they can do. The therapists who have successfully combated the phenomenon of "Verweichlichung" (the German word is the most descriptive by far, "pampering" or "coddling" seem to apply chiefly to the bringing-up of children and "effeminate" is a libel to women!) are unanimous in the opinion that the circumstances counteracting it must emanate from the impersonal environment and not from any human agency. Helmut Schulze, in his book *Der progressiv domestizierte Mensch* has pointed out some very interesting possibilities of therapy, and long before him Kurt Hahn applied the same principle.

The nature of the therapy illuminates the primary root of the disturbance: the essence of all countermeasures consists in getting the "patient" into *real* trouble which, if possible, concerns not only himself but is strongly evocative of social responses. The most effective therapy for "blasé" adolescents which Kurt Hahn could devise, was to set them the task of saving life at some danger of their own. Helmut Schulze came to identical conclusions on the basis of the paradoxical observation that some of his patients, who had lived in concentration camps and who had, under these dreadful circumstances, proved to be heroes of courage and altruism, became neurotic or went to pieces in other ways as soon as they had regained the security of a soft civilized life. Another illustration of the same paradox is furnished by the not infrequent cases of young people who find the softness of modern civilized life boring to the point of attempting suicide, succeed in hurting themselves badly and afterwards, amazingly, go on living happily with a broken back or with their optic nerves shot through. Now they have a real trouble to face and to conquer, they find life worth living.

To sum up: the cause of the symptoms hitherto discussed is, at least to a great extent, to be found in the fact that the mechanisms equilibrating pleasure and displeasure are thrown off balance because civilized man *lacks obstacles* which force him either to accept a healthy amount of painful, toilsome displeasure, or perish.

VIII. Disequilibration of Mechanisms Preserving and Adapting Culture

I now turn to the description of another set of symptoms, those which I believe to be caused by the unbalancing of that system of behavior whose function it is to transmit tradition from one generation to the next and, simultaneously, to eliminate obsolete and to acquire new and adaptive information. All these phenomena add up to a most alarming hostility which the younger generation bears the older and which is characteristically reciprocated only halfheartedly and only by a small proportion of the adults. A very small part of this hostility may be caused by the ill-advised attempt on the part of the older generation, to act the part of the proverbial "Spartan father" in regard to the softening process already discussed. The young might forgive us our admonitions to take some exercise, they might even condone our earning the money on which they live. They hate us for other reasons and I am afraid they hate us very deeply indeed. It is not only the "rockers" who

do so, though others do not go to the extreme of tortur-
ing people just because they are old. An ambivalent element of hate is noticeable, to the initiated, even in the
behavior of sons who are overtly and consciously quite
fond of their parents. Their hate is not *personal*, it is
directed at *cultural* properties of the older generation.
They hate our mode of life, our attitudes, the way we
dress, wash and shave, they distrust us and refuse to
believe anything we say. They think that they are
gloriously free from parental influence while in reality
they are copying the preceding generation slavishly, if
with a negative sign. When Hippies wear elaborate vel-
vet waistcoats and long, gloriously curling locks, skin-
tight trousers and chains round their necks, they don't
do it because they really like it, but because *we dislike
it.* All this is done to spite us, and the horrible thing is
that we react exactly in the way we are expected to do.
At least, I myself have to confess to a desire to kick the
behinds of the languidly pretty young men, and slightly
less of the bearded unwashed type. I am very angry
with myself because I cannot prevent myself from getting angry, which is quite unworthy of the initiated
ethologist—but there it is! Other old men, more dig-
nified than I am and less prone to subject their own motives to a self-ridiculing ethological analysis, simply get
uninhibitedly furious with the younger generation and
this mutual hostility, by a process of escalation, can
reach dangerous levels wherever the younger and the
older generation are thrust upon each other, as they are,
for instance, at schools and universities.

The enmity which so many members of the younger
generation bear the older has a lot in common with that
which can be observed between two hostile ethnic
groups. The term "ethnic group," is here meant to describe a very wide concept: that of any community
whose individuals are kept together by their *regard for
common symbols* rather than by personal friendship.

The budding of an ethnic group begins with the first occurrence of *culturally ritualized norms of behavior* which are specific to the group. These ritualized norms may consist at first of quite inconspicuous mannerisms, in an accent, in ways of dressing etc., as can be observed in schools, military units and similar small communities.

These group-specific ritualized norms play a most important part in keeping the group together. They are *valued* by all its members. "Good manners" are, of course, the manners of one's own group, its ways of dressing are those that are considered "elegant." Deviations from the rules set by these ritualizations are regarded as contemptible and *socially inferior*. Therefore, two comparable groups of this kind, each being aware of the contempt in which it is held by the other, will show a quick escalation of hostility. Hostile contact of this kind enhances the value which each group attributes to its specific ritualizations. Ethnologists have known for a long time that the etiquette and the old modes of peasant dresses, which otherwise are rapidly disappearing all over Europe, retain their traditional force in localities where different ethnic groups are in direct contact with each other, for instance, in Hungary wherever Slovakian and Hungarian villages border on each other.

Ethnic groups developing independently of each other become more and more different with the lapse of time. In other words, their distinguishing properties permit deductions concerning their age and history much in the same way as the genetically fixed properties of animal and plant species permit the reconstruction of their genealogical tree. The *comparative* method is equally applicable in the elucidation of cultural and of phylogenetical history. Of course, one must be conversant with the subtleties and the pitfalls of this method, in particular, one must know how to exclude convergent adaptation as a source of error. Of these methodological necessities, few ethnologists seem to be aware. Divergent cultural development erects *barriers* between ethnic groups much as divergent evolution tends to separate species.

It was Erik Erikson who first drew attention to this phenomenon and coined for it the term of *cultural pseudo-speciation.* In itself, it is a perfectly normal process, and even a desirable one, because a certain degree of isolation from neighboring groups may well be advantageous to a quick cultural development, analogous to the reasons why geographical isolation facilitates the evolution of species. There is, however, a very serious negative side to it: pseudo-speciation is the cause of *war.* The group cohesion effected by the common esteem of group-specific social norms and rites is inseparably combined with the contempt and even hate of the comparable, rival group. If the divergence of cultural development has gone far enough, it inevitably leads to the unfortunate consequence that one group does not regard the other as quite *human.* In many primitive languages the name of one's own tribe is synonymous with that of Man—and from this viewpoint it is not really cannibalism if you eat the fallen warriors of the hostile tribe! Pseudo-speciation suppresses the instinctive mechanisms which normally prevent the killing of fellow-members of the species while, diabolically, it does not inhibit intraspecific aggression in the least.

There is no doubt that the younger generation responds to the parent generation *of the same community* with all the typical patterns of hostile behavior which are normally elicited in the interaction with a *strange and hostile* group. Our deplorable familiarity with the phenomenon prevents us from realizing what a bizarre distortion of normal cultural behavior it really represents.

At this point let us ask Ronald Hargreaves' first question: what is the mechanism which we find disturbed and what is its normal function in the service of the survival of the species? Obviously, the functions concerned are those which normally ensure an ethnic group's continuance in time. I have already said that, in the continued existence of a culture, all those mechanisms which preserve and hand down from one generation to the next all the culturally ritualized rites and norms of social behavior, are performing functions which are closely analogous to those which the mechanisms of inheritance perform in the preservation of a species. They *store* knowledge (*not* simple information in the sense of information theory) and pass it on from generation to generation. In my paper "Innate Bases of Learning" I explained what happens to a species or a culture when stored knowledge gets *lost,* and I shall try to sum up what I said there as concisely as I can. If details drop out of the genetic "blueprint" of the general, large-scale structure of an organism, the consequence is a malformation; if the loss concerns the microstructure of tissues, the result is very often a regression to an ontogenetically or phylogenetically *more primitive* type of structure. Between these two, all kinds of intermediates are possible. If the loss of knowledge goes so far that, in the body of a multicellular organism, some cells altogether "forget" that they are parts of an adult metazoan, they will naturally revert to the behavior of unicellular animals or of embryonic cells, in other words they will begin uninhibitedly to multiply by division. This is how a tumor originates and, for obvious reasons, its malignity is in direct proportion to the extent of the regression, to the *immaturity*—as pathologists call it—of its tissue.

If only in parenthesis, I must here mention an old hypothesis of mine which contends that some of the phenomena under discussion have a *genetic* basis. In all these alarming symptoms I cannot help feeling a strong undercurrent of *infantilism*. Diligence, long-term striving for future goals, patient bearing-up under hard labor, the courage to take the responsibility for calculated risk and, above all, the faculty of compassion are all characteristic of the *adult*, in fact they are so uncharacteristic of children that, in them, we all are ready to condone their absence.

We know from the work of Bolck and others that man owes some of his specifically human properties to what he has called "retardation," in terms of common biological parlance, to neoteny. In my contribution to Herberer's book on evolution, I myself have tried to show that this permanent retention of infantile characters in man has its parallel in many domesticated animals, also that one of these retained characters, infantile *curiosity*, has been one of the essential prerequisites for the genesis of man. I have a shrewd suspicion that mankind has to pay for this gift of heaven by incurring the danger that a further process of progressive self-domestication might produce a type of man whose genetic constitution renders him incapable of full maturation and who, therefore, plays the same role in the context of human society which immature cells, by their infiltrating proliferation, play in the organization of the body. It is a nightmare to imagine that the disintegration of society might be caused by the genetic disintegration of its elements, because education—which is our hope otherwise—would be powerless against it!

Still, I believe that the bulk of the disintegration phenomena here under discussion are "only" cultural. A culture however, is nothing but a living system, and a highly complicated and vulnerable one at that! As I have already pointed out, its structure is in many points analogous to that of systems of less high integration. The blueprint of the program which, in pre-cultural systems, is stored in the genome, is contained, in the case of human culture, in all the ritualized norms of social behavior, in all the symbols on which the cohesion of a culture is dependent, in the logic of language, in adherence to certain values, in short in everything that is handed down in tradition from one generation to the next. While genetic knowledge is present in coded form in every single individual of a species, so that in the case of a catastrophe one survivor is, in principle, in possession of all the knowledge necessary to build the species up again, knowledge of cultural tradition depends on a far more extensive and more vulnerable repository. Cultural knowledge—and with it a whole culture—can be snuffed out in the interval from one generation to the next. The individuals who have lost the traditional knowledge of the culture from which they stem very often behave in a manner analogous to that of tumor cells. Being unable to fend for themselves, they fall back on parasitism.

It cannot be my task here to convince readers of the fact that our culture is in immediate danger of extinction. I can refer them to the work of people like Kurt Hahn, Max Born, John Eccles, Paul Weiss and many others. That a sudden collapse of culture has not happened in previous history is no legitimate reassurance. There is no more blatant untruth than Rabbi Ben Akiba's alleged wisdom that everything that happens has happened before. Nothing has, and I am setting out to demonstrate that the sudden break in cultural tradition is threatening just *now*. With that I proceed to Hargreaves' second question, concerning the causes which effect a malfunction, or even the cessation of function, in the mechanism of passing-on tradition.

I must begin by describing a few functional properties of this mechanism. Though human intelligence and inventiveness "enter into" its results, the growth of a human culture produces something that is not "man-made" in the sense that a bridge or an airplane is. In my papers on phylogenetic and cultural ritualization, I have explained in detail why this is so. Like a forest, a culture needs a long time to grow and, like a forest, it can be annihilated in one short holocaust. Unlike a forest, however, it does not leave behind it fertile soil, on which new plants can grow quickly, but a barren land devoid of all fertility. To believe that a culture can be "made," starting from scratch, by one generation of men, is one of the most dangerous errors, not only of juveniles, but of many adult anthropologists. As Karl Popper has pointed out, the total destruction of our world of culture, Popper's "third world," would set us back to the Palaeolithicum.

The ritualized norms of social behavior which are handed down by tradition represent a complicated supporting skeleton without which no culture could subsist. Like all other skeletal elements, those of culture can perform their function of *supporting* only at the price of *excluding* certain degrees of *freedom*. The worm can bend wherever it wants to, we can only bend a limb where a joint is provided. Any change of structure necessitates dismantling and rebuilding, and a period of increased vulnerability intervening between these two processes. An illustration of this principle is the crustacean which has to cast its skin-skeleton in order to grow a larger one. The human species is in possession of a very special mechanism, providing the possibility of change in cultural structure. At the approach of puberty, young people begin to loosen their allegiance to the rites and social norms of behavior handed down to them by family tradition and, at the same time, to cast about for new ideals to pursue and new causes to embrace. This "molt" of traditional ideas and ideals is a period of true crisis in the ontogeny of man, it implies hazards quite as great as those threatening the newly-mounted soft-shelled crab.

It is at this phase of man's ontogeny that changes are wrought in the great inheritance of cultural tradition. The pubertal "molt" is the open door through which new ideas gain entrance and become integrated into a structure which otherwise would be too rigid. The culture-preserving and hence, species-preserving function of this adaptive mechanism presupposes a certain balance between the old traditions that are to be retained and adaptive changes which make it necessary to discard certain parts of traditional inheritance.

In my opinion it is certainly this mechanism which sifts and hands down tradition and whose disturbance creates all the symptoms just described. We can proceed to Hargreaves' second question concerning the nature of the disturbance, before putting a third one: what are its causes?

The essence of the disturbance indubitably lies in the fact that the process of *identification* by which the younger generation normally accepts and makes its own the greatest part of the rites and norms of social behavior characteristic of the older, is seriously impeded or entirely obstructed. Excellent books have been written on this subject by Erik Erikson, Mitscherlich and others, so I need not enlarge on it.

However, it must be emphasized that this failure to identify with the social norms of the parental culture is the direct cause of truly pathological phenomena. The urge to embrace some sort of cause, to pledge allegiance to some sort of ideal, in short to *belong* to some sort of human group, is as strong as that of any other instinct. Like any other creature which, under the imperative drive of an instinct, cannot find its adequate object, the deracinated adolescent searches for and invariably finds a *substitute object*. Here, the pathological disfunction is particularly significant for the analysis of the underlying phylogenetically programmed mechanism. The diagram of the social situation for which the unrequited instinct is pining appears to be simple, as all those stimulus situations tend to be which form the goal of appetitive behavior. The adolescent must have at his disposal a group with which to identify, some simple rites and social norms to perform, and some sort of enemy group to release communal militant enthusiasm. If you have seen the psychologically excellent musical *West Side Story*, you have a perfect illustration of how all the social virtues of courage, unselfishness, friendship and loyalty reach the highest, most glorious peaks in a gang war, entirely devoid of any higher aims or values, in an absolutely senseless orgy of mutual killing.

Art representing these deplorable disfunctions would not move us as deeply as it does if it did not strike a chord which is still responsive in most of us. The very simplicity, the almost diagrammatic character of the sketch constitutes an appeal to very deep layers of our souls, to neither more nor less than the phylogenetic program of tribal warfare. What we observe in practically all the juvenile groups which break with tradition and take a hostile attitude to the older generation, is the more or less complete realization of this program. The Hamburg rockers who declare open war on older people represent the most clear-cut paradigm, but even the most emphatically non-violent groups are constituted on essentially the same principles. All of them are constructed as surrogates to assuage the burning need of adolescents who, by the processes described, are deprived of a natural group whose causes they can embrace and for whose values they can fight.

Considering all this we are, I think, justified in our assumption that it is quite particularly the failure of normal identification which causes the alarming breakdown of the mechanism whose important survival function lies in the sifting as well as in the handing-down of cultural tradition from one generation to the next.

We now come to the question: What are the causes contributing to the erection of an apparently unsurmountable obstacle to normal identification? We can name a number of them, but we cannot be sure that we know them all.

Optimists, who believe that men and women are reasonable beings, tend to assume that rebellious youth is impelled by rational motives. There are indeed many good reasons to revolt against the older generation. It is perfectly true that practically all "establishments" on all sides of all curtains are committing unpardonable sins against humanity. I am not speaking only of actual cruelties, of the political suppression of minorities, like the Czechoslovakians, or of the mass murder of innocent Indians by the Brazilians, but also of the deadly sins against the biology and ecology of mankind which are consistently being perpetrated by all governments: of the exploitation, pollution and final destruction of the biosphere in and on which we live, of the constantly increasing hustle of commercial competition which deprives man of the time in which to be human, and of similar phenomena of dehumanization. The young do indeed have good reason to take issue with the goals for which the majority of the older generation is striving, and I think that they do indeed recognize the intrinsic worthlessness of utilitarian aims.

There are several circumstances which tend to raise our hope that there is an element of intelligent rationality in the rebellion of youth. One is its ubiquity: the young protest against Stalinistic orthodoxy in communist countries, against race discrimination in Berkeley, against the utilitarianistic and commercial "American way of life" all over the United States, against the antiquated tyranny of professors at German universities etc. Another reason for optimism is that never, so far as I know, have the young exerted their powers in the wrong direction, never have they demanded a more effective commercial system, better armament, or a more nationalistic attitude of their government. In other words, they seem to know—or at least feel—quite correctly what is wrong with the world. A third reason for assuming that there is a considerable rational element in the rebellion of youth is a very special one: rebelling students of biology are far more accessible to intelligent communication than are those of philosophy, philology and (I am sorry to say) of sociology.

We do not know how great a part of the rebellion of youth is motivated by rational and intelligent considerations. I must confess that I am afraid it is only a very small part, even with those young people who profess— and honestly believe—that they are fighting for purely rational reasons. The main roots of the rebellion of youth are to be found in wholly irrational, ethological causes, as I hope to demonstrate. Many adults have found, to their cost, that it is useless to try reasoning with rebellious young people. In many countries, left-oriented professors have attempted, rather pathetically, to propitiate rebel students by making all possible concessions to their demands. As the German sociologist, F. Tenbruck, has pointed out, this endeavor led, in every single case, to a concentration of attack on the would-be peacemakers who were insulted with particular rancor and actually booed in exactly the same manner as a bull who refuses to fight is booed in the corrida. Political opinions play no role at all: Herbert Marcuse, extreme communist and advocate of completely scratching all tradition, was insulted by Cohn-Bendit and his young people, not because he held other opinions—which he did not—but because he was nearly seventy years old. Anyone familiar with ethological facts needs only to observe the hate-distorted faces of the more primitive type of rebel students in order to realize that they are not only unwilling, but quite unable to come to an understanding with their antagonists. In people wearing that kind of facial expression, the hypothalamus is at the helm and the cortex completely inhibited. If a crowd of them approaches you, you have the choice of either running away or fighting, as your temperament and the situation may demand. In order to avoid bloodshed, a responsible man may be forced to do the first—and be accused of cowardice in consequence. If he sees fit to fight, he will be accused of brutality, so whatever he does will be considered wrong. Yet it seems nearly hopeless to argue, as it appears impossible to reach the cortex across the smoke screen of hypothalamic excitation. However, what else should an old man do who is neither a coward nor brutal?

However, we must face the sad and highly alarming fact that, whatever the rebel young *say* concerning their reasons for rejecting everything the older generation stands for, their *actions* prove, to anybody with some knowledge of neuroses, that their real motivation is to be sought in much deeper and more archaic disturbances. When rebelling students resort to defecating, urinating and masturbating publicly in the lecture theaters of the university, as they have been known to do in Vienna, it becomes all too clear that this is not a reasoned protest against the war in Vietnam or against social injustice, but an entirely unconscious and deeply infantile revolt against all parental precepts in general, right down to those of early toilet training. This type of behavior can only be explained on the basis of a genuine regression causing the recrudescence of ontogenetic phases of earliest infancy, or, from the historical viewpoint, precultural states of affairs far below those of palaeolithic times. This alone is a sufficient reason to suspect strongly that the foundation of this type of neurosis is laid very early in life. The alarming fact is, not that this type of mental illness does indeed occur, but that its overt symptoms evidently pass unnoticed or at least unrebuked by intelligent and otherwise responsible young people.

We are safe in concluding that a large part of the factors which, by preventing normal cultural identification, cause hostility in the young, is strictly nonrational. We may divide these factors roughly into three groups. The first are those which enlarge the gap which is to be bridged between two generations; the second are those which impede the processes which normally effect the bridging; the third and most interesting are those which make the present-day young people of different cultures more similar to each other than to their own parents.

The rapid change which the explosion of technology, impelled by irresistible technocracy, forces on human ecology and sociology has the unavoidable consequence that cultural norms of social behavior are becoming obsolete at an ever-increasing rate. In other words, the proportion between those traditional norms which are still valid and those which have become obsolete, is changing, with increasing velocity, in the direction of the latter.

Thomas Mann, in his marvelous historical and psychoanalytical novel about Joseph and his brothers, has shown most convincingly how complete the identification of a son with his father could be, could *afford* to be in biblical times, for the simple reason that the changes needing to be effected between one generation and the next were negligibly small. I believe that humanity has now reached the critical point at which the changes in social norms of behavior demanded within the time period between two generations has begun to exceed the capacity of the pubertal adapting mechanisms. The ever-increasing gap between the social norms which circumstances dictate to each generation, has suddenly attained a size which the powers of filial identification fail to bridge. From the point of view of the young, their parents are hypocrites and liars. In a rapid escalation of hostility, they are even now beginning to treat each other as enemy groups.

The discrepancy between the rapidity of ecological change which technological development forces on humanity, and the relative slowness of the adaptive change possible to traditional culture, would alone be a sufficient explanation for the breaking-off of tradition. There are, however, a number of further causes contributing to the same effect. The indispensable process of *identification* is severely hindered by the *lack of contact* between the generations. Lack of parent-child contact even during the first months of life can cause inconspicuous but lasting damage: we know, from the work of René Spitz, that it is in earliest infancy that the faculty to develop human contacts passes through its most critical period. It is one of the functions that are dangerously prone to *atrophy* if not thoroughly used. The lamentable syndrome which Spitz has called "hospitalization" consists of an "autistic" unwillingness to form human contacts at all, accompanied by a complete cessation of exploratory behavior, as well as by a "negativistic" response to external stimulation in general. The child literally turns its back on the world, lying in its crib with its face turned to the wall. This unfortunate effect can be caused by the seemingly innocuous change of personnel which takes place in most hospitals. The baby begins, at the age at which it becomes able to recognize persons, to form a personal bond to one of its nurses and would be ready to enter into a near-normal child-mother relationship with her. When this bond is severed by the routine change of personnel, the infant will try to form a second attachment and, halfheartedly, a third or even a fourth, but finally it resigns itself to an autism which is in its external symptoms very similar to infantile schizophrenia—whatever that may be.

Mothering a baby is a full-time job. The silly baby games are the beginning of cultural education and very probably its most important part. I do not know the English equivalent to "Bocki, bocki stoß," or "Hoppe, hoppe Reiter," "Guck guck—Dada" can, I think, be translated by "Peek-a-boo." Have you ever seen a baby's face light up when it has just grasped the *communicative* character of such a game and starts to join in it actively? If you have, you will have grasped the importance of this first establishment of mutual understanding on a cultural basis. Nowadays young mothers all too often have no time for this kind of nonsense, many of them would feel self-conscious in doing such a silly thing as gently butting a baby with her head or hiding behind a curtain and popping out again, crying "peek-a-boo." I think they are afraid of treating a small baby too anthropomorphically.

It may seem surprising to some, though really it is not, that this early education is obviously indispensable. It represents the infant's first introduction to *ritualized forms of communication,* and it would seem that, if this is not effected at the correct sensitive phase of the child's ontogeny, permanent damage is done to the development of its faculty to communicate at all. In other words, we have to face the fact that the majority of present-day babies are slightly, but noticeably "hospitalized." They talk later and they become toilet-trained much later, as is witnessed by the huge, diaper-distorted behinds of quite big children. On the principle of distrusting anybody over thirty, their mothers flatly disbelieve me when I tell them the age at which my children were toilet-trained. Today's children are literally "uneducated," they do not "know the first things." How should they, as nobody takes the time to tell them? So the basis for later phenomena of dehumanization is laid down at an early age, by diminishing the readiness for contact and compassion as well as by dampening the natural curiosity of man.

I am aware that the precept that all young mothers should spend most or all of their time with their babies is one that cannot be followed. The scarcity of mother-child contact is a consequence of the scarcity of time which, in turn, is caused by intraspecific competition and ultimately by crowding and other effects of overpopulation. The same fundamental evils have, with equally disastrous results, wrought profound changes in the sociological structure of the family. The preindustrial family was lucky in respect to several prerequisites of the successful handing-down of tradition. The family worked together striving for common aims intelligible to the children. These helped their father at his work and, in doing so, not only learned his craft but also developed a healthy respect for his powers and abilities. Mututal help engendered not only respect, but love as well. Very little disciplining and certainly no thrashings were needed to impress the children with the superior position which the parents held in the social rank order of the group. Even the gradual taking-over of the leading position by the son was a frictionless ritualized procedure which generated as little hostility as possible. Except in certain lucky, old-fashioned peasant families in some parts of Europe, I do not know where these happy circumstances prevail any more. This is just too bad, because they are the indispensable prerequisites for the younger generation's readiness to accept the tradition of the older!

How many children of today ever see their father at work, or help him in such a manner as to be impressed by the difficulty of what he is doing and his prowess in mastering it? Tired Pa, coming home from his office, is anything but impressive and if there is anything he wants to do less than talk about his work, it is to discipline a naughty child. He may even irritably shout at Ma when she—with full justification—thinks it necessary to do so. There is nothing to admire in her either, in fact she is the lowest-ranking creature within the child's horizon, because she is evidently rank-inferior to the char-lady whose favor she is currying in an abjectly submissive manner for fear that this all-important person might give notice.

In addition to these hardly avoidable evils, the parents may have heard the "environmentalistic" theory that human aggression is engendered by frustration and may try to spare their unlucky offspring the necessity of overcoming any kind of obstacle, including, of course, any kind of contradiction from their parents. The result is intolerably aggressive, and, at the same time, neurotic children. Quite apart from the fact that trying to raise unfrustrated human beings is one of the most cruel deprivation experiments possible, it puts its unfortunate victim in a position of tormenting insecurity. Nobody, not even an all-loving saint, can ever *like* a nonfrustration child, and the latter, with the great sensitivity which young children have for nonverbal expression, are very receptive to the suppressed hostility they arouse in every stranger with whom they come into contact. Defended by two despicable weaklings who do not even dare to slap back at a tiny child when slapped by it, and surrounded by a multitude of strangers who dearly would like to give them a sound thrashing, these children live in an agony of insecurity. Small wonder if their world breaks down and they become openly neurotic when they are suddenly exposed to the stress of public opinion, for instance, on entering college.

Young people are able to accept tradition only from a person or persons of the older generation whom they respect *and love*. It is as simple as that! When the family environment fails to produce these conditions, which very often coincides with a degree of early hospitalization, there is only a small chance that the adolescent may find in some other person, for instance, in a teacher, a father figure with whom to identify himself. If this tenuous chance, too, is lost, the unlucky juvenile, in the phase of searching for new ideals, is completely at a loss, more than a little demoralized and highly vulnerable to all the dangers of accepting an unworthy substitute object of his or her loyalty. From this, there are all possible gradations to outright neurosis.

A third set of factors which, while enhancing the cultural break between generations, might nevertheless prove beneficial in the end, consists of all those which tend to minimize the differences between cultures. The mass media, the increasing facility of transportation, the all-embracing spread of fashion and other things, all tend to make the representatives of the young generation more similar to each other than their parents had been, and indeed more similar to each other than to their widely divergent parents. Those who were reared since the last war were reared under circumstances and in an atmosphere entirely different from that of their parents' childhood. In this respect, their relation to their parents has been rightly compared to the one existing between the children of immigrants into a new country and these immigrants themselves. This, in fact, represents a silver lining in an otherwise very dark cloud: if the break of traditional knowledge is not so complete as to cast humanity back to a precultural state of affairs, one might cherish a faint hope that the young of the whole world, while waging war upon the older generation, might become less prone to do so on each other.

IX. Conclusions and Outlook

Our culture is in an unbelievably paradoxical situation. Here, on the one hand, we have an established culture, assiduously committing suicide in seven different ways. First, there is the population increase which will soon suffocate, if not our actual species, all that is really human about it. Second, the rat-race of modern commercialism threatens, in a truly satanic vicious cycle, to accelerate to the point of insanity. Third, man is progressively destroying nature, devastating the biotope in and on which he lives. Fourth, there is the progressive "Verweichlichung" of which I have spoken which is the death of human emotionality and, therewith, of all truly human relationships. Fifth, an imminent danger of genetic deterioration of mankind is due to the fact that common decency in every civilized community is at a negative survival premium. Sixth, and quickest, is nuclear warfare, yet I believe it is the least dangerous, because of its obviousness. Everybody understands the threat of the atom bomb, but who cares about disintegration of culture or genetic deterioration, and who will even believe that insecticides can endanger the world in which we live?

The powers that be flatly ignore all these dangers—except where soil erosion or other consequences of over-exploitation become financially disturbing. Yet any man of average intelligence and tolerably good education cannot fail to see them. This irresponsibility of the responsible is due neither to their being stupid or immoral, but to their *indoctrination*. Indoctrination may be regarded as public danger number seven. Fundamentally identical with superstition, it is camouflaged under pseudo-scientific terminology and grows apace with the absolute number of people that can be influenced by the so-called mass media. The function of

all doctrine, as Philip Wylie puts it, is to explain everything. Where doctrine rules, all possibility of truth is
gone and, with it, all hope for an intelligent consensus.
Indoctrination is, I think, the very worst of humanity's
deadly vices!

On the other side, there are the rebelling young. At
least some of them, and the best among them, are
gloriously free from indoctrination and commendably
distrustful of all doctrines; also, they are yearning for a
just cause for which to fight, for real obstacles to overcome. There is no dearth of dangers to humanity which
must be fought, and our attempt to save mankind meets
with a number of great obstacles which ought to be
quite sufficient to keep the most ebullient militant enthusiasm of the young happily occupied for a long time.

The young *say* that they want to save mankind. We
may be convinced that they are honest about this, and I
even believe that some of them have a real understanding of the predicament of man. But do they, collectively, show any promise of ever accomplishing their
great task?

At present, they are indulging in the archaically instinctive pleasure of tribal warfare. The instinct of militant enthusiasm is not a whit less seductive than that of
sex, nor less stultifying. And hate is the most absolutely
stultifying emotion of all, as it precludes all communication, all acceptance of the kind of information
that might tend to abate it. This is why hate is "blind"
and why it is so dangerously prone to escalate.

We must face the truly horrible fact that the hate
which the young bear us, is of the same nature as national or tribal hate. It bears all its earmarks, the
haughtiness of only regarding one's own party as quite
human, the tendency to discredit and vilify the enemy
("Never trust a man over thirty"), the honest conviction
that it is a moral duty to stamp out the enemy's culture
as completely as possible, etc. etc. All these are atti-

tudes and slogans which we know only too well as the tools of demagogues well-versed in the technique of rousing one nation against another.

Of course, there is a certain danger that the older generation might reply in kind, in other words that there might be an escalation of the enmity between the generations. It is a fact that the young revolutionaries are actively striving to be as revolting to the older generation as they possibly can contrive to be. I know a number of highly intelligent and altogether admirable old gentlemen who are neither hide-bound nor etiquette-ridden, but who would find it absolutely impossible to take seriously what a man dressed up as a hippie or a communarde has to say. I myself confess I should find it difficult to listen to M. Cohn-Bendit in his pretty blue blouse, or to suffer having flowers heaved at me by flower-power. I honestly feel I should be in greater sympathy with Papuans throwing spears at me, and all this in spite of the fact that I know about my own instinctive responses and do my very best to suppress them. Professionally disciplined not to bite back when being bitten by a subject of my studies, I still doubt that I could keep up my readiness to communicate with APO students when hit full in the face by a paint-bag, as recently happened to an 80-year-old colleague in my presence in Göttingen.

Yet I do not think that there is any danger of the old ever hating the young in the manner in which the young hate the old. We of the older generation are prevented from doing so by the most archaic of instinctive responses, those of parental care. Among the rebelling young there are our own children or grandchildren, and we find it impossible to cease loving them, let alone to hate them. This creates a queerly unbalanced situation of being hated, yet being quite unable to reciprocate hate, and it seems to be human nature to react to the conflict thus produced in a very specific and unexpected manner. If somebody we love dearly suddenly flies into an apparently justified rage against us, we automatically and subconsciously assume that we have inadvertently given good cause for that rage. In other words, we react by feeling *guilty*. Highly social animals, such as dogs and certain species of geese, show an analogous response. When unexpectedly attacked by an otherwise friendly companion they act "as if" it were their own fault, or else a mistake. In other words, they "react by not reacting," submitting to the attack by simply ignoring it whereupon the attacker regularly ceases to be aggressive. In terms of observable behavior, the human "guilt response" is strictly analogous, whatever the accompanying emotions may be. I am sure that part of the feeling of guilt which at present is weighing down many people of the older generation, has its source in the paradoxical reaction just described, and that this is particularly true of the almost masochistic attitude assumed by some university teachers towards the rebelling young.

To sum up: our culture is threatened with immediate destruction by a breakdown of cultural tradition. This threat arises from the danger of what amounts to a tribal war between two successive generations. The causes of this war, from the viewpoint of the ethologist as well as from that of the psychiatrist, appear to lie in a mass neurosis of the worst kind.

This diagnosis, though matter-of-fact, is pessimistic only in appearance, because any neurosis can, in principle, be cured by raising its subconscious and unconscious causes above the threshold of consciousness. In respect to the neurotic war between the generations, it should not be too difficult to do just that. It ought to be quite easy to make those among the rebelling students who are neither hopelessly indoctrinated nor stupid, understand the few biological facts of which I could give some idea, even in one short presentation. The young *have* already grasped the one fundamental fact that humanity is going to the dogs at a rapid rate unless some vicious cycles like population growth, destruction of the biotope and accelerating commercial competition are stopped, and *soon* at that.

They still have to understand a few further truths. One is that, even if their whole generation consisted of nothing but blessed geniuses, they could not build up a culture from scratch, but would be back at Neanderthal if they followed Marcuse's precepts of destroying all tradition: tradition is to a culture what the genome is to a species. Another fact they must comprehend is that they should not give way to hate. Hating the older generation prevents them from learning anything from it, and there is a lot to learn. It is hate that makes them so stupidly haughty, that creates, in them, that exasperating inverted "mother-knows-best-attitude" which makes them impermeable to advice and renders them actually paranoiac because everything one tells them is automatically interpreted as an attempt to uphold the so-called establishment. (If one criticizes the establishment, one is suspected of being a particularly insidious and clever supporter of it.) Finally they should come to understand in all fairness that, if we of the older generation, on being hated, don't reciprocate with hate, this is not because we are guilt-ridden, having perpetrated nameless crimes against them, but because, being their parents, we cannot help loving them.

I am admittedly an incurable optimist and I believe that the young can be made to understand all this, and that, if they once have grasped the simple ethological facts underlying it, they will not only be able to save and retain everything worth preserving of our present-day culture, but that they might even do more: they are, as I said, even today loosening their allegiance to their several established cultures, and they are becoming increasingly similar to each other, independent of their provenance. Provided they do not, by jettisoning the accumulated knowledge of their culture, relapse to Neanderthal, provided they attain power when they attain maturity, provided they do not then forget their present aims and provided they do not get caught, as they are all too likely to be, in the orthodoxy of some doctrine or other (it does not matter in the least which), they really might be successful in getting mankind out of the horrible mess it is in at present.

All these high hopes depend, of course, on education, and if I have seemed overly optimistic just now, I have occasion to counteract that impression at once. One of the ugliest facts in the social life of present-day humanity is that the decision concerning what to teach the young and what to withhold from them, still rests almost exclusively with those who are in power politically. What is to be taught and what is to be withheld, is therefore mainly dependent on what the politicians deem advisable in the interests of their own, shortlived political aims, and not on any consideration of what will be necessary for the present-day young people to know when, a few years hence, they will have to shoulder the responsibility for the survival of mankind. The teaching of Charles Darwin's discoveries is still legally prohibited in the state of Indiana, a few miles from Chicago. Biology, and particularly Ecology and Ethology, are regarded as subversive sciences in many parts and the teaching of biology in German middle schools has been cut down to a ridiculous minimum.

Furthermore, the technique of all teaching, particularly in the United States, is still founded on the assumption that the pseudo-democratic doctrine is absolutely true. This results in a purely utilitarian teaching which leaves entirely out of consideration the fact that man possesses certain species-specific programs of behavior, the suppression of which inevitably leads to neurosis and contributes to the mass neurosis with which we are confronted nowadays. In other words, the usual kind of education intentionally or unintentionally ignores the fact that the realization of certain phylogenetically evolved programs of human behavior constitutes an inalienable human *right*. So far from being a mere quibble, the question whether a certain pattern of human social behavior is determined by a phylogenetically adapted program or by cultural ritualization becomes of supreme importance the very moment we have to deal with a pathological disfunction. Its correction requires entirely different steps in each of the two cases. If the disturbance has its source in cultural tradition alone, education alone ought to be capable of dealing with it. If the central cause of the disturbance lies in a phyletic program which, by remaining unfulfilled, causes malaise and even neurosis, educative measures will only serve to make matters worse by destroying what faith in the educator is still left. One cannot *teach* a man to remain happy, to retain his love for his neighbor, to avoid developing neuroses, high blood pressure and heart attacks under the stressful conditions of crowded commercial city life, which is exactly what present-day education is persistently and unavailingly trying to do.

Even from the full recognition of the *cause* of certain pathological phenomena, it does not follow that a means of combating them is automatically apparent. There are many examples in medical science demonstrating this sad fact. However, I believe that an increased emphasis on teaching biology, in particular ecology and ethology, on teaching young people to think in terms of systems rather than in those of atomism, together with a certain amount of tuition in pathology and psychopathology, would help enormously to make young people understand the real predicament of mankind. This considered opinion of mine is founded on what I regard as a highly suggestive fact. Among the rebelling students there is a clear positive correlation of their knowledge of biology and the constructiveness of their demands. The deepest malaise, the most un-compromising enmity against the teachers, the deepest confusion of the intentions of the teachers and those of the politicians in power, in short the greatest amount of general disorientation is to be found among the students of sociology, of a science which I reproach for being still too much under the influence of the pseudo-democratic doctrine. In a discussion of three hours duration which I had late at night with APO students in the streets of Göttingen, a discussion which began in hostility and ended in friendship, I could not offer any better suggestions for the solution of the problems of education just mentioned than I have to offer now. Politicians can only be influenced by the pressure of public opinion. There is only one way to gain their attention for our problems, and that is by *infiltrating public opinion* with the knowledge of the real causes of man's predicament and trusting in the public to force politicians to do the right things. It is an error common among scientists to underrate the intelligence of the public, and that is why all-too few scientists regard it as their duty to write generally intelligible books, leaving this task to popularizers who rarely accomplish it in a satisfactory manner. If science is ever to gain that kind of influence on politics which is obviously necessary to save mankind, it can only do so by educating the public independently of accepted political doctrines.

Major Published Works
of Konrad Lorenz

References

Index

Major Published Works
of Konrad Lorenz

1927 "Beobachtungen an Dohlen." *Journal für Ornithologie*, 75, 511–519.

1931 "Beiträge zur Ethologie sozialer Corviden." *Journal für Ornithologie*, 79, 67–127.

1932 "Beobachtungen an Schwalben anlässlich der Zugkatastrophe im September 1931." *Der Vogelzug*, 3, 4–10.

1932 "Betrachtungen über das Erkennen der arteigenen Triebhandlungen bei Vögeln." *Journal für Ornithologie*, 80, 50–98.

1933 "Beobachtetes über das Fliegen der Vögel und über die Beziehungen der Flügel—und Steuerform zur Art des Fluges." *Journal für Ornithologie*, 81, 107–236.

1933 "Fliegen mit dem Wind und gegen den Wind." *Journal für Ornithologie*, 81, 596–607.

1934 "Betrachtungen an freifliegenden zahmgehaltenen

Nachtrethern." *Journal für Ornithologie*, 82, 160–161.

1934 "A Contribution to the Comparative Sociology of Colonial-nesting Birds." *Proceedings of the 8th International Ornithological Congress*. London: Oxford University Press, 207–218.

1935 "Der Kumpan in der Umwelt des Vogels." *Journal für Ornithologie*, 83, 137–215, 289–413.

1936 "Über eine eigentümliche Verbindung branchialer Hirnnerven bei Cypselus apus." *Gegenbaurs Morphologisches Jahrbuch*, 77, 305–325.

1937 "Über den Begriff der Instinkthandlung." *Folia Biotheoretica*, Serie B, 2, *Instinctus*, S. 17–50.

1937 "Biologische Fragestellungen in der Tierpsychologie." *Zeitschrift für Tierpsychologie*, 1, 24–32.

1937 "Über die Bildung des Instinktbegriffes." *Die Naturwissenschaften*, 25, 289–300, 307–308, 324–331.

1937 "The Companion in the Bird's World." *The Auk*, 54, 245–273.

1937 "Tiere beobachten besser als wir." *Königsberger Allgemeine Zeitung*, vom 15. January 1937.

1938 "Taxis und Instinkthandlung in der Eirollbewegung der Graugans" (zusammen mit N. Tinbergen). *Zeitschrift für Tierpsychologie*, 2, 1–29.

1938 "Über Ausfallserscheinungen im Instinktverhalten von Haustieren und ihre sozialpsychologische Bedeutung." 16. Kongress der Deutschen Gesellschaft für Psychologie in Bayreuth. Leipzig: Johann Ambrosius Barth, S. 139–147.

1939 "Vergleichende Verhaltensforschung." *Verhandlungen der Deutschen Zoologischen Gesellschaft. Zoologischer Anzeiger*, Supplementband 12, 69–102.

1939 "Vergleichendes über die Balz der Schwimmenten" (Graugansfilm). *Journal für Ornithologie*, 87, 172–174.

Major Published Works of Konrad Lorenz

1940 "Die Paarbildung beim Kolkraben." *Zeitschrift für Tierpsychologie*, 3, 278–292.

1940 "Systematik und Entwicklungsgedanke im Unterricht." *Der Biologe*, 1/2, 24–36.

1940 "Durch Domestikation verursachte Störungen arteigenen Verhaltens." *Zeitschrift für angewandte Psychologie und Charakterkunde*, 59, 1–81.

1941 "Kants Lehre vom Apriorischen im Lichte gegenwärtiger Biologie." *Blätter für Deutsche Philosophie*, 15.

1941 "Vergleichende Bewegungsstudien an Anatiden." *Journal für Ornithologie*, 89, Ergänzungsband 3, Festschrift O. Heinroth, 194–293.

1941 "Oskar Heinroth 70 Jahre." *Der Biologe*, 2/3, 45–47.

1942 "Induktive und teleologische Psychologie." *Die Naturwissenschaften*, 30, 133–143.

1943 "Psychologie und Stammesgeschichte." In G. Heberer, *Die Evolution der Organismen*. Jena: G. Fischer, 1. Auflage, 105–127.

1943 "Die angeborenen Formen möglicher Erfahrung." *Zeitschrift für Tierpsychologie*, 5, 235–409.

1949 "Literarisches Subjekt und angeborener auslösender Mechanismus." *Wiener Literarisches Echo*, 1, Heft 2.

1949 "Der sonderbare Dativ." *Umwelt*, 2, 1.

1949 "Tierbücher." *Umwelt*, 2, 2.

1949 "Was ist vergleichende Verhaltensforschung?" *Umwelt*, 2, 3.

1949 "Über die Beziehungen zwischen Kopfform und Zirkelbewegung bei Sturniden und Ikteriden." In *Festschrift für Stresemann*, 1949, 153–157.

1949 *Er redete mit dem Vieh, den Vögeln und den Fischen*. Wien: Verlag Borotha-Schoeler.

1950 "Ganzheit und Teil in der tierischen und menschlichen Gemeinschaft." *Studium Generale*, 9, 455–499.

1950 "Die zeitlosen Gesellen." *Du* 4, 11–12, 17–18.

1950 "The Comparative Method in Studying Innate Behaviour Patterns." Symposia of the Society for Experimental Biology, 4, *Animal Behaviour*. Cambridge: University Press, 221–268.

1950 "Ethologie der Graugans: Beiheft zum gleichnamigen." Film, Hochschulfilm C 560.

1950 "Über das Töten von Artgenossen." In E. Dennert (Ed.), *Die Natur, das Wunder Gottes*, 5. Auflage. Bonn: Athenäum.

1950 *So kam der Mensch auf den Hund.* Wien: Verlag Borotha-Schoeler.

1950 "Ausdrucksbewegungen höherer Tiere." *Verhandlungen der Gesellschaft Deutscher Naturforscher und Ärzte*, Berlin, 96. Versammlung in München, vom 22.–25. Oktober. Berlin: Springer, 84–87.

1951 "Ausdrucksbewegungen höherer Tiere." *Die Naturwissenschaften*, 38, 113–116.

1951 "Über die Entstehung auslösender 'Zeremonien.'" *Die Vogelwarte*, 16, 9–13.

1951 "Comparative Studies on the Behaviour of Anatinae." *Avicultural Magazine*, 57.

1951 "The Role of Gestalt Perception in Animal and Human Behaviour." In C. C. Whyte (Ed.), *Aspects of Form*. London: Bradford, 157–178.

1952 "Ehe- und Familienleben im Tierreich." *Basler Nachrichten*, vom 6. Februar (Nr. 56), 2. Beilage.

1952 "Balz und Paarbildung bei der Stockente" (Anas plathyrhynchos L.). Begleitheft zum gleichnamigen Film des Instituts für den wissenschaftlichen Film, Hochschulfilm C 626.

1952 "Comparative Studies on the Behaviour of the Anatinae." *Avicultural Magazine*, 58 (Fortsetzung von 44).

1952 "Über tanzähnliche Bewegungsweisen bei Tieren." *Studium Generale*, 5, 1–9.

1952 "Angeborenes Können und Erkennen im Tierreich." *Orion*, 7, 716–720.

Major Published Works of Konrad Lorenz

1952 *King Solomon's Ring.* New York: Crowell, 1952.

1952 "Die Entwicklung der vergleichenden Verhaltensforschung in den letzten 12 Jahren." *Zoologischer
Anzeiger,* 1952 Supplementband, 36–58.

1953 "Comparative Studies on the Behaviour of the Anatinae." *Avicultural Magazine,* 59 (Fortsetzung von
48).

1953 "Scientific Value of a Group Collection of Live Animals." *The Wilson Bulletin,* 65/1, 59–62.

1953 "Über angeborene Instinktformeln beim Menschen."
Deutsche medizinische Wochenschrift, 78, 45–46.

1953 "Die Verständigung unter Tieren." *Das Interna-
tionale Forum,* 1.

1953 "Können Tiere sprechen?" *Sie und Er,* 19/20, vom 14.
März.

1953 "Die Welt des Tieres I und II." In Sendereihe: *Hier
spricht die Wissenschaft.* UKW-Programm Hessi-
scher Rundfunk Frankfurt, vom 2. und 16. Januar.

1954 "Psychologie und Stammesgeschichte." In G. Heberer (Ed.), *Die Evolution der Organismen.* Jena: G.
Fischer, 2. Auflage, 131–172.

1954 "Über angeborene Instinktformeln beim Menschen."
*Zur menschlichen Vererbungs—und Konstitutions-
lehre,* 32, 385–389.

1954 "Das angeborene Erkennen." *Natur und Volk,* 84: 9,
285–295.

1954 "Moralanaloges Verhalten geselliger Tiere." *Forschung und Wirtschaft,* IV, 1–23.

1955 "Morphology and Behavior Patterns in Closely Allied
Species." First Conference on Group Processes,
Princeton, N.J.: Transactions of the Josiah Macy Jr.
Foundation.

1955 *Les Animaux ces Inconnus.* Paris, 156 S.

1955 "Über das Töten von Artgenossen." Göttingen: *Jahrbuch der Max-Planck-Gesellschaft,* 105–140.

1956 "The Objectivistic Theory of Instinct." In *L'Instinct dans le Compartement des Animaux et de l'Homme.* Paris: Masson et Cie., 51–76.

1956 "Plays and Vacuum Activities." In *L'Instinct dans le Compartement des Animaux et de l'Homme.* Paris: Masson et Cie., 633–645.

1956 "Zur Entwicklungsgeschichte einer neueren Forschungsrichtung der Biologie." Aus der Deutschen Forschung der letzten Dezennien, Festschrift für Dr. Telschow. Stuttgart: Georg Thieme, 208–214.

1956 "Moralanaloges Verhalten geselliger Tiere." *Universitas,* 11: 7, 691–704.

1957 "Über das Töten von Artgenossen." In E. Dennert (Ed.), *Die Natur, das Wunder Gottes,* 6. Auflage. Bonn: Athenäum-Verlag, 262–281.

1957 "Methoden der Verhaltensforschung." In Kükenthals, *Handbuch der Zoologie,* VIII, T. 10. Berlin: Walter de Gruyter.

1957 "Companionship in Bird Life." In C. H. Schiller (Ed.), *Instinctive Behavior.* New York: International Universities Press, 83–128.

1957 "The Nature of Instinct." In C. H. Schiller (Ed.), *Instinctive Behavior.* New York: International Universities Press, 129–175.

1957 "Taxis and Instinct" (zusammen mit N. Tinbergen). In C. H. Schiller (Ed.), *Instinctive Behavior.* New York: International Universities Press, 176–208.

1957 "Comparative Study of Behavior." In C. H. Schiller (Ed.), *Instinctive Behavior.* New York: International Universities Press, 239–263.

1957 "The Past Twelve Years in the Comparative Study of Behavior." In C. H. Schiller (Ed.), *Instinctive Behavior.* New York: International Universities Press, 288–310.

1958 "Nachruf auf Oskar Heinroth." Der Zoologische Garten.

1958 "The Evolution of Behavior." *Scientific American,* 199: 6, 67–76.

1959 *Methods and Approach to the Problems of Behavior.* The Harvey Lectures. New York: Academic Press, 60–103.

1959 "Gestaltwahrnehmung als Quelle wissenschaftlicher Erkenntnis." *Zeitschrift für experimentelle und angewandte Psychologie,* 6: 1, 118–165.

1959 "Gustav Kramer." *Journal für Ornithologie,* 100, 265–268.

1959 "Otto Koehler 70 Jahre." *Zeitschrift für Tierpsychologie,* 16, 641–646.

1959 "Das Woher, Warum und Wozu unserer Forschung." Göttingen: *Mitteilungen aus der Max-Planck-Gesellschaft,* 2, 105–119.

1959 "Beiträge der Zoologie zum Selbstverständnis des Menschen." In *Das ist der Mensch. Sendereihe des Süddeutschen Rundfunks;* in Buchform: Stuttgart: Alfred Kröner, 23–34.

1959 "Comments on Professor Piaget's Paper." *Child Development,* 4, 28–34.

1959 "The Role of Aggression in Group Formation." 4th Conference on Group Processes, 1957. Princeton, N.J.: Transactions of the Josiah Macy Jr. Foundation.

1960 "Die Ausdrucksbewegungen der Sichelente Anas falcate" (zusammen mit W. von de Wall). *Journal für Ornithologie,* 101, 50–60.

1960 "Erwin Stresemann zum 70 Geburtstag." *Journal für Ornithologie,* 101, 3–6.

1960 "Prinzipien der vergleichenden Verhaltensforschung." *Fortschritte der Zoologie,* 12, 265–294.

1961 "Phylogenetische Anpassung und adaptive Modifikation des Verhaltens." *Zeitschrift für Tierpsychologie,* 18, 139–187.

1962 "Erich von Holst zum Todestag." *Die Naturwissenschaften,* 49, 385–386.

1962 "Naturschönheit und Daseinskampf." *Kosmos,* 58, 340–348.

1962 "Der Kampf ums Dasein auf dem Korallenriff." Göttingen: *Mitteilungen aus der Max-Planck-Gesellschaft*, 4, 195–206.

1962 "Kant's Doctrine of the A Priori in the Light of Contemporary Biology." *General Systems*, New York, 7, 23–35.

1962 "Gestalt Perception as Fundamental to Scientific Knowledge." *General Systems*, New York, 7, 37–56.

1962 "The Function of Color in Coral Reef Fishes." *Proceedings of the Royal Institution of Great Britain*, 39, 282–296.

1963 "Die räumliche Orientierung von Paramecium aurelia" (zusammen mit W. Rose). *Die Naturwissenschaften*, 19, 623–624.

1963 "Die Erfindung von Flugmaschinen in der Evolution der Wirbeltiere." *Therapie des Monats* (Mannheim-Waldhof: C. F. Boehringer & Soehne), 13, 138–148.

1963 "Die Konstruktion von Flugmaschinen in der Evolution der Wirbeltiere." *Therapie des Monats* (Mannheim-Waldhof: C. F. Boehringer & Soehne), 13, 186–195.

1963 "Das sogenannte Böse." *Zur Naturgeschichte der Aggression*. Wien: Verlag Borotha-Schoeler.

1963 "Die Hoffnung auf Einsicht in das Wirken der Natur." In *Die Hoffnung unserer Zeit*. München: Piper, 142–159.

1963 "Haben Tiere ein subjektives Erleben?" München: *Jahrbuch der Technischen Hochschule*.

1963 "A Scientist's Credo." In *Counterpoint. Libidinal Object and Subject. A Tribute to René Spitz on his 75th Birthday*. New York: International Universities Press.

1964 "Moralanaloges Verhalten von Tieren—Erkenntnisse der Verhaltensforschung." *Universitas*, 19, 43–54.

1964 "Über die Wahrheit der Abstammungslehre." In *Medico Europa-Ausgabe*, Heft 1, 9. Mannheim-Waldhof: C. F. Boehringer & Soehne.

Major Published Works of Konrad Lorenz

1964 "Erich von Holst, Seher und Forscher." 4. *Biologisches Jahresheft des Verbandes Deutscher Biologen.*

1964 *Darwin hat recht gesehen.* Pfullingen: Verlag Neske.

1964 "Ritualized Fighting." In *The Natural History of Aggression.* New York: Academic Press.

1965 "Moralanaloges Verhalten von Tieren—Erkenntnisse der Verhaltensforschung." In *Naturwissenschaften heute.* Gütersloh: H. Walter Bähr.

1965 "Dank an Otto Koehler." *Zeitschrift für Tierpsychologie*, 22, 1–5.

1965 "Über die Entstehung von Mannigfaltigkeit." *Die Naturwissenschaften*, 12, 319–329.

1965 "Zur Naturgeschichte der Aggression." *Neue Sammlung*, 4, 296–308.

1965 "Eine Lanze für das Aquarium." *Die Natur*, 4, 163–164.

1965 "Über tierisches und menschliches Verhalten. Aus dem Werdegang der Verhaltenslehre." *Gesammelte Abhandlungen*, Band I. München: Piper.

1965 "Über tierisches und menschliches Verhalten. Aus dem Werdegang der Verhaltenslehre." *Gesammelte Abhandlungen*, Band II. München: Piper.

1965 *Evolution and Modification of Behavior.* Chicago: University of Chicago Press.

1965 "Alfred Seitz 60 Jahre." *Zeitschrift für Tierpsychologie*, 22, 600–602.

1965 *Der Vogelflug.* Neudruck von Nr. 5. Pfullingen: Verlag Neske.

1966 "Stammes- und Kulturgeschichtliche Ritenbildung." München: Mitteilungen aus der Max-Planck-Gesellschaft, 1, 3–30. *Naturwissenschaftliche Rundschau*, 19, 361–370.

1966 "Über gestörte Wirkungsgefüge in der Natur." Hannover: *Naturschutz in Niedersachsen*, 11/12, 9–18.

1966 *On Aggression.* New York: Harcourt, Brace & World.

1966 "Evolution of ritualization in the biological and cultural spheres. A discussion on ritualization of behaviour in animals and man." London: *Philosophical Transactions of the Royal Society.*

1967 "Zanclus cornutus der Halfterfisch." *Aquarienmagazin,* 1, 19–22.

1967 "Die instinktiven Grundlagen menschlicher Kultur." *Die Naturwissenschaften,* 54, 377–388.

1968 "Die Entwicklung des Spießens und Klemmens bei der drei Würgerarten Lanius collurio, L. senator und L. excubitor" (zusammen mit U. v. Saint Paul). *Journal für Ornithologie,* 109, 2, 137–156.

1968 Neudruck von Nr. 1 und Nr. 20 in *Mensch und Tier.* München: Deutscher Taschenbuch Verlag.

1968 "Vom Weltbild des Verhaltensforschers." Drei Abhandlungen aus: *Über tierisches und menschliche Verhalten.* München: Deutscher Taschenbuch Verlag.

1968 *Antriebe tierischen und menschlichen Verhaltens. Gesammelte Abhandlungen* (zusammen mit P. Leyhausen). Neudruck von Nr. 18. München: Piper.

1969 "Innate Bases of Learning." In Karl H. Pribram: *On the Biology of Learning.* New York: Harcourt, Brace & World.

1970 "Der ethische Wert des Naturschutzes." *Wiener Naturschutznachrichten,* 13–21.

1970 "The Enmity between Generations and Its Probable Ethological Causes." In *The Place of Value in a World of Facts.* Nobel Symposium 14, Stockholm, 385–418. *Studium Generale,* 23, 963–997. *The Psychoanalytic Review,* 57, 3, 333–377.

1970 "Die Hoffnung auf Einsicht in das Wirken der Natur." Neudruck von Nr. 100. *Universitas,* 25, 12, 1291–1304.

1970 "On Killing Members of One's Own Species." Übersetzung von Nr. 64. *Bulletin of Atomic Scientists,* 26, 8, 2–5.

Major Published Works of Konrad Lorenz

1971 "Naturschutz und Ethik." *Blätter für Naturschutz*, 51, 1, 31–33.

1971 "Der Sinn für Harmonie." Neudruck von Nr. 133. *Kosmos*, 67, 187–191.

1971 "Der Mensch, biologisch gesehen." *Studium Generale*, 24, 495–515.

1971 "Die acht Todsünden der zivilisierten Menschheit." In *Sozialtheorie und soziale Praxis*. Verlag Anton Hain: Meisenheim, 281–340.

1971 "Blind für das Schöne, blind für das Gute." *Wochenpress*, Wien, 28.4.71. *Architekt*, 9/10, 3–4.

1971 "Knowledge, Beliefs and Freedom." In *Hierarchically Organized Systems in Theory and Practice*. By Paul A. Weiss. Hafner: New York, 231–262.

1972 "Vom Auftrage der Vergleichenden Verhaltensforschung." In *15 Jahre Gesellschaft der Freunde des Biologischen*. Station Wilhelminenberg, 6–8.

1972 "Wissenschaft, Ideologie und das Selbstverständnis und Gesellschaft. Kritische Anmerkungen zur 'empty organ' Doktrin der behavioristischen Schule." In *Mannheimer Forum*, 72. Herausg. Hoimar v. Ditfurth. Boehringer: Mannheim, 9–27.

1973 Rede auf der 10. Hauptversammlung des Verbandes Deutscher Biologen. *Mitteilungen des Verbandes Deutscher Biologen, Bei Naturwissenschaftliche Rundschau*, 1, 903–905.

1973 "Die Naturwissenschaft vom menschlichen Geiste." *Mitteilungen der Humboldt-Gesellschaft*, 5, 117–127.

1973 "Die acht Todsünden der zivilisierten Menschheit." Piper: München. Verbesserte Neuauflage, von Nr. 136.

1973 "The Fashionable Fallacy of Dispensing with Description." *Naturwissenschaften*, 60, 1–9.

1973 *Civilized Man's Eight Deadly Sins*. New York: Harcourt Brace Jovanovich, 1973.

References

Ardrey, Robert. *The Territorial Imperative.* New York: Atheneum, 1966.

Ashby, W. R. *Design for a Brain.* New York: Wiley, 1952.

—— *An Introduction to Cybernetics.* New York: Wiley, 1956.

Bandura, A. "Vicarious processes: a case of no-trial learning." In L. Berkowitz (Ed.), *Advances in Experimental Social Psychology,* Vol. 2. New York: Academic Press, 1965.

—— *Principles of Behavior Modification.* New York: Holt, Rinehart & Winston, 1969.

Bateson, P. P. G. "Effect of similarity between rearing and testing conditions on chicks' following and avoidance responses." *Journal of Comparative Physiological Psychology,* 1964, 57, 100–103.

Bergson, H. L. *Creative Evolution.* New York: Holt, 1911.

Berkowitz, L. *Aggression: A Social Psychological Analysis.* New York: McGraw-Hill, 1962.

Bernard, L. L. *Instinct: A Study in Social Psychology.* New York: Henry Holt, 1925.

Bertalanffy, L. von. "An essay on the relativity of categories." *Philosophy of Science,* 1955, 22, 243–263.

Bischof, N. "Aristoteles, Galilei, Kurt Lewin, und die Folgen." *Zeitschrift für Sozaipsychologie* (in preparation).

Campbell, D. T. "Methodological suggestions from a comparative psychology of knowledge processes." *Inquiry*, 1959, 152–182.

—— "Variation and selective retention in socio-cultural evolution." In H. R. Barringer, G. I. Blanksten, and R. W. Mack, (Eds.), *Social Change in Developing Areas.* Cambridge, Mass.: Schenkman, 1965.

—— "Ethnocentric and other altruistic motives." In D. Levine (Ed.), *Nebraska Symposium on Motivation 1965.* Lincoln: University of Nebraska Press, 1965, 283–311.

—— "Pattern matching as an essential in distal knowing." In K. R. Hammond (Ed.), *The Psychology of Egon Brunswik.* New York: Holt, Rinehart & Winston, 1966, 81–106.

—— "On the genetics of altruism and the counter-hedonic components in human culture." *Journal of Social Issues,* 1972, 28, 21–37.

—— "Making the case for randomized assignment to treatments by considering the alternatives: Six ways in which quasi-experimental evaluations in compensatory education tend to underestimate effects." Paper presented to Conference on Central Issues in Social Program Evaluation, C. A. Bennett and A. Lumsdane, Coordinators, Battelle Human Affairs Research Center, Seattle, Washington, July 1973. (*Publication pending.*)

—— "Evolutionary Epistemology." In P. A. Schilpp (Ed.), *The Philosophy of Karl Popper.* Vol. 14, I and II. *The Library of Living Philosophers.* LaSalle, Ill.: Open Court Publishing, 1974, 413–463.

—— and Erlebacher, A. E. "How regression artifacts in quasi-experimental evaluations can mistakenly make compensatory education look harmful." In J. Hellmuth (Ed.), *Compensatory Education: A National Debate.* Vol. III. *Disadvantaged Child.* New York: Brunner/Mazel, 1970, 185–210.

—— and Frey, P. W. "The implications of learning theory for the fade-out of gains from compensatory education."

In J. Hellmuth (Ed.), *Compensatory Education: A National Debate.* Vol. III. *Disadvantaged Child.* New York: Brunner/Mazel, 1970, 455–463.

Coser, L. A. *The Functions of Social Conflict.* New York: Free Press, 1956.

Craig, W. "Appetites and aversions as constituents of instincts." *Biological Bulletin,* 1918, 34, 91–108.

Darwin, C. *On the Origin of Species by Means of Natural Selection or the Preservation of Favored Races in the Struggle for Life.* London: Murray, 1859.

Darwin, C. G. "Can man control his numbers?" In S. Tax (Ed.), *Evolution After Darwin.* Vol. II. Chicago: University of Chicago Press, 1960.

Driesch, H. *The History and Theory of Vitalism.* London: Macmillan, 1914.

Eccles, J. S. "Some implications of the scientiae for the future of mankind." *Studium Generale,* 1970, 23, 917–924.

Erikson, Erik. *Childhood and Society,* 2nd Ed. New York: W. W. Norton, 1963.

—— *Identity: Youth and Crisis.* New York: W. W. Norton, 1968.

—— "Ontogeny of ritualization in man." *Philosophical Transactions of the Royal Society of London,* Series B, 772, 251, 1966, 337–349.

Evans, R. I. *Conversations with Carl Jung and Reactions from Ernest Jones.* New York: D. Van Nostrand, 1964.

—— *Dialogue with Erich Fromm.* New York: Harper & Row, 1966.

—— *B. F. Skinner: The Man and His Ideas.* New York: E. P. Dutton, 1968.

—— *Dialogue with Erik Erikson.* New York: E. P. Dutton, 1969a.

—— *Psychology and Arthur Miller.* New York: E. P. Dutton, 1969b.

—— *Gordon Allport: The Man and His Ideas.* New York: E. P. Dutton, 1971.

—— *Jean Piaget: The Man and His Ideas.* New York: E. P. Dutton, 1973.

Fisher, R. A. *The Genetical Theory of Natural Selection.* Oxford: Clarendon Press, 1930.

Freyer, H. *Theorie des gegenwärtigen Zeitalters.* Stuttgart: Deutsche Verlagsanstalt, 1955.

Fromm, Erich. *Escape from Freedom.* New York: Farrar & Rinehart, 1941.

———— *The Anatomy of Human Destructiveness.* New York: Holt, Rinehart and Winston, 1973.

Haldane, J. B. S. *Heredity and Politics.* New York: Norton, 1938.

Hall, Elizabeth. "Konrad Lorenz." *Psychology Today,* November 1974.

Harlow, H. F. "The nature of love." *American Psychologist,* 1958, 13, 673–685.

———— "Sexual behavior in the rhesus monkey." In F. Beach (Ed.), *Sex and Behavior.* New York: Wiley, 1965.

Harlow, M. K., and Harlow, H. F. "Affection in primates." *Discovery,* 1966, 27, 11–17.

Heinroth, O. "Über bestimmte Bewegungsweisen der Wirbeltiere." *Sitzungsberichte der Gesselschaft der Naturforschenden Freunde,* Berlin, 1930.

Hermstein, R. J. *IQ in the Meritocracy.* Boston: Little, Brown, 1973.

Hess, E. H. *Imprinting. Early Experience and the Developmental Psychology of Attachment.* New York: D. Van Nostrand Company, 1973.

———— "Ethology." In R. Brown, et al. (Eds.), *New Directions in Psychology.* New York: Holt, 1962.

Hinde, R. A. "Ethological models and the concept of drive." *British Journal of Philosophical Science,* 1956, 6, 321–331.

Hull, C. L. *Principles of Behavior.* New York: D. Appleton-Century, 1943.

Huxley, A. *Brave New World.* New York: Harper, 1932.

———— *Brave New World Revisited.* New York: Harper, 1958.

Jacobson, A. L., Babich, F. R., Bubash, S., and Jacobson, A. "Differential approach tendencies produced by injection of ribonucleic acid from trained rats." *Science,* 1965, 150, 636–37.

James, W. "Great men, great thoughts and the environment." *Atlantic Monthly,* 1880, 46, 441–459.

——— *Principles of Psychology.* Vol. II. New York: Holt, 1890.

Jensen, A. R. "How much can we boost IQ and scholastic achievement?" *Harvard Educational Review,* 1969, 39, 1–123.

——— "Input: Arthur Jensen replies." *Psychology Today,* 1969, 3, 4–6.

——— "Reducing the heredity-environment uncertainty: a reply." *Harvard Educational Review,* 1969, 39, 449–483.

——— "Rejoinder." *Journal of Social Issues,* 1969, 25, 212–217.

Kelman, Herbert C. "Violence without moral restraint: reflections on the dehumanization of victims and victimizers." *Journal of Social Issues,* 1973, 29, 25–61.

Kinsey, A. C., Pomeroy, W. B., and Martin, C. E. *Sexual Behavior in the Human Male.* Philadelphia: W. B. Saunders, 1948.

——— and Gebhard, P. H. *Sexual Behavior in the Human Female.* Philadelphia: W. B. Saunders, 1953.

Klineberg, O. *Characteristics of the American Negro.* New York: Harper, 1944.

Koehler, O. "Die Ganzheitsbetrachtung in der modernen Biologie." *Verhandlungen der Königsberger Gelehrten Gesselschaft,* 1933.

Konishi, Mark. "Effects of deafening on song development in two species of junco." *Condor,* 1966, 66, 85–102.

Krafft-Ebing, R. V. *Psychopathica Sexualis.* New York: Pioneer Publications, 1950.

Kropotkin, P. *Mutual Aid: A Factor in Evolution.* New York: Dial, 1902.

——— *Ethics: Origin and Development.* New York: Dial, 1924.

Kuhn, T. S. *The Structure of Scientific Revolutions.* Chicago: University of Chicago Press, 1962.

Kuo, Z. Y. "Ontogeny of embryonic behavior in aves, I and II." *Journal of Experimental Zoology,* 1932, 61, 395–430; 62, 453–489.

——— "Ontogeny of embryonic behavior in aves, III and IV." *Journal of Comparative Psychology,* 1932, 13, 245–272; 14, 109–122.

Laing, R. D. *The Divided Self.* Baltimore: Penguin, 1965.

Lehrman, Daniel S. "A critique of Konrad Lorenz's theory of instinctive behavior." *Quarterly Review of Biology*, 1953, 28, 337–363.

LeVine, R. A., and Campbell, D. T. *Ethnocentrism: Theories of Conflict, Ethnic Attitudes and Group Behavior.* New York: Wiley, 1972.

Lorenz, K. A. "Kant's Lehre vom apriorischen im Lichte gegenwärtiger Biologie." *Blätter für Deutsche Philosophie*, 1941, 15, 94–125. Translated as "Kant's doctrine of the a priori in the light of contemporary biology." In L. von Bertalanffy and A. Rapoport (Eds.), General Systems: *Yearbook of the Society for General Systems Research.* Vol. VII, New York: Society for General Systems Research, 1962, 23–35.

——— "The rule of Gestalt perception in animal and human behavior." In L. L. Whyte (Ed.), *Aspects of Form.* New York: Pellegrini & Cudahy, 1951.

——— *King Solomon's Ring.* New York: Crowell, 1952.

——— "Gestaltwahrnehmung als Quelle wissenschaftlicher Erkenntnis." *Zeitschrift für experimentelle und angewandte Psychologie*, 1959, 6, 118–165. Translated as "Gestalt perception as a source of scientific knowledge." In K. Lorenz, *Studies in Animal and Human Behavior*, Vol. II. Cambridge: Harvard University Press, 1971, pp. 281–322.

——— "Haben Tiere ein subjectives Erleben?" *Jahrbuch der Technischen Hochschule München*, 1963, 57–68. Translated as: "Do animals undergo subjective experience?" In K. Lorenz, *Studies in Animal and Human Behavior*, Vol. II. Cambridge: Harvard University Press, 1971, pp. 323–337.

——— *Man Meets Dog.* Baltimore: Penguin, 1964.

——— *Evolution and Modification of Behavior.* Chicago: University of Chicago Press, 1965.

——— *On Aggression.* New York: Harcourt, Brace & World, 1966.

——— "Evolution of ritualization in the biological and cultural spheres." *Philosophical Transactions of the Royal Society of London*, 1966, 251 (Series B), 273–284.

———— "Innate bases of learning." In K. H. Pribram (Ed.), *On the Biology of Learning*. New York: Harcourt, Brace & World, 1969, 13–93.

———— "The enmity between generations and its probable ethological causes." *Studium Generale*, 1970, 23, 963–997.

———— *Studies in Animal and Human Behavior*. Cambridge, Mass.: Harvard University Press. Vol. I, 1970, 23, 963–967.

———— *Civilized Man's Eight Deadly Sins*. New York: Harcourt Brace Jovanovich, 1973.

———— *Die Rückseite des Spiegels*. Munich: Piperverlag, 1973.

McConnell, J. V., Jacobson, A. L., and Kimble, D. P. "The effects of regeneration upon retention of a conditioned response in the planaria." *Journal of Comparative and Physiological Psychology*, 1959, 52, 1–5.

McDougall, W. *An Introduction to Social Psychology*. London: Methuen, 1908.

Mallick, S. K. and McCandless, B. R. "A study of catharsis of aggression." *Journal of Personality and Social Psychology*, 1966, 4, 591–596.

Marler, P., and Griffin, D. K. "The 1973 Nobel Prize for Physiology or Medicine." *Science*, 1973, 182, 464–466.

Maslow, A. *Motivation and Personality*. New York: Harper & Row, 1954.

Masters, W. H., and Johnson, V₁ E. *Human Sexual Response*. Boston: Little, Brown, 1966.

Miller, N. E. "Liberalization of basic S-R concepts: extensions to conflict behavior, motivation, and social learning." In S. Koch (Ed.), *Psychology: A Study of Science*. Vol. II. *General Systematic Formulations, Learning, and Special Processes*. New York: McGraw-Hill, 1959, 196–292.

Monod, J. *Chance and Necessity*. New York: Knopf, 1971.

Morris, Desmond. *The Naked Ape*. New York: McGraw-Hill, 1968.

National Commission on the Causes and Prevention of Violence. *To Establish Justice, To Insure Domestic Tranquility*. New York: Award Books, 1969.

Olds, J. "Self-stimulation of the brain: its use to study local effects of hunger, sex and drugs." *Science*, 1958, 127 (3294), 315–324.

Pastore, N. *The Nature-Nurture Controversy*. New York: King's Crown Press, Columbia University, 1949.

Pavlov, I. P. *Conditioned Reflexes*. Translated by G. V. Anthrep. London: Oxford, 1927.

Pearson, K. "The moral basis of socialism." In K. Pearson (Ed.), *The Ethic of Free Thought*. London: T. Fisher Unwin, 1887, 317–345.

―――― "Socialism and natural selection." In K. Pearson (Ed.), *The Chances of Death*. London: Edward Arnold, 1897, 103–139.

Polanyi, M. *Personal Knowledge*. London: Routledge & Kegan Paul, 1958.

―――― "Life's irreducible structure." In M. Polanyi, *Knowing and Being*. London: Routledge & Kegan Paul, 1969, 225–239.

―――― "Why did we destroy Europe?" *Studium Generale*, 1970, 23, 909–916.

Popper, K. R. *The Logic of Scientific Discovery*. New York: Basic Books, 1959.

―――― *Conjectures and Refutations*. New York: Basic Books, 1963.

Powers, K. T. *Behavior: The Control of Perception*. Chicago: Aldine, 1973.

Quine, W. V. *Ontological Relativity*. New York: Columbia University Press, 1969.

―――― *Report of the Commission on Obscenity and Pornography*. New York: Bantam, 1970.

Rosenblatt, P. C. "Origins and effects of group ethnocentrism and nationalism." *Journal of Conflict Resolution*, 1964, 8, 131–146.

Roszak, T. *The Making of a Counter Culture*. Garden City, New York: Doubleday, 1969.

Schutz, F. "Objektfixierung geschlechtlicher Reaktionen bei Anatiden und Hühnern." *Die Naturwissenschaften*, 1963a, 50, 624–625.

―――― "Über geschlechtliche unterschiedliche Objektfixierung sexueller Reaktionen bei Enten im Zusammenhang mit dem Prachtkleid des Männchens." *Verhandlungen der Deutschen Zoologischen Gesellschaft*, 1963b, 282–287.

Sheffield, F. D. and Roby, T. B. "Reward value of a non-nutritive sweet taste." *Journal of Comparative and Physiological Psychology*, 1950, 43, 471–481.

Sherif, M. and Sherif, C. W. *Groups in Harmony and Tension*. New York: Harper, 1953.

Spitz, René A. *The First Year of Life*. New York: International Universities Press, 1965.

Storr, A. *Human Aggression*. New York: Atheneum, 1968.

Sumner, W. G. *Folkways*. New York: Ginn, 1906.

Thorpe, W. H. *Learning and Instincts in Animals*. London: Methuen, 1956.

—— *Science, Man and Morals*. London: Methuen, 1965.

Tinbergen, N. "Social releasers and the experimental method required for this study." *The Wilson Bulletin*, 1948, 60, 6–51.

—— "The hierarchical organization of nervous mechanisms underlying instinctive behavior." *Symposia of the Society of Experimental Biology IV* (Physiological mechanisms in animal behavior), 1950, 305–312.

—— *The Study of Instinct*. Oxford: Clarendon Press, 1951.

—— *Social Behavior in Animals*. New York: Wiley, 1953.

—— *Animal Behavior*. New York: Time, Inc., 1965.

Toulmin, S. E. *Foresight and Understanding: An Inquiry into the Aims of Science*. Bloomington: Indiana University Press, 1961.

—— *Human Understanding*. Vol. I. *The Evolution of Collective Understanding*. Princeton, N.J.: Princeton University Press, 1972.

Tryon, R. C. "Genetic differences in maze-learning abilities in rats." *Yearbook of Natural Social Studies Education*, 1940, 39, 111–119.

Uexküll, J. von. *Theoretical Biology*. New York: Harcourt, Brace, 1926.

—— "Streifzüge durch die Umwelten von Tieren und Menschen." Berlin: Springer, 1934. Translated as "A stroll through the worlds of animals and men." In C. H. Schiller (Ed.), *Instinctive Behavior*. New York: International Universities Press, 1957, pp. 5–80.

Ungar, G. (Ed.) *Molecular Mechanisms in Memory and Learning*. New York: Plenum, 1970.

Veblen, T. "The intellectual pre-eminence of Jews in modern Europe." *Political Science Quarterly*, 1919, 34, 33–42.

Vollmer, G. *Evolutionäre Erkenntnistheorie*. Freiburg: Physikalisches Institut der Universität, 1974.

Wallraff, C. F. *Philosophical Theory and Psychological Fact*. Tucson: University of Arizona Press, 1961.

Washburn, S. L. and DeVore, E. "The social life of baboons." *Scientific American*, 1961, 204, 62.

Weiss, P. "The living system: determinism stratified." In Koestler and Smythies (Eds.), *Beyond Reductionism*. London: Hutchinson, 1969.

——— "Depolarisation: pointers to conceptual disarmament." *Studium Generale*, 1970, 23, 925–940.

——— "The basic concept of hierarchic systems." In P. Weiss (Ed.), *Hierarchically Organized Systems in Theory and Practice*. New York: Hafner, 1971.

Whitman, C. O. "Animal Behavior." 16th lecture, Biological Lectures from the Marine Biological Laboratory. Woods Hole, Mass., 1898.

Whyte, L. L. (Ed.) *Aspects of Form*. New York: Pellegrini and Cudahy, 1951.

Wiener, N. *Cybernetics: Or Control and Communication in the Animal and the Machine*. New York: Wiley, 1948.

Windelband, W. *Geschichte und Naturwissenschaft*, 1894.

Wynne-Edwards, V. C. *Animal Dispersion in Relation to Social Behavior*. Edinburgh and London, 1962.

Index

Index

habituation, 237–38
Hahn, Kurt, 232, 233, 242, 249
Haldane, J. B. S., 109, 110
Hall, Clark, 21
Hall, Elizabeth, xv
Hargreaves, Dr. Ronald, 175, 176, 230, 231, 234, 237, 247, 249, 251
Harlow, Harry, 19, 30–32
Hassenstein, Bernhard, 135
hate, 41–42, 55–56, 144, 264–65, 266
Heinroth, Oskar, xiii, 6–7, 12, 80, 132–33, 135, 166
Heinz, Professor, 47
Heisenberg, Werner, 153
Hellmann, Bernhard, 173, 176, 229–30
Helmholtz, Hermann, 188
Herberer, J., 248
Herrnstein, Richard, 74, 110
Hess, E. H., 9, 13
Hinde, Robert, 53
Hitler, Adolf, 45–46, 47
homosexuality, 64, 70–72
Horney, Karen, 51, 55–56
Hull, C. L., 59, 163
Hume, David, 94, 187, 188, 189
hunger, 19, 21–22, 25, 92
Huxley, Aldous: *Brave New World*, 123, 162; *Brave New World Revisited*, 123
Huxley, Sir Julian, 40, 133, 136, 140, 159
Huxley, Thomas, 81

imprinting, xiii, 3, 12–15
individual differences, 10–12, 105, 109, 122–23
innate behavior, xiii, 12, 24, 26–29, 38–39, 58–59, 60–61, 62, 77, 80, 81, 88, 91, 99–100, 135, 183, 189, 193, 202, 212, 215, 221
inorganic matter, 152, 153–55, 177, 223, 262
insects, 6, 30, 101
instinctive behavior, xiv, 7, 19, 20, 22–23, 24, 25–27, 40, 52, 55, 81, 92, 93, 99, 129, 133, 134, 137, 139, 142, 146, 150, 162, 197, 220, 246, 251–52, 264
Institute for Comparative Behavior Research, 91
intelligence, 74–75, 109–10, 114–18; testing, 69, 115–17

intuition, 172, 182, 184, 186, 188, 191, 192–93, 201

Jacobson, A. L., 75
James, William: *Principles of Psychology*, 89–90
Jensen, Arthur, 69, 74
Jones, Ernest, xvi, xvii, xviii
Joule, James, 211
Journal of the New York Academy of Sciences, xiv
Jung, Carl, xvi, xvii, xviii, 51, 57–59

Kant, Immanuel, 94, 181–217, 227; *Prolegomena*, 187 n., 188
Kelman, Herbert C., 102
Kinsey Report, 41
Klineberg, Otto, 115
knowledge, 89, 93–94, 126, 185, 198, 199, 200, 215, 224–26, 231–32, 234–35, 242, 243, 247, 249–50; *see also* epistemology
Kocher, Dr. E. T., 174, 231
Koehler, Otto, 131, 169
Konishi, Mark, 13
Krafft-Ebing, Richard von, 14–15
Kropotkin, P., 109
Kuhn, T. S., 94
Kuo, Z. Y., 81

Laing, R. D., 30
language, 141, 175–76, 226, 249
leadership, 77–78
learning, 20, 22, 23, 24, 27, 28–29, 75–76, 81–82, 89, 91–92, 108, 234; *see also* intelligence
Lehrman, Daniel, xiv, 79, 81–82
Leyhausen, Paul, 178
Locke, John, 94
Loeb, Jacques, 170
Lorenz, Konrad, xi–xvi, xviii–xix, 3, 6, 80–83, 88, 128; criticism of, xiii–xvi, 47, 81–83, 98, 118; influences on, 80–81
Lorenz, Konrad, writings of, xviii; *Civilized Man's Eight Deadly Sins*, xiv, 88, 102, 104, 106, 111; "Do Animals Undergo Conscious Experience?", 90, 97; "Enmity Between Generations and Its Probable Ethological Causes," 87, 88, 102, 104, 111, 118, 120, 218–69; *Evolution and Modification of*

Index

302